T0323486

# PARETO
## *on*
# Policy

# PARETO
## *on*
# Policy

## WARREN J. SAMUELS

### With a new introduction by Steven G. Medema

Routledge
Taylor & Francis Group

LONDON AND NEW YORK

To Sylvia, Kathy, and Susan

Originally published in 1974 by Elsevier Scientific Publishing Company.

Published 2012 by Transaction Publishers

Published 2017 by Routledge
2 Park Square, Milton Park, Abingdon, Oxon OX14 4RN
711 Third Avenue, New York, NY 10017, USA

*Routledge is an imprint of the Taylor & Francis Group, an informa business*

Library of Congress Catalog Number: 2012007458

Library of Congress Cataloging-in-Publication Data

Samuels, Warren J., 1933-
    Pareto on policy / Warren J. Samuels ; with a new introduction by Steven G. Medema.
        p. cm.
    "Originally published in 1974 by Elsevier."
    Includes bibliographical references and index.
    ISBN 978-1-4128-4751-3
        1. Pareto, Vilfredo, 1848-1923. Trattato di sociologia generale. 2. Sociology. I. Title.
    HM477.I8P378 2012
    301--dc23

                                                    2012007458

ISBN 13: 978-1-4128-4751-3 (pbk)

# Contents

# Introduction to the Transaction Edition

**Steven G. Medema**

When the economist of today contemplates the other social sciences, it is usually as economist *qua* economist—looking at political activity, sociological phenomena, the law, etc. through the lens of rational choice theory with the goal of providing new frameworks for analysis that challenge or support (but perhaps with a "superior" perceived grounding) the received views in these other disciplines. Rare is the economist whose approach is truly that of a multidisciplinary social scientist, one who draws on the insights of a range of disciplines to develop sophisticated insights into social issues or broad-based frameworks for the analysis thereof. But it was not always so. Intellectual history is littered with polymaths who not only made fundamentally important contributions to a range of disciplines, but who saw them as necessarily interrelated and as constituent elements for doing social science. Vilfredo Pareto was one of these; Warren Samuels was another. The present volume, originally published in 1971 and reissued here by Transaction, brings them together in Samuels' profound and insightful commentary on Pareto's monumental *Trattato di Sociologia Generale (Treatise on General Sociology*, hereinafter, the *Trattato*), published in four volumes in 1916.

For Samuels, as for Pareto, economics is first and foremost a policy science. But each of these men was of the mind that the economy is not and cannot properly be conceived of an independent subsystem—hence the need for the broader social science view. While Pareto's *Trattato* attracted a great deal of attention among sociologists, political scientists, psychologists, and economists, much of the discussion was grounded in the disciplinary approach of the commentator and thus, for Samuels, missed out on the larger threads that unified Pareto's system. Samuels' goal in *Pareto on Policy* was to rise above narrow disciplinary confines to get at Pareto's larger message and, in doing so, reveal the inherent complexity of policy analysis and the need for a deep and comprehensive approach to the subject—an approach of the sort revealed by Pareto in the *Trattato*, and which defined Samuels' own perspective on the theory of economic policy.

## About the Author

The passing of Warren J. Samuels on August 17, 2011 brought to a close what was perhaps the most prolific modern career in the study of the history of economics. Whether it was through one of the hundreds of articles that he authored, the innumerable volumes that he edited or co-edited, through his work as a founder of the History of Economics Society and of the journal, *History of Political Economy*, or as the founding editor of *Research in the History of Economic Thought and Methodology*, Samuels left almost no aspect of the history of economics untouched by his efforts. His wide-ranging intellectual curiosity was matched only by his capacity for hard work, and the combination plays out over a vita that runs to 87 pages.[1]

Samuels' passing brought with it more than the loss of a valued colleague. It also provided another signal of the end of an era—that of the generalist historian of economics who makes important scholarly contributions across the spectrum of the history of economic ideas, with those ideas laid out against the contextual backdrops that span the humanities, social sciences, natural sciences, and events of the period in question. In recent decades, historians of economics have followed the lead of their economist brethren in becoming ever more narrowly specialized. While they reach beyond the confines of economics to draw on literary theory, intellectual historiography, the sociology of knowledge, and so on, those tools are applied to a relatively narrow slice of the history of economics. The modern historian of economics is the craftsman who remodels kitchens or handcrafts furniture. The giants of the past built and furnished the entire house. Adam Smith has told us that the modern way is a good thing—that the division of labor is the source of all improvements.

But some historians of economics transcend Smith's point. Warren Samuels was one. Mark Blaug, Bob Coats, Denis O'Brien, Lionel Robbins, and George Stigler were others. Of these, only O'Brien still walks among us.

Born in 1933, Warren Samuels earned his B.B.A. from the University of Miami in 1954 with majors in economics, accounting, and political science, and a minor in philosophy—an early indication of the breadth of scholarly interests that would define his career. He went on to pursue graduate work at the University of Wisconsin, turning down offers from Harvard and Duke because of his interest in further immersing himself into the Wisconsin-J.R. Commons institutionalist tradition, to which he had been exposed while an undergraduate at Miami. Samuels earned his M.S. in economics from Wisconsin in 1955, and his Ph.D. in economics in 1957. He held positions at the University of Missouri, Georgia State University, and the University of Miami before moving to Michigan State University in 1968. He officially retired from MSU with emeritus status in 1998 but continued to teach for several years thereafter, until relocating permanently to Gainesville, Florida with his wife, Sylvia.

Though most closely identified with the institutionalist branch of economics—and, specifically, its Wisconsin variant dominated by the work and legacy of John R. Commons—Samuels was a true eclectic, finding relevance and inspiration in the work of scholars as diverse as Adam Smith, Karl Marx, Frank Knight, Thorstein Veblen, F.A. Hayek, and Paul Samuelson. Indeed, this very eclecticism was the source of no small amount of interesting commentary and even controversy throughout his career. Samuels was referred to as an institutionalist and even a Marxist by those on the right and as a neoclassical economist and even a libertarian by those on the left. He often remarked that people have a deep-seated desire for a world of certainty, determinacy, and uniformity, and become very uncomfortable with one characterized by uncertainty, indeterminacy and heterogeneity. Samuels was perhaps most at home in the latter world, and his scholarly career—from the courses he taught to his published writings to his editorial work—is in many ways representative of these themes. This is also the perspective that drew him to Pareto.

Given his prolific output, it may surprise the reader to hear that while Samuels received his Ph.D. in 1957, his first publication did not appear until 1961, with the intervening period having been spent reading widely across the many literatures that interested him. It goes almost without saying that such a career path would be professional suicide in the current age, where "publish or perish" is the scholar's credo. A further sign of the transformation in the profession since that time is that Samuels' first two publications, "The Physiocratic Theory of Property and State" (1961) and "The Physiocratic Theory of Economic Policy" (1962), appeared in the *Quarterly Journal of Economics*—thus illustrating that there was a time when the leading journals of the economics profession saw fit to publish important work in the history of economics and that the profession actually took such work seriously as an important component of economic analysis.

The breadth of perspectives that informed Samuels' work was match by the spectrum of subjects upon which and areas within which he worked. His books and articles dealt with, *inter alia*, subjects including François Quesnay, Adam Smith, Thomas Robert Malthus, Benjamin Jowett, the Duke of Argyll, Henry George, Friedrich von Weiser, Vilfredo Pareto, Alfred Marshall, John Bates Clark, F.Y. Edgeworth, William Ashley, Frank Taussig, Joseph Schumpeter, Thorstein Veblen, Robert Lee Hale, John R. Commons, John Maurice Clark, Edwin Witte, Isaiah Berlin, Sergius Bulgakov, Gardiner Means, John Maynard Keynes, John R. Hicks, Daniel Ellsberg, Kenneth Boulding, and Ronald Coase. Reflecting his view that the history of economics is very much a story of battles over ideas contending for dominance in the professional and public minds, he was also very interested in schools of thought—their formation, evolution, and influence—and broader questions of how scholars throughout the ages have approached the task of "doing economics." Thus, we find among Warren's publications works on classical economics, Chicago economics, institutional economics, post-Keynesian economics, and Austrian economics, as well as the historical analysis of larger disciplinary movements and trends such as equilibrium theory, economic methodology, law and economics, the scope of economics, and the teaching of economics.

Though perhaps best known as a historian of economics, Samuels published widely in fields as diverse as law and economics, public finance and public choice, regulatory analysis, macroeconomics, income distribution, labor economics, comparative economic systems, welfare economics, and economic methodology. His was perhaps the last generation whose economic theorizing was informed by a close acquaintance with the history of economics, though, unlike some of those in whose theoretical writings the history of economics loomed so large—e.g., George Stigler and Paul Samuelson—Samuels never acquiesced in the view that a graduate student would be better served by replacing core coursework in the history of economic thought with additional courses in mathematics or econometrics.

Recent decades have witnessed a significant evolution in how historians of economics practice their trade, attended by a number of historiographic debates. Samuels, as it happens, was in many ways a pioneer on these fronts. On the historiographic front, he was (along with Donald Winch and Bob Coats) an early advocate for viewing the history of economic thought as intellectual history (Samuels 1974b), as against the rational reconstructivism and Whiggish tendencies that tended to dominate scholarship in the field at that time. One facet of this was his extraordinary interest in archival materials of all sorts and in promoting archival research by making these materials more accessible to scholars. Toward that end, he inaugurated a series of "Archival Supplements" to *Research in the History of Economic Thought and Methodology*, whose contents ranged from lecture notes to unpublished manuscripts to correspondence, accompanied by enlightening introductory materials by the individual who had unearthed them or by Samuels himself. He was also among the first to train the historian's lens on "modern" economics. While this area of research is gaining only gradual (and in some quarters, grudging) acceptance even today, Samuels was both doing and promoting such work as early as the 1960s, with his most significant stimulus to such scholarship coming via *Contemporary Economists in Perspective*, a two-volume collection that he co-edited with Henry Spiegel in 1984. But it would be incorrect to lump Samuels in with the crowds that decry particular ways of writing history in favor of their own. In this, as in so much else, Samuels was an eclectic—a firm believer that there are many good and useful ways of writing history and that we would all be best off if we would check our prejudices at the door and let a million flowers bloom.

One significant manifestation of Samuels' wide-ranging interests and eclectic nature was his extensive program of editing—a program that included the editorship of journals, but also of books and book series'. One of those series is that in which the present volume appears, Transaction's Classics in Economics series. This series is indicative of Samuel's eclectic nature, as it includes both canonical works in the history of economics and what one might call "heterodox" classics—each one presented with an original introduction by a leading specialist in that area. Through these efforts, Samuels brought to the contemporary reader important but difficult to access slices from the history of economics. His interest in this series was partly historical or antiquarian—that is, keeping alive important and interesting ideas from the past—but was also driven by his view that economics itself will flourish going forward if the marketplace of ideas contains the broadest possible array of insights and perspectives, including those of past thinkers. There are certainly more than a few people who would say the same in light of economists' performance leading up to and during the recent economic crisis.

## The Economic Role of Government

Samuels' deep philosophical and practical interest in the analysis of the economic role of government, particularly within a capitalist market system, was perhaps *the* defining theme of his scholarly career—both as historian of economics and as economist *qua* economist. And the University of Wisconsin in the 1950s was the right place for a graduate student to be pursuing this interest. His major professor, Edwin Witte, had been a student of John R. Commons, was one of the leading labor policy economists of his generation, and was the man primarily responsible for developing the Social Security Act of 1935. The interplay of economic analysis and economics policy making evidenced in Witte's career had for decades been a hallmark of the Wisconsin approach. Samuels was profoundly influenced by Witte in many ways, the evidence for which is perhaps nowhere more clear than in his 1967 essay on Witte's view of the economic role of government.

It was Witte who reinforced in Samuels the view that government and the economy are inseparable—that it is wrongheaded to speak of markets versus government when government, in fact, defines the legal framework within which the economy (including businesses, consumers, labor, etc.) operates. The economy, here, is not some self-subsistent sphere. As such, economics was, for Witte and for Samuels, "political economy" and could not be otherwise, in that to understand the economy one must, of necessity, understand government and the various ways that government inherently controls the operation of the economic system. When one understands the matter in this way, the issue becomes not one of more versus less government, or of government versus the market, but of the *form* of government action *vis-à-vis* the market and the interests the government supports, or is used to support, against other interests. The introduction of workplace safety regulations, for example, is not a government "intrusion" into the marketplace. Rather, the introduction of such regulations represents a change in the interests supported by government—from those of business owners to those of the workers. Government is present in the employer-employee relationship regardless of the direction of liability for these workplace accidents.

In focusing much of his life's work on the economic role of government, Samuels was picking up one of the bright threads in the carpet that is the history of economic ideas. But whereas most economic analysis in this vein is about what government *should or should not do*, or what it (in the post-Robbins 1932 era) *could or could not do* (with the "coulds" often influenced by the "shoulds"), Samuels took a rather different approach. His interest was in some sense that of the impartial spectator, one who observed and wrote about how economists, and others, talked about the economic role of government—discourse analysis, if you will, but informed by his own particular view of the role that government *does* play in a market system.

Samuels' first foray into this area came in his Ph.D. dissertation, which took as its subject the question of how big businesses and labor unions viewed the economic role of government. Where others were writing on impact of actual and prospective government policies that affected business—a prominent topic during this heyday of traditional industrial organization, before it became a branch of game theory in many quarters—Samuels wanted to know how the affected entities themselves viewed the state and what they thought its proper role in a market system. Toward that end, Samuels interviewed a wide range of business and labor leaders—a leap into the "empirical" realm that was a very rare moment in Samuels' career. Though most of Samuels' subsequent scholarship on economic role of government dealt with economists and their views, he remained very interested in popular discussions of this topic, and a perusal of his articles will reveal regular references to statements made by politicians, newspaper columnists, and others.

But it was in the analysis of economists musings on the role of the state in the economic system where Samuels was most at home, and this line of inquiry permeates his three major treatises in the history of economic thought: *The Classical Theory of Economic Policy* (1966), *Pareto on Policy* (1974a), and *Erasing the Invisible Hand: Essays on an Elusive and Misused Concept in Economics* (2011).

The first of these works, *The Classical Theory of Economic Policy*, is in some sense a philosophically oriented complement and response to Lionel Robbins's classic book, *The Theory of Economic Policy in English Classical Political Economy* (1952). Where the latter is (in relative terms) a breezy read that looks at the roles that various of the classical economists ascribed to the state and successfully debunks the notion that the classical economists were die-hard adherents of *laissez-faire*, Samuels' book is a much more dense effort, and also more sophisticated in its approach.

While Samuels applauded Robbins's effort and, in particular, his move to couch the classical theory as a "market-plus-framework" approach to economic policy and the role of the state, he was of the mind that Robbins did not go far enough. Yes, as Robbins pointed out very clearly, the classicals did not conceive of the market operating *in vacuo*. Instead, said Robbins, the classicals were very clear that, if the "invisible hand" result claimed for the market were to work its magic, the market must be set within an appropriate legal framework. Thus we see Robbins suggesting that the invisible hand is "the hand of the lawgiver, the hand which withdraws from the sphere of the pursuit of self-interest those possibilities which do not harmonize with the public good" (1952, 56).

While this would seem to be music to the ears of an institutionalist such as Samuels, he in fact found the tune incomplete, and in important ways. Robbins's account, he said, left out of the story several key facets by (i) neglecting to analyze non-legal forces of social control, such as religion, morals, custom, and education; (ii) failing to get into the specifics of the framework-providing functions filled by government, and (iii) inadequately examining the role played by law as a mechanism for social change. Samuels' goal in his book, then, was to set matters right through an examination of these issues. The messages of the tale that Samuels tells are far too extensive and nuanced to get into here, but two things stand out for this author. The first is that the classical theory of economic policy is just that—a theory, or, perhaps, a model. That is, it is a framework for policy analysis rather than a set of prescriptions about what the state should and should not do. Second, the framework employed by the classicals was far more sophisticated—involved many more elements—than traditional histories allowed, something that was a function both of the relatively broad backgrounds of the giants of classical economics and the economic pluralism that informed their policy analysis.

Samuels' final publication, *Erasing the Invisible Hand*, is in some sense the *magnum opus* that ties together many of the strands that made up his life's work. He takes as his subject matter here the concept of the invisible hand—one of the most important and controversial ideas in the history of economics—exploring both its genesis in economic thinking at the hands of Adam Smith and its use by economists over the ensuing two-plus centuries. As such, this work combines Samuels' interest in the market-state interplay (which he often referred to as the "legal-economic nexus"[2]), the history of ideas, and the uses to which ideas are put by scholars, politicians, the media, and the average citizen.

The reader who turns to this book in the hopes of learning exactly what is meant by this elusive concept that permeates the last two-plus centuries of economic thinking will be sorely disappointed. Instead, the reader is treated to a series of essays on the meaning given to the invisible hand throughout the recorded history of ideas—the primarily focus, of course, being on the history of economics from Adam Smith onward. For Samuels, the invisible hand was a concept that had taken on a life of its own, and *Erasing the Invisible Hand* is in some sense the biography of an idea. Yes, we are treated to an in-depth exploration of the use of that term by Smith, one grounded in the economic, philosophical, social, and religious milieu of the period, but I believe that, for Samuels, this is the least interesting aspect of the discussion—and would have formed a very minor part of it had he lived long enough to complete the three-volume work that he had contemplated.

What attracted Samuels to this subject was the use made of the invisible hand concept by economists after Smith—devotees and critics alike—and not least the several dozen different things identified in the literature as "the invisible hand." This focus on economists' use of the term makes *Erasing the Invisible Hand* both an exercise in intellectual history and a slice into the sociology of the economics profession over the last 200 years. Samuels' interest in the history of economics was fueled in no small part by an unwavering belief in the power of ideas and, as he read the historical record, the invisible hand was perhaps the most powerful of economic ideas. And what gave it, and gives so many ideas, their power is the *uses to which they are put* rather than anything that inheres in the ideas per se. To use modern economic terminology, ideas become vehicles for rent seeking of various sorts, used to support certain interests at the expense of others, but often cloaked in the rhetoric of the larger social interest. They function as mechanisms for social control and as psychic balm (the latter a Samuels favorite, owing to G.L.S. Shackle); they are the objects of ideology and myth-making; they have linguistic, ontological, epistemological, and theological significance; they are emblematic of tensions between the individual and the social, the problem of order in society, the conflicting interests for continuity versus change, and attempts to obfuscate the use of power. This is all very heady stuff, but it was exactly Samuels' type of stuff. And the invisible hand story has it in spades. To even begin to tell this story requires a breadth that few can muster, and though Samuels did not live to tell the entire story that he wished to tell (the raw materials for which filled many file cabinets and boxes in his home), it is clear that this was the type of story that Samuels, with his vast command of the literature and amazing synthetic powers, was uniquely equipped to tell.

## Pareto on Policy

Though Vilfredo Pareto is best known among economists today for his *Manual of Political Economy* (originally published in 1906), as the developer of the ordinal theory of utility, and for devising the conception of economic efficiency that bears his name and has become central to modern economic analysis, it may surprise the economist reader to know that Pareto considered the *Trattato di Sociologia Generale* (1916) to be his most important work. But this reflects nothing more than the fact that Pareto was not, as some would make him out to be, a modern neoclassical economist. Where the modern economist sees economics as a self-contained discipline—one that, for many, intersects with the other social sciences by bringing its insights *to them*, Pareto believed that a good economics was one that drew on a broad range of social science insights and remained, as it were, close to the ground. That said, he was also convinced of the power of mathematical analysis to provide important insights and so was somewhat unique in the history of economics for his melding of highly sophisticated mathematical analysis with attention to larger social and other forces.

Pareto was born in Paris in 1848 as the son of an Italian in exile. The family returned to Italy in 1852 and Pareto entered the University of Turin at the age of 16, studying mathematics as an undergraduate before pursuing a Ph.D. in engineering. His doctoral thesis, *"Principi fondamentali della teoria della elasticita dei corpi solidi e ricirche fondamentali sulla integrazione delle equazione diffenziali che ne differiscono l'equilibrio,"* was a harbinger of the economics that occupied much of his career, dealing, as the title notes, with the notion of equilibrium—here, in a physical system. His early career was spent in Florence, working as an engineer for a railway company and then as the technical director of an ironworks, but this was also the period when he began the serious study of economics that would occupy much of the rest of his life. His membership in the *Accademia dei Georgofili*, a society to promote the study of agriculture, forestry, geography, and economics, was both a reflection of this interest and a stimulus to his writings in the field. Pareto was an ardent proponent of free trade in particular (though he moderated his stance here later in life) and of minimizing the extent of direct government interference in the economy in general, attitudes that he attempted to popularize through his role as a co-founder of the Adam Smith Society in Ferrara and as an unsuccessful (twice!) candidate for the Italian Parliament.

Of the numerous contacts that Pareto made during the early stages of his career, perhaps the most important was with Maffeo Pantaleoni, the Italian economist who, among other things, played a major role in the development of *La Scienza delle Finanze*, the distinctive Italian approach to public finance that has certain interesting commonalities with the modern public choice approach. It was Pantaleoni who introduced Pareto to Leon Walras and later recommended him as the successor to Walras at Lausanne—a position that Pareto took up in 1893. Pareto was a natural successor to Walras in that, like Walras, he believed that the economy should be contemplated in its totality—that is, via a general equilibrium approach. His *Cours d'économie*

*Politique,* (published in two volumes in 1896-97), *Manuale d'economia Politica* (1906) and his 1911 encyclopedia essay on "Economie Mathématique" are illustrative both of his basic approach and of the evolution of his thinking on this score. The general equilibrium emphasis helps to account for why Pareto's influence (like that of Walras) was so much delayed in the United States and Britain, where the influence of Alfred Marshall and his partial equilibrium system carried the day until the middle of the twentieth century.[3]

It is Pareto's *Trattato* and the theory of social-economic policy embodied therein, though, that Samuels takes up in *Pareto on Policy.* Samuels' interest in and attraction to Pareto's system sprung from several sources, two of which are worth noting here. One was Pareto's conception of sociology as "a general, that is abstract ..., synthesis of all the disciplines studying human society" (1974a, p. 8)—economics, sociology, psychology, political science, law, political economy, political history, the history of religions, and so on. This clearly resonated with Samuels' institutionalist leanings. A second source of attraction was Pareto's insistence on developing "a general equilibrium model of the total socio-politico-economic decision-making or policy process" (pp. ix-x). Within this system, power, knowledge, and psychology played central roles, and the general equilibrium nature of the model conceptualized their fundamental interdependence. Given his view that the economy is not an independent, self-subsistent sphere, Samuels, like Pareto, believed that the analysis of it and of the attendant policy-making process demands an approach that draws on the larger base of social-scientific thought.

At the center of Pareto's theory of economic policy, for Samuels, is the issue of power, with both economy and society being systems of power or, differently put, political processes. Those classes that have "the greater strength, intelligence, ability, and shrewdness" effectively call the shots (p. 88). This makes the social process one of power struggle, where equilibrium outcomes result in a ruling class and a class subjected to the rule of others. But there is also circulation among the classes, meaning that both the ruling class itself and the social equilibrium are continually evolving. And, at any given time, competing interests are jockeying for position through a process of mutual coercion and mutual manipulation, all with the goal of enhancing their opportunities for gain. Policy making, then, is, at its heart, the exercise of power play.

Knowledge and psychology enter Pareto's system because knowledge is both an instrument of power and a function of psychology. For Pareto, much of what humans take to be knowledge is non-logico-experimental, supported by faith or conviction rather than being potentially verifiable. Because policy is a function of knowledge and non-logico-experimental knowledge is pseudo-knowledge, much of policy is, for Pareto, based on pseudo-knowledge. This, then, is where psychology comes into focus. That which people are willing to accept as knowledge (the non-verifiable variant) is a function of their sentiments—that is, of psychology—and it is on this basis that choices are made. Power, then, allows for the manipulation of these sentiments in such a way that what passes for knowledge are a body of ideas more or less in accord with what those in power would like to see accepted as truth to get their desired results via the collective decision process. As Samuels puts it, "knowledge is manipulated by power to work upon the sentiments as an alternative to the use of force" (p. 133).

It was Pareto's approach, rather than his policy stances per se, that appealed to Samuels' tastes. Indeed, though Samuels and Pareto were clearly kindred spirits when it came to the subject of interdisciplinary social science, their politics were rather different. In Samuels' hands, Pareto was one for whom economic policy was about "more than market allocation of resources, that is, more than the market, more than resource allocation, and more than micro-economic equilibrium" (p. 199), its attention to equilibrium states of the world notwithstanding. And so Pareto

analyzed the forces governing the distribution of power in society, and economy, the operation of the institutional and motivational forces and framework within which market activity takes place, and the interaction between market, institutions, and socio-economic forces. Moreover, he analyzed the institutional and motivational framework not just as it bears on the allocation of resources, but primarily as it constitutes the structuring of the economic decision-making process, that is, the power structure (p. 199).

The system was one of marginal adjustments, within which all variables are manipulable and manipulated, and in which institutions, including government, economy, social utility, truth, knowledge, psychology, and power are both independent and dependent variables. This emphasis on the larger institutional structure within which policy making proceeds, and especially the power structure and its role in determining economic outcomes, both allocative and distributive, was, for Samuels, a central but all-too-neglected aspect of economic analysis—where the term "economic analysis" is defined as the attempt to come to grips with or understand the operation of the economic system and to devise and assess the potential impacts of economic policy.

All of this led Samuels to identify Pareto with the American Institutionalist tradition, in contrast to the standard historian of economics propensity to lump him in with neoclassical economics in general and the Lausanne school in particular. (Samuels did the same with the classical economists and with Frank Knight, the latter no doubt displeasing both Chicagoans and institutionalists.) In Samuels' hands, the Pareto of the *Trattato* adds to and complements neoclassical theorizing (and its microeconomic and welfare theory aspects in particular) with a theory of institutions and their influence not unlike what institutionalists added to the neoclassical approach. The result was the development of a broader framework for the study of the organization and control of the economic system and thus the theory of economic policy.

## Complexity and Indeterminacy

Samuels' emphasis on the desire of individuals for simplicity rather than complexity, for determinacy rather than indeterminacy, pervades his approach to economics, whether one is "doing economics," elaborating a theory of economic policy, or studying the history of economic ideas. Though his eclecticism and willingness to learn from all manner of approaches to the subject kept him from preaching (other than, perhaps, for openness), Samuels was clear about the benefits that a focus on these dichotomies would have for the economist and for the historian of economics, and the need for both to take a non-traditional (for them) approach to the subject to get at these issues and their influence. As he noted in his 1974 essay on "The History of Economic Thought as Intellectual History,"

> The belabored human mind tends to prefer simplicity and unity to complexity and diversity and thereby to perceive only burdensomeness in the latter. But complexity and diversity are not only a correct description of

the reality of intellectual systems but more importantly they represent opportunity, indeed challenge, to the intellectual historian. The opportunities are real and important; all involve research leading to depth and breadth of perception and understanding. The fact of and the opportunities accorded by complexity and diversity relate to what is perhaps the most profound objective of the history of economic thought. On the one hand, it is that of broadening the mind, providing a sense of the deeper and broader facets of seemingly narrow or minor points and issues, an appreciation of the meaning of other approaches to a problem, indeed, an understanding of meaning in terms of fundamental problems and not particular solutions or positions; on the other hand, it is the combination of a critical posture toward all thought and meaning with the ability to think in terms of different intellectual systems and the mastery of a degree of intellectual and emotional distance with regard to one's own mode or system of thought. In one respect the objective is breadth and depth of perspective; in the other, it is critical ability; in both respects, assuming mastery of substance and technique, it is a sense of distance without alienation. Needless to say, the accomplishment of this objective is both difficult and deceptive, though it is very rewarding. In any event, it is a major task and opportunity accorded by the subject matter (1974b, pp. 307-308).

Samuels' objection to Whig history as *the* mechanism for studying the history of economics was not that it is wrong, but that it is seriously incomplete: it focuses on content at the expense of form; on one particular strand of the history of ideas rather than the "kaleidoscopic blend of types of social thought" which it embodies (p. 309); on the influence of received cognitive systems on the development and reception of ideas, on the tendencies to confuse positive and normative, value and fact; on the basis upon which ideas are declared to be "knowledge;" and so on.

For Samuels, these facets of intellectual history were important because he stood with Keynes in emphasizing the importance of ideas to shape individual and social consciousness and, with them, individual and social action. As Keynes put it so well in 1936,

the ideas of economists and political philosophers, both when they are right and when they are wrong, are more powerful than is commonly understood. Indeed the world is ruled by little else. Practical men, who believe themselves to be quite exempt from any intellectual influences, are usually the slaves of some defunct economist. Madmen in authority, who hear voices in the air, are distilling their frenzy from some academic scribbler of a few years back. I am sure that the power of vested interests is vastly exaggerated compared with the gradual encroachment of ideas.

Not, indeed, immediately, but after a certain interval; for in the field of economic and political philosophy there are not many who are influenced by new theories after they are twenty-five or thirty years of age, so that the ideas which civil servants and politicians and even agitators apply to current events are not likely to be the newest. But, soon or late, it is ideas, not vested interests, which are dangerous for good or evil (1936, pp. 383-84).

In the conclusion to *Erasing the Invisible Hand*, Samuels writes along similar lines and, in the process, makes a case for the instrumental benefits associated with the study of the history of economics as intellectual history—not to promote one particular set of ideas, whether victorious or defeated in the intellectual battles of the past, but to *understand* the force that ideas have in society, to grapple with the use of those ideas by scholars or groups of scholars who would promote particular agendas and to, in some sense, rescue those ideas from those who would use them ill and to restore them to a more appropriate epistemological status:

> It has not been my purpose in this book to foster a particular agenda for government. My objective has been to help put an end to the false beliefs about government and the use of those beliefs in manipulating people's perceptions and attitudes. ... People should understand what government does, how it does it, in what ways government is important, and the significance of that knowledge. The premise of that objective is the value of knowledge that is as nonnormative as possible for democratic decision-making, as free of error and pretense as possible (2011, p. 295).

This is surely a sentiment with which Pareto would have strongly concurred. Though this sentence was written when Samuels was in his late seventies, the perspective that it embodies has its roots in his undergraduate days, when he learned from Miami professor Gerald Franklin that "one could study ["Government and Business," the course he took with Franklin] in a meaningful and useful abstract, theoretical way that was overwhelmed by neither ideological preconceptions and agendas nor the issues of the day" (1996, p. 38). For Samuels, openness and honesty were both paramount virtues of the scholarly life and habits that should be central to the policy-making process. In the last, at least, we have a long way to go.

# Notes

1. The interested reader can find Samuels' vita online at http://econ.msu. edu/faculty/samuels/vita.pdf.
2. On Samuels' view of the legal-economic nexus, see Samuels (1989).
3. It is also the case that most economists could not understand the mathematics of Walras and Pareto during their own lives and for many decades thereafter—economics only becoming a more highly mathematical science in the post-World-War II period.

# References

Cohen, W.J. 1960. "Edwin E. Witte (1887-1960): Father of Social Security." *Industrial and Labor Relations Review* 14: 7-9.

Keynes, John Maynard. 1936. *The General Theory of Employment, Interest and Money*. London: Macmillan.

Pareto, Vilfredo. 1896-1997. *Cours d'économie politique 2 vol.* Lausanne: Rouge.

_____. 1906. *Manuale d'economia Politica*. Milan: Societa Editrice Libraria.

_____. 1909. *Manuel d'Économie Politique*. Paris: V. Giard and E. Brière. Translated as *Manual of Political Economy* by A. S. Schwier. New York: Augustus M. Kelly, 1971.

_____. 1911. "Economie mathématique." In *Encyclopédie des sciences mathématiques* 4(1). Paris: Gauthier-Villars. Translated by J.I. Griffin as "Mathematical Economics," *International Economic Papers* 5 (1955): 58–102.

_____. 1916. *Trattato di Sociologia Generale*, 4 vols. Florence: Barbera. Translated as *The Mind and Society*, edited by Arthur Livingston; translated by Andrew Bongiorno and Arthur Livingston, with the advice and active cooperation of James Harvey Rogers. New York: Harcourt Brace & Co., 1935.

Robbins, Lionel. 1932. *An Essay on the Nature and Significance of Economic Science*. London: Macmillan.

_____. 1952. *The Theory of Economic Policy in English Classical Political Economy*. London: Macmillan.

Samuels, Warren J. 1961. "The Physiocratic Theory of Property and State." *Quarterly Journal of Economics* 75 (February): 96-111.

_____. 1962. "The Physiocratic Theory of Economic Policy." *Quarterly Journal of Economics* 76 (February): 145-62.

_____. 1967. "Edwin E. Witte's Concept of the Role of Government in the Economy." *Land Economics* 43: 131-47.

_____. 1966. *The Classical Theory of Economic Policy*. Cleveland: World.

_____. 1974a. *Pareto on Policy*. Amsterdam: Elsevier.

_____. 1974b. "The History of Economic Thought as Intellectual History." *History of Political Economy* 6: 305-323.

_____. 1989. "The Legal-Economic Nexus." *George Washington Law Review* 57: 1556-78.

_____. 1996. "My Work as a Historian of Economic Thought." *Journal of the History of Economic Thought* 18: 37-75.

_____. 2011. *Erasing the Invisible Hand: Essays on an Elusive and Misused Concept in Economics*. Cambridge: Cambridge University Press.

Samuels, Warren J. and Henry W. Spiegel, eds. 1984. *Contemporary Economists in Perspective*, 2 vols. Greenwich, CT: JAI Press.

# Preface

This book is devoted to an interpretation of Vilfredo Pareto's *Treatise on General Sociology* in terms of a general equilibrium model of policy. There are three themes and one conviction running throughout the study. The first theme is a model of policy making involving three sets of variables, namely, power, knowledge, and psychology. The second is a general equilibrium approach to the study of these variables emphasizing fundamental interdependence. The third theme is the importance of Pareto's work. The conviction concerns the importance and possibility of an objective or positive approach to deep problems of policy. Pareto's *Treatise* is analyzed, interpreted, and critically evaluated in terms of these themes and this conviction.

Pareto is one of the few individuals whose work has had enormous influence in not one but at least three social sciences in the twentieth century. In the areas of economics, sociology, and political science — wherein, for example, S. E. Finer says "it claims to rank as the most pregnant work of political science in the last half century," (Finer, 1966, p. 87) — Pareto either made seminal contributions or re-enforced the work of others to produce major trends of analysis and interpretation. Yet, notwithstanding Pareto's explicit attempt in the *Treatise* to produce a general sociology (as he called it) encompassing all of these sciences, together with psychology, Pareto's work has been treated almost completely from the individual perspectives of the various disciplines. The unique feature of this volume is an interpretation consonant with Pareto's intention, namely, to provide a general equilibrium model of the total socio-politico-economic decision-making or policy process in terms of power, knowledge, and psychology as so many sets of interdependent variables.

The study shows, through the Paretian vision, the diverse processes of and interactions between individual and social choice. It emphasizes how the very structure of power, that is, of economic decision making, is itself the most fundamental problem of policy, a problem that is taken for granted in partial equilibrium models. It demonstrates the critical role of information systems and of what is taken as knowledge in the formation of man's definitions of reality and values, and therefore of the communication processes of society. It raises fundamental and continuing questions of both policy making and policy analysis which must be confronted if we are to see the social world as it is and if we are to acquire greater realism with regard to the possibilities and conditions of change, continuity, order, freedom, and so forth.

The book is therefore directed at those who would better comprehend society, polity, and economy as policy processes; that is, as processes whose structure, conduct, and performance are a function of complex decision making. There is a growing community of social scientists and policy analysts who are disturbed at the limits of presumptively normative and/or partial equilibrium models which take for granted the solutions to variables or problems which are themselves worked out through policy making in the real world. The approach taken here will be of interest to those who, for example, are interested in pursuing the implications of such propositions as (1) the working rules of law and morals govern the distribution and exercise of power *and* the distribution and exercise of power govern the development of the working rules, (2) values depend upon the decision-making process *and* the decision-making process depends upon values, and, *inter alia*, (3) government is an instrument available for the use of whoever can get into a position to control it.

The author's fellow economists are most in need of the insight provided by the interpretation here accorded to Pareto. Contemporary criticism of economic theory by both theorists and nontheorists and by both orthodox and heterodox economists very often points to the importance of the topics of this book for the conventional problems of economic theory and for the even deeper problem of the organization and control of the economic system. The allocation of resources can be explained in terms of the forces of demand and supply, but the thrust of much historical and recent criticism of traditional theory is that the explanation can and need be driven much deeper. The allocation of resources can be shown to be a function of demand and supply, but the latter can be shown to be a function, in turn, of power, rights, law, and the use of government. Moreover, the problem of power, namely, the organization and control of the economic system, may be investigated and theorized about on its own merits. The market in many ways only gives effect to the institutions and power structure which form and work through it.

The limits of formal microeconomic theory, and of the related new welfare economics, especially of what has come to be called Pareto optimality (Samuels, 1972b) are subtle and very profound. What irony lies in the fact that the narrowest elements of formal economic theory have been re-enforced by — indeed, have been legitimized by reference to — the welfare economics of the same Pareto who examined the widest possible model of factors and forces governing the actual operation of the economy and distribution of economic welfare! Pareto's own work demonstrates the importance of power in economic affairs, whereas orthodox economic theory proceeds as if the economy was a neutral black box devoid of power. Pareto's work demonstrates the presumptive and narrow character of the new welfare economics which pretends to speak in terms of the Pareto rule; he demonstrates how the actual economic world is, as a matter of fact, almost exactly opposite to the picture conveyed by that rule and the microeconomics supporting it.

This book shows Pareto to have been a major contributor to an understanding of the broadest problems of economic policy and policy analysis (Samuels, 1972a). It suggests how these problems can be schematically examined in terms of a general equilibrium model of power, knowledge, and psychology. The ambition of the book is limited, however, in that it attempts these suggestions only in terms of a reinterpretation of Pareto's *Treatise*. Although it does not attempt to present a new, complete, or modern statement of a model, it does indicate the major outlines, variables, and interrelationships thereof. Furthermore, it does suggest that Pareto was the author of a hitherto celebrated treatise whose enormous heuristic value and seminal quality have yet to be completely realized. Indeed, the text, which follows the argument of Pareto's *Treatise* very closely, will show the faulty and narrow interpretation of Pareto dominant among economists and something of how those errors can be remedied.

I would like to acknowledge the assistance of Terry Hull, my research assistant when most of the research and writing were undertaken, and Betsy Johnston, who removed much infelicity of style from a difficult manuscript. I am indebted to numerous colleagues, past and present, for their help and support, and to several secretaries and librarians for devoted aid.

I conclude with a note about myself. In researching and writing this volume I believe that I have not been captivated by Pareto. It is striking that so many commentators upon Pareto have been either outspoken disciples or outspoken antagonists. I would make it clear from the beginning that I consider some of his formulations and emphases rather distasteful. I do recognize however, indeed, I insist, that the problems which Pareto unveils are some of the most difficult yet important in social philosophy, social science, policy analysis, and ethics. In studying policy, and perhaps especially Pareto on policy, one learns a great deal not only about the world of policy but also about oneself.

# Chapter 1.

# Introduction

## 1. Objectives

Vilfredo Pareto has a secure albeit controversial place in the history of social thought. He was a seminal figure who influenced the direction of both economic and sociological theory. His contributions to economic analysis consisted primarily of his treatment of general economic equilibrium, including its extension to non-competitive conditions and variable coefficients of production; his ordinal-utility and indifference approach to the theory of demand; and his notion of welfare-economic optimality (or, more accurately, ophelimity). Sociologists have been primarily interested in his analysis of society as a system; his attempt at a positivist logico-experimental science of society; his theories of non-logical conduct, the residues, and derivations; and the circulation of the elite. As political sociologist, Pareto is one of the leading theoreticians and exponents of the theory of a ruling class. In addition, economists have shared with sociologists an interest in Pareto's "law" of income distribution. In almost every aspect of his work Pareto has been penetratingly criticized, from his major substantive theorems to his concept and practice of science. On a different but not unrelated plane, many critics have been disturbed by Pareto's relation to Mussolini and to the theory and genesis of fascism in general.

Interest in Pareto among social scientists, however, has been essentially dichotomized. In particular, there has been a substantial neglect of Pareto's sociological analyses among economists. This neglect is regrettable, especially in light of the historical hia-

1

tus between orthodox neoclassicist and heterodox institutionalist economists. Pareto considered that market forces were part of a larger process and that the economic man was only a convenient, although important and necessary methodological, and to some extent substantively justified, abstraction. To Pareto, economics — particularly pure economic theory — was part of a larger general sociology; economic equilibrium was one facet of a more complex general social equilibrium; and economic ophelimity was one facet of generalized utility. Pareto, then, was not satisfied with analyzing the market as a self-contained process. He examined the operation of the forces and institutions of the market and the interaction between them and other social forces, institutions, and processes without making either artificially rigid. He attempted in his sociology to do for the larger matrix of forces what he had done earlier with respect to the economic. The larger general sociology, the general social equilibrium, and the model of generalized utility were developed by Pareto in the major work he produced after leaving economic theory for sociology, his *Treatise on General Sociology.* [1] Yet there is also the complaint by several sociologists, perhaps most recently Lopreato, (1965, p. 2 and *passim*), that Pareto's central analytical system — as distinct from the particular theories — has been neglected and/or misunderstood among sociologists themselves.

What strikes me as being of great significance is that the general social equilibrium analysis of the *Treatise* may be interpreted as a particular theory of socio-economic policy and thereby is at least suggestive of the outline of a general model of socio-economic policy. The application of the Walras-Pareto general equilibrium model to micro-economics is a representation of the forces through which the economic decision-making process allocates resources through a market. Pareto's model of the social process can be interpreted as a broader general model of policy encompassing both nominally market and socio-political forces, with greater attention given in the *Treatise* to the sociological than to the economic forces. Pareto's general social system in the *Treatise* is an equilibrium model with an admixture of elements of both organic and mechanistic theories. But his model, generally functionalist in character, is readily restated in terms of the central problems of a general model of policy. Such a restatement is the rationale of this volume.

The objectives of this study, then, are, first and most immediately, to identify and restate the main themes of Pareto's *Trea-*

2

*tise on General Sociology* as a particular theory of socio-economic policy, and second and of broader significance, to derive insight into the fundamentals of a general model of policy. With respect to the former objective, one by-product should be a more thorough and systematic statement of Pareto's system than is generally to be found in the sociological literature, however much the distinctive feature of the statement will lie in its interpretation as a model of policy. With respect to the latter objective, broader insight should be gained concerning the elements of a more complete general model of the economic decision-making process, and of the scope of both policy and policy participation. Incidentally with respect to the latter objective, additional insight should be gained, first, about the artificiality of a strict market-plus-framework dichotomy for policy analysis and, second, about the relation of neoclassical to institutional analysis generally.

## 2. Theory of Economic Policy

The concept, theory of economic policy, emphasizes that policy is essentially choice and that the economy may be interpreted as a policy or decision-making, that is, a choosing process. Choices may be envisioned as emanating from businesses, families, universities, churches, and governments, or from particular individuals or subgroups therein. Decisions may also be envisioned as society's effective or composite choices produced through the interaction of those institutions. Society's economic policy issues from the total economic decision-making process. The economy, like the larger society itself, is a process through which effective decisions are reached or worked out in a continuing manner.

The scope of economic policy includes the three conventionally recognized basic economic problems of resource allocation, income distribution, and the determination of the aggregate level of income, output, employment, and prices. The economy may be functionally defined, *pro tanto*, in terms of the forces and institutions participating in the decision-making resolution of those problems. But the scope of economic policy also encompasses the fourth and more fundamental problem of the structuring of the economic decision-making process itself. In this and other connections the following arguments may be made: the market, considered separately, is itself a policy or decision-making process; policy encompasses more than *government* policy; the economic decision-making process — more extensive than the market and government — includes all forms of non-market and institutional participation; and the structuring of the economic decision-making process is a matter of policy. This latter is indeed, the fundamental level of policy.

With the scope of policy including the structuring of the decision-making process itself, the scope of policy participation encompasses nominally private-market, legal, and non-legal forces. Although traditional economic theory has been limited generally to the analysis of market forces, other bodies of thought, including institutional economics, have been attentive to the participation of both market and non-market institutions and forces in the resolution of the basic economic problems.

The problem of structuring the decision-making process is one facet of the more pervasive problem of order, which may be functionally defined as the continuing resolution of the dual basic social problems of freedom (or autonomy) and control and of continuity and change (Spengler, 1948). Indeed, in the economic realm, the problem of freedom and control takes the form of structuring the economic decision-making process, and the problem of continuity and change often reduces to the problem of restructuring the decisional process. In this and in other respects, economic policy analysis thus necessarily encompasses a theory of social control and a theory of social change. That analysis is made even more complicated inasmuch as the process frequently must at least tend to involve both a theory of society and a theory of history (that is, of social change).

Consequently, the deepest issues of economic policy are inevitably concerned with such elemental questions of policy as whose interests, whose freedom, whose capacity to coerce, who may injure whom, whose rights, and who decides? Moreover, there is the question of specific content: the problem of applying general propositions, rules, or categories to specific instances.

One fundamental dimension pervading the nature of policy, the scope of policy and of policy participation, and the elemental questions of policy is *power*. The problem of structuring and restructuring the economic decision-making process — the problem of the organization and control of economic activity — is essentially a problem of the distribution of power in society. A corollary of that proposition is that the economy is essentially a system of power play, mutual coercion, or jockeying for position. Effective social choice ultimately governs the distribution of power both in

4

society as a whole and in the institutions and relationships that comprise it.

But power is but one of three dimensions of policy. A second is *knowledge*. Policy is a partial function of knowledge of both reality and of values. A theory of economic policy must necessarily include a theory of the organization and application of knowledge in society and a theory of both the determination and the role of knowledge in respect to social or economic policy.

A third dimension of policy is *psychology*. It may be asserted simply that the participation of individuals and groups in the decision-making process is a partial function of complex individual and collective psychic states and motivations and that the effective policies that issue from the decision-making process are, *pro tanto*, a function of the interplay of those psychic states or postures. These conditions hold whether in the context of a corporation, a corporate board of directors, a church, a university, a university department, a family, or, *mutatis mutandis*, a single individual.

Policy (or decision-making), it may be said, is a function of *power*, *knowledge*, and *psychology*. The economist who is concerned with both the evolving structure of the economic system and the allocative and distributional consequences of the economic process must be concerned with policy as to the structure of the economic system and its operational consequences investigated in terms of power, knowledge, and psychology.

It is the premise of this study that the social equilibrium analysis of Pareto's *Treatise on General Sociology* may be interpreted as a theory of economic policy. Accordingly, the nature of policy is choice, the socio-economic system is essentially a decision-making process, the choices are effective choices (as well as incrementally contributing individual choices), the scope of policy includes the structuring of the decisional process itself, and the scope of policy participation includes both market and social forces. Moreover, Pareto's analysis may be interpreted in terms of the dual basic social problems of freedom and control and of continuity and change as they relate to the economic decisional process. In addition, the elemental questions of policy also will be seen to emerge in the context of the foregoing. Finally, and with appropriate credit to the genius of Pareto, it will be seen that his social equilibrium system, interpreted as a theory of economic policy, postulates policy as a function of power, knowledge, and psychology. There are, therefore, in Pareto's *Treatise* the basic problems, ele-

5

mental questions, and general dimensions of a theory or model of economic policy.

In the remaining section of this chapter, Pareto's general system in the *Treatise* will be characterized and outlined. Part One (chapters two through four) will attempt to identify the three dimensions of policy as derived from Pareto's system. Chapter five of Part Two will attempt to chart the making of policy through the interaction of power, knowledge, and psychology as developed in the *Treatise*. Chapters six and seven, also in Part Two, will survey the problems of freedom and control and of continuity and change as they are manifest in the *Treatise* and in the foregoing analysis. Chapter eight will present a partial summary and conclusions.

Before proceeding, a brief digression will be taken. It is one which is highly appropriate in view of the marginalist and equilibrium character of Pareto's economic and social analysis.

The making of policy, including society's economic policy, is a complex process. Policy questions are not generally solved either *in toto* or once and for all time. One does not solve the farm problem, poverty, or air pollution, at one fell swoop; nor does one establish "freedom," "justice," or "security" in one blow. The latter are, for example, problems of policy on an abstract level. Although they are frequently discussed and argued in absolutist and universalist language, in the real world they are multifaceted and are worked out or resolved only incrementally, gradually, and contingently. Economic policy making thus may be characterized as a multivariable system of interdependent variables with magnitudes of possible marginal adjustments (both intensive and extensive) and equilibrium positions theoretically approaching infinity. As Lindblom (1958) has pointed out definitively, policy *making* is in fact incremental, and policy *analysis* accordingly should be incrementalist.

The present author is in definite accord with this view. The opinion that there are certain abstract problems (freedom and control and continuity and change), certain elemental problems, and certain dimensions of policy generic to policy *qua* policy is supplementary not contradictory to the view of Lindblom. The incrementalist analysis of policy can be, and should be, conducted in terms of the problems, elemental questions, and dimensions of a general model of policy; that is, analysis along the lines of such a general model of policy usually must be incrementalist or as incrementalist as the situation warrants or allows. Incremental analysis

6

in the context of such a general model of policy will be seen below to be highly appropriate to the social equilibrium theory of Pareto's *Treatise*.

In addition, it should be pointed out that Pareto attempted in his *Treatise* to create what appears to be a rather grandiose general schema. It is a general social equilibrium model of rather delusive grandeur. In economics, the Walrasian and Paretian general equilibrium model provided an integrating vehicle for many hitherto divergent strands of microeconomic theory. It also provided an heuristic organon for the exploration of new fields and new aspects of old fields. Insofar as traditional economic theory is itself a general model for policy analysis, those roles of general equilibrium theory are even more significant (Lindblom, 1958, p. 299). Another and particularly instructive example, found in sociology, is the effort of Talcott Parsons (among others) to construct a general theory of action. It is particularly instructive because Parson's (1937) initial effort in this cause involved an integration of the work of several forerunners, including Pareto (the others being Alfred Marshall, Emile Durkheim, and Max Weber). Such general models, far from necessarily precluding or hindering, enhance the development of what Merton calls middle-range theories through provision of integrative and interpretive insight (Merton, 1949). Moreover, they are important on their own level of generality.

Still, a sense of perspective and proportion must be retained. In studying any particular theory of economic policy it must be recognized that very real difficulties exist for at least two reasons. First, the construction and interpretation, if not the application, of a theory of policy strongly tends to involve both a theory of society and a theory of history. Second, no theory of policy can be fully specified (Samuels, 1966, pp. 215ff, 286ff). The world is comprised of more specifics than any general theory or model of policy can incorporate, and policy ultimately is a matter of specific content (Samuels, 1966, pp. 129 - 135, 146, 171 - 172, 209 - 223, 263 - 264, 285 - 286). That content is worked out in the real world of decision-making, which is to say, in the interrelations of power, knowledge, and psychology.

## 3. Pareto's General System

Pareto's general aim in the *Treatise* was in principle rather ambitious. His objective was to identify the "forms" that society takes (that is, the basic organization and structure of society), how those forms are determined, and the manner in which variations in the form of society take place (Secs. 15, 145, 1770). The *Treatise* was an attempt to develop a general theory of society and a general theory of social change and to integrate them so as to throw in relief the major variables operating upon the organization of society over time. According to Pareto, earlier sociologists and other writers ignored or neglected these fundamental subjects, and their systems and theories, accordingly, are deficient, incomplete, and superficial. It will be seen below that Pareto sketched a general model of the forces or variables involved in the organization and reorganization of society and then concentrated on the several variables which he considered most important to the sociologist.

In Pareto's view, sociology was a general, that is abstract (Sec. 144; *cf.* Lopreato, 1965, p. 28), synthesis of all the disciplines studying human society: law, political economy, political history, the history of religions, etc. Pareto thought it would be impossible and perhaps even undesirable to specify any very strict definition. Nomenclature and compartmentalization are matters of convenience and, therefore, arbitrary, and change over time (Sec. 1). But the basic objective of Paretian sociology is clear. General sociology would have its own distinctive problem and heuristic function: to construct a general model of social organization and change which was important in its own regard and level of abstraction and which would function as a framework within which the more specialized disciplines could be developed.

Pareto never denigrated economics; he stressed its importance as a separate science (Pareto, in Hamilton, 1962, p. 49). Economics concerns "interests," which relate to material well-being, and is an appropriate subject for abstract analysis, to wit, pure economics (*cf.* Bell, 1967, pp. 467 - 470; Pareto, 1910, p. 139; and Pareto, in Gherity, 1965, p. 413). But Pareto eventually concluded that he had to supplement economics with the results yielded by the other sciences of man and society, since the subject matter of those other sciences bear on problems only nominally economic. Late in life Pareto wrote:

"Having arrived at a certain point in my researches in political economy, I seemed unable to continue ahead. Many obstacles confronted me ... and among these was the truly interdependent relationship which exists among the social phenomena of all sorts. Just as in our times it has come to be realized that the theory of chemistry is linked with that of electricity, and vice

8

versa, so also it is evident that no single social study can progress far without the aid of all the others" (Bell, 1967, p. 466; *cf.* secs. 2408 - 2410).

It is interesting to compare Pareto with Adam Smith. Whereas Smith wrote his *Moral Sentiments* before the *Wealth of Nations*, Pareto's *Cours* and *Manuale* both antedate his *Treatise*. Whereas the *Moral Sentiments* developed the non-legal forces of social control within which market activity is undertaken, the *Treatise* was a theory of society and social structure within which economic interests operate and with which those interests interact.

To Pareto, the relation of economics (particularly but not exclusively pure economics) to sociology was this. Economics must be part of a larger general sociology, ultimately because of the interdependence of nominally economic and sociological variables. Pareto gave the following reasons: economics alone gives only a very incomplete picture of the organization of society; economics is incomplete even with respect to nominally economic problems because economics includes a limited number of variables; man is more than economic man; economic dynamics merge into sociology; the social optimum encompasses more than the economic optimum; and social equilibrium likewise encompasses more than economic equilibrium. The task of general sociology was to supplement the analyses of each of the specialized disciplines with those of the others and thus to create a synthetic theory of the social system and its change. In addition, but to the same effect, Pareto, whose attention was directed equally to the practical (and thus to the manipulative) and to the abstract, also wrote: "Science proceeds by analysis, whereas synthesis is required where practice is concerned" (Pareto, in Hamilton, 1962, p. 48, *cf.* secs. 1919 - 1920).

The central substantive and methodological premise of the *Treatise* — as with Pareto's economics before that — is, then, that society is or may be treated as if it were a multivariable system of interdependent variables. It rests ultimately upon a pervasive interaction between individuals, groups, forces, and so on (sec. 1732). Pareto never tired of reminding his reader of the erroneousness of presuming simple cause - and - effect relationships where, in reality, there are spatial and temporal interdependence, simultaneous and mutually dependent variation, and functional correlation or correspondence (secs. 829, 861, 1731, 2061, and p. 1919; *cf.* Pareto, in Gherity, 1965, p. 378). Henderson wrote earlier that the

9

"central feature" of Pareto's general sociology was "the analysis of mutually dependent variations of his variables" (Henderson, 1937, p. 18; *cf.* p. 13 and *passim*, *cf.* Homans and Curtis, 1934, pp. 33ff). It was Muller's judgment that "Pareto's awareness of intricate interdependencies, multiple causes and effects, endless action and reaction, is one of the soundest and clearest of his perceptions."[2] More recently, Lopreato has stressed that "The central feature of [Pareto's] approach is the analysis of mutually dependent variations of the variables with which he focuses on the social system, together with the analysis of the functions that these variables or 'elements', singly and in combination, discharge for the social system and for various units implicated in it" (Lopreato, 1965, pp. 5 - 6). Several facets noted by Lopreato will be discussed at some length below, but it should be acknowledged at this point that "interdependence and autonomy must, of course, be viewed in relative terms. The units or parts of a social system are not all equally interdependent with, or autonomous from, each other" (Lopreato, 1965, p. 16 n. 21; *cf.* DeVoto, 1933b, .p. 579). The differential character of interdependence, spatially and temporally, is a main theme of Pareto's general premise of interdependence, in sociology as well as economics.

On the basis of the presumption of the interconnectedness and interdependence of social phenomena, in both his economics and his sociology Pareto erected an equilibrium system. In his view, society was or could be analyzed as such a system. As Homans and Curtis expressed it, "Equilibrium is a form that a state of Mutual Dependence may take" (1934, p. 271; *cf.* Lopreato, 1965, p. 5). Consequently, general sociology should and can meaningfully analyze the movement of equilibrium — and the forces of disequilibrium — in human societies. Equilibrium generally was seen by Pareto as a state or position from which there was no tendency to move (*cf.* Pareto, in Gherity, 1965, p. 376), a condition of more or less temporarily (or theoretically) exhausted mutual impact between variables. The economist and sociologist would analyze the theoretical effects of a change in one variable upon other variables, the forces restorative of equilibrium, the correspondence of movements away from and toward equilibrium and the marginal variations in variables. Problems of such a nature would "constitute, at bottom, the theory of the social equilibrium" (Sec. 1586).

It is important to recognize that Pareto's conception was one of a moving equilibrium. Social equilibrium was a function of a continually changing array of forces (to be called "elements") and Pareto's general sociology is an analysis of "society in terms of a moving equilibrium" (Perry, 1935, p. 97). As Amoroso pointed out, Pareto's concept is not one of an ideal configuration "around which the real configuration oscillates now in one direction and now in another." Paretian equilibrium rather is one in which the configurations are open and dynamic, characterized by incessant movement (Amoroso, 1938, p. 6). In addition, Pareto's view is that of a multiequilibrium model, with each of the various "elements" in the social system tending toward its own theoretical equilibrium and all differing from the theoretical general social equilibrium.

"The state of concrete equilibrium observable in a given society is a resultant of all these effects, of all these actions and reactions. It is, therefore, different from a state of theoretical equilibrium obtained by considering one or more of the elements $a$, $b$, $c$, $d$ instead of considering all. Political economy, for instance, deals with category $b$, and one of its branches is pure economics. Pure economics yields a theoretical equilibrium that is different, still within category $b$, from another theoretical equilibrium yielded by applied economics; and different from other theoretical equilibria that could be obtained by combining $b$ with some of the elements $a$, $c$, $d$; and different, again, from the theoretical equilibrium that most nearly approximates the concrete and is obtained by combining all the elements $a$, $b$, $c$, $d$" (Sec. 2207).

The conception of society as an equilibrium of forces was not new, of course, with Pareto (House, 1935, p. 82; cf. Russett, 1966). Timasheff (Timasheff, 1957, pp. 159, 165, 166) nevertheless, has written that Pareto's most important contribution to sociological theory was his conception and elaboration of society as a system in dynamic, imperfect equilibrium. Yet as Perry has pointed out, while Pareto correctly emphasized the importance of the concept of *equilibrium* (and also *system*), he "does not give anything like an adequate analysis" of it.[3] In particular, it will be seen below in chapter seven that Pareto, notwithstanding the dynamic character of equilibrium in his analysis, attributed in his sociology a markedly restrictive and conservative meaning to *equilibrium*, a meaning which confuses but does not destroy his general use of an equilibrium model.

The fundamental thrust of Pareto's equilibrium treatment of interdependence is the identification and analysis of the social system *as a system* (Henderson, 1935, p. 4; Lopreato, 1965, pp. 5, 6, 13, 20). Pareto was one of the first to conceptualize society as a system, one property of which was interdependence. In his view, society is characterized by forces, or "elements," and these elements "constitute a system, which we may call the 'social system'." [4] As such, it is the product of "all the elements in it acting upon it and upon each other and it in turn reacting upon them" (MacPherson, 1937, p. 464). Pareto's attempt to delineate society as a system was undoubtedly one of his most seminal contributions. [5] No small quantum of sociological theory reflects the significance of this attempt, most particularly that of Talcott Parsons who deliberately used and transformed Pareto's analysis in his own studies (Parsons, 1951, p. vii; *cf*. Martindale, 1960, pp. 485, 499). Parsons, for example, found in the *Treatise* the germ of what he called "the sociologistic theorem, that society is a reality *sui generis*; it has properties not derivable from those of its constituent units by direct generalization" (Parsons, 1937, p. 248; *cf*. pp. 459, 464, and *passim*). The remainder of this section will be primarily devoted to a specification of the elements which comprise Pareto's general social model. The additional property of the social system developed by Pareto at great length, namely, utility (Sec. 2105ff and *passim*), will be discussed in chapter two.

It may be reiterated at this point that Pareto's analysis of the social system was an admixture of organicist, mechanistic, and functionalist theorizing. Controversy exists as to whether and on what terms Pareto may be classified as one or the other and, particularly, on how far he transcended biological organicism for mechanism and/or, ultimately, functionalism. [6] There can be little question that Pareto treated words, religion, socialism, theories, and the like in terms of their more or less ambiguous social function. He differentiated between subjective and objective and between truth value and social utility in such a manner that, generally considered, objective social utility in some contexts is a rough equivalent to social function, (Secs. 7, 13, 14, 69, 81, 259 - 260, 304, 346, 366, 615 - 616, 1695, 1859, 1932n.2, and *passim*) for example "relating to the doctrines as viewed in connexion with individuals and their functions in society" (Sec. 1896). Although a clear formulation of functional prerequisites was not presented in the *Treatise* one was implied, and implied so clearly that Pareto's analysis has been and may still be restated in terms of several (as is done, in effect, below). The same is true of the distinction between latent and manifest function (Lopreato, 1965,

12

pp. 15 - 22). But Pareto's *Treatise* also has or reflects strains of organicist and, particularly, mechanistic (or physicalistic) theorizing. [7]

The controversy is difficult to resolve because all three elements are manifest in the *Treatise* and because the controversy is largely retrospective and exegetical. It is further difficult to resolve because it is still an open-ended matter as to just what makes a theory or model "functionalist." Furthermore, both mechanistic and organicist theorizing, on the one hand, and functionalist theorizing, on the other, need not be mutually exclusive (*cf.* Nagel, 1961, chapters 12, 14). The controversy need not be resolved — if that be possible — for present purposes. Suffice it to say that Pareto deliberately attempted to consider social phenomena from what has been called a functionalist perspective in some if not many respects; that he was impressed with and tried to emulate, analogize with, and structure his system along the general lines of mechanistic or physicalist models; and that in both respects his analysis evidences at least some vestiges of organicism. [8]

Transcending all such disputation, however, is the fact of Pareto's attempt to construct an empiricist or positivist — he called it "logico-experimental" — *science* of society. This attempt greatly impressed those who were quite early intoxicated with the *Treatise*, although the extent of Pareto's success in this respect — even by his own criteria — has long been open to question. Pareto's approach to science is an important facet of his theory of knowledge and its role and determination in society, and it will be discussed *in extenso* below, beginning with chapter two.

The substance of Pareto's analysis in the *Treatise* is comprised of what he called the "elements." As already has been seen, there is a reciprocal and interdependent relationship between the form of society and the elements and within and between the elements themselves (Sec. 2060). Equilibrium in the Paretian general social system is a function of the interaction between and within the elements. In the context of the present study, social policy results from the interplay of the forces and other factors subsumed under the several classes of elements. These are, in principle, rather all-encompassing and exhaustive and incorporate what is normally within the scope of all physical and social sciences, including both those variables possibly considered as policy or choice variables (for example, psychological, economic, political, and sociological factors) and those variables typically considered as (at least short run) constraints upon choice (for example, geographic and natural resource factors). As already indicated, Pareto examined several of these selectively and intensively, having treated the economic — the interests — in the *Cours* and *Manuale*, and only acknowledged the remainder. It should perhaps also be reiterated that "Pareto's basic model is of a very general nature," however much "it was intended to be widely applicable in the analysis of the social phenomenon" (Lopreato, 1965, p. 28).

In Pareto's general model there are three broad classes of elements: *physical conditions, external elements,* and *internal elements.* By *physical conditions* Pareto had in mind the terrestrial physical and nonhuman environment of man, epitomized by him as "soil, climate, flora, fauna, geological, mineralogical, and other like conditions." By *external elements* Pareto specified the "elements external to a given society at a given time, such as the influences of other societies upon it — external, therefore, in space; and the effects of the previous situation within it — external, therefore, in time." By *internal elements,* Pareto meant the forces contemporarily within any society, "chief among them" being what he called race, residues, proclivities, aptitudes for thought and observation, the state of knowledge, and derivations (Sec. 2060), as well as social heterogeneity and class circulation.

Through what may be called a triple filtering or reduction process, Pareto tended to narrow his focus progressively so as to concentrate more intensively on certain of the elements and their components. First, he excluded the physical conditions. While their influence "is undoubtedly very important," he made "no direct examination" (Sec. 2064) of them in the *Treatise,* acknowledging their relevance only as he considered necessary and as points through which other elements had their effect. So also with external elements.

Second, in analyzing the class of internal elements, Pareto concentrated upon four: residues, derivations, social heterogeneity, and class circulation. About the others — race, proclivities, aptitudes for thought and observation, and the state of knowledge — Pareto had little to say. He generally passed over them, except, of course, for interests, which he discussed but did not examine thoroughly in the *Treatise.* In a moment, the four internal elements upon which Pareto concentrated, together with interests, will be briefly identified.

Third, with respect to the residues, Pareto identified and examined intensively six classes. When he focused upon the forces governing the form of society — one of which is the residues generally

— he filtered out four of these, maintaining that these four are so constituted as to have their impact or influence exercised largely through one of the other two. These two residues are thus analyzed as interacting with social heterogeneity and class circulation (frequently considered together), as well as with the derivations and the interests. Indeed, it will be seen below that Pareto *tended* to concentrate on the interests and the residues (and here only the two classes of the six), "on the ground that many of the other elements have their influence on society only through their influence on residues and interests, and that, therefore, in studying the residues and interests you are studying all the other elements as well, at the point where they have their effect on the form of society" (MacPherson, p. 464; *cf.* p. 463).

There is some exaggeration in the foregoing, for in the *Treatise* Pareto did not discuss the interests as intensively as he did the residues. In addition, power play — through social heterogeneity and class circulation — was a main dimension of his analysis (although not given a distinctive name). Yet it may be said with some accuracy that, to Pareto, power play was a "point where" interests and residues "have their effect on the form of society." Moreover, it is important to recognize that in Pareto's system of mutual interdependence, the reverse is also true. For example, in writing of "the influence upon a given people of other peoples," Pareto maintains that the "military, political, intellectual, economic, and other kinds of power through which those influences have been exerted depend upon elements such as sentiments, state of knowledge, and interests; and the influences, therefore, may be inferred, in part at least, from those elements" (Sec. 2065). However, the same may be said of each of the three main variables of Pareto's general model of policy. Power, knowledge, and psychology are each points, or vectors, through which the others have their effect.

Pareto thus concentrated his attention and analysis upon four internal elements — residues, derivations, social heterogeneity, and class circulation — together with a fifth, less intensively analyzed internal element, interests. Before briefly identifying these five as background for the following chapters, it should be pointed out that Pareto differentiated between logico-experimental and non-logico-experimental knowledge, and between logical and non-logical conduct. It will be seen in chapter two that, to Pareto, knowledge was broadly of two kinds: first, logico-experimental, or scientific, a blend of theory and empirical verification; and, second, non-logico-experimental, or metaphysical, or non-verifiable, pseudo-knowledge. What Pareto meant by "the state of knowledge" was logico-experimental or scientifically demonstrated knowledge. Most of what men accept as "knowledge," according to Pareto, is not of this type. What he meant by the "derivations" was pseudo-knowledge, that is, rationalizations, pseudo-explanations, and the like. Belief in the derivations was held by Pareto to be a matter of their accordance with sentiments manifest in the residues. Conduct was logical when, generally, it proceeded from an objective assessment of means and ends; it was non-logical when it was dominated or governed by the emotions (that is, the residues). Most of human conduct, according to Pareto, was of the latter type. With these distinctions and emphases in mind, attention may be directed to a brief identification of the five primary elements in Pareto's general system, four of which will necessarily be developed intensively in the following chapters. Only interests need be examined in some detail at this point.

In the Paretian system, *interests* are what Lopreato calls "largely the logical, goal-oriented elements of conduct that provide the basic data for the science of economics" (Lopreato, 1965, p. 7). In the words of Pareto in the *Treatise*

"Individuals and communities are spurred by instinct and reason to acquire possession of material goods that are useful — or merely pleasurable — for purposes of living, as well as to seek consideration and honours. Such impulses, which may be called 'interests,' play in the mass a very important part in determining the social equilibrium" (Sec. 2009).

Clearly, Pareto included in *interests* not only material well-being, capital and wealth accumulation, and consumer satisfaction, but also such traditionally non-economic ends as status and honor. But, he continued, "That mass of interests falls in very considerable part within the purview of the science of economics..." (Sec. 2010). Indeed, "... it has been possible to constitute a general science of interests, the science of economics, which assumes that logico-experimental reasonings exclusively are used in certain branches of human activity." (Sec. 2146). Thus, economics proceeds by virtue of the economic man or rationality assumption, (Secs. 262 - 263, 2146, and *passim*), although Pareto explicitly recognized that *interests* (for example, consumer demands) are a function of taste and, therefore, are non-logical: "In the economic system the non-logical element is relegated entirely to tastes and

16

disregarded, since tastes are taken as data of fact" (Sec. 2079). Status and honor are also relevant because, on the same level as given tastes, "the objective is known and the quest is for the means best suited to reaching it" (Sec. 2146).

Ultimately, then, *interests* have to do with wealth (economic welfare) and power, as well as status and honor (Parsons, 1937, p. 298, Spengler, 1944, p. 124 n. 1). The production of wealth is thus a conspicuous criterion of judgment and valuation, indeed of objective social utility (Secs. 1779, 2301, 2316, and *passim*). Generally speaking, however, following DeVoto (1933b, p. 579) *interests* relate to human interests as citizen of a particular country, as head of a particular family, as member of a particular political party, as taxpayer, as one engaged in a particular economic pursuit or occupation. The policy process, to transfer from Amoroso's context to that of the present study, is a process in which there is the play and pushings of this or that private interest, whether it be in the market or in politics (Amoroso, 1938, pp. 13 - 16).

Pareto has already been quoted to the effect that *interests* are a function of "instinct and reason." It will be seen in a moment that the *residues* are considered by Pareto to be manifestations of underlying *sentiments*. Upon what do the *interests* rest? According to Pareto, these also are a function of sentiments. [9] "But they are of such great intrinsic importance in the social equilibrium that they are best considered apart from residues" (Sec. 1207). As Parsons pointed out, "Pareto treats the interests as variable independently of the residues and the sentiments they manifest." (Parsons, 1937, p. 609; *cf.* Spengler, 1944, p. 124 n. 1). This is largely because of the greater play of logico-experimental reasonings and logical conduct in the identification of and quest for attainment of *interests* (Aron, 1970, pp. 171 - 173). *Interests* are a function of sentiments and reason; residues are a manifestation of *sentiments*. (There are also what Pareto called "simple appetites" and "inclinations;" like tastes and the residues they are also a function of the sentiments, and like tastes they are taken as data by the sociologist and economist (Secs. 851, 2013)).

Of the four main elements developed at length in the *Treatise*, the *residues* were beyond doubt the most important to Pareto. He understood that human beings are complex personalities with complex motivations. Underlying behavior were what he called the residues, or identifiable manifest psychic tendencies or personality components. The residues, in turn, were held to be the manifestation of underlying *sentiments*, which are unconscious or subcon-

17

scious and non-operationally determinable drives. Together, the residues and sentiments comprise what may be called the complex psychic states or postures which delineate the motivational personality of the human being. It is one of the main themes of Pareto's *Treatise* that both social equilibrium and the form of society are a function of the aggregate interplay of human sentiments manifest in the residues, that is, of psychic states. In terms of policy analysis, the thrust of Pareto's argument is that policy is, *pro tanto*, a function of psychology.

The *derivations* are the arguments, rationalizations, justifications, reasoning, ideologies, and pseudo-demonstrations by which non-logico-experimental explanations for natural phenomena are maintained and by which statements of value are presented as statements of fact. The derivations function to mask non-logical belief and conduct, to make both *appear* as logical. Moreover, appearance is functional both *vis-a-vis* other persons and to assuage one's own compulsions. Derivations are essentially secondary to the residues. Behavior is held by Pareto to be a function of the sentiments and not the derivations. The relationship, in Pareto's analysis, as will be seen below, is much more complicated than this. In any event, the thrust of Pareto's analysis, in this and other respects, is that policy is, *pro tanto*, a function of knowledge of one sort or another.

By *social heterogeneity* Pareto meant simply, yet profoundly, that "Human societies are essentially heterogeneous," (Sec. 2172; *cf.* 1882) "that individuals are physically, morally, and intellectually different" (Sec. 2025). Amplified, social heterogeneity connotes, first, social stratification and differential mobility (Lopreato, 1965, p. 7); second, differential abilities, including intelligence (Perry, 1935, p. 99; Borkenau, 1936, pp. 106ff); and third, differential interests and attachments by virtue of family, occupation, and institutional involvements (Henderson, 1937, p. 16). Social heterogeneity signifies, further, both individual and class differences. On the level of the individual, it reflects Pareto's emphasis that individuals are complex personalities variously motivated, such that individual differences reflect or correspond with differences in the relative intensity or strength of the various residues (or the sentiments which give rise to them), particularly the first two classes of residues (Ginsberg, 1936, pp. 240 - 241). But there is also the impact of environment,[10] as one would expect given Pareto's system of general interdependence.

On the level of social class, the element of class *circulation*

18

derives from the fact that society is divided into more or less ambiguous social classes, ultimately into elite and subject classes, and that over time there is interclass interaction which results in, ultimately, the circulation of the elite, that is, the movement of individuals and their progeny from one class to another. Social heterogeneity and class circulation thus are integrally related, and Pareto eventually considered them as one combined element for model-building and analytical purposes (Secs. 2205ff). The significance of both elements, perhaps particularly when seen in combination (*Treatise*, chapter 12), is the jockeying for position and power which enables the proposition that policy is, *pro tanto*, a function of power (or power play).

As an overview, it should be clear that Pareto's general sociological model encompassed both market and non-market activity and decision-making; that it was an equilibrium model based upon a set of interdependent variables or elements; that it delineated society as a system; and that in developing the foregoing he utilized strains of functionalism, mechanism, and organicism to describe and analyze society as a continuing process. In addition, Pareto's model incorporated three classes of elements: physical, external, and internal. With respect to the latter category, the primary internal variables were interests, residues, derivations, social heterogeneity, and class circulation.

To somewhat the same effect but elaborating slightly, one generally may state the major theorems of Pareto's sociology. Society is an equilibrium system of interdependent parts or variables with an inherent tendency for the restoration of equilibrium through the role of the sentiments (or, more directly, the residues). The non-logical (belief and action) predominates in social life. Justification-explanation is caused by and is not causative of behavior (with the corollary that the substance of derivations is essentially accidental *vis-a-vis* the behavior whose justification-explanation is involved), although with some qualifications. Finally, society generally is stratified into classes, with a ruling or elite class, and with a circulatory movement in and out of the elite class (Timasheff, 1957, pp. 158 - 166).

In terms of a general model of policy, Pareto's general social model may be interpreted in terms of the fundamental proposition that socio-economic policy is a function of knowledge, psychology, and power. Insofar as it involved a theory of society and a theory of history, [11] Pareto's model further may be specified in terms of the dual basic social problems of freedom and control and of continuity and change. As already indicated, the procedure here will be to develop Pareto's theories concerning, first, the three dimensions of knowledge, psychology, and power; second, their interaction; and third, the meaning of the foregoing in terms of freedom and control and of continuity and change.

One final consideration. Pareto's general social model in the *Treatise* (considering that it assumed and extended his earlier economic model) is a sociology, a psychology, and an economics. Whether the *Treatise* is primarily a sociology or a psychology will be examined in the next chapter. As an economics, the *Treatise* has been interpreted by some as evidencing economic determinism. Suranyi-Unger (1931, p. 141; *cf.* Clerc, 1942, p. 591), for example, points out that "one can detect a flirtation with historical materialism." There is no question that the interests (that is, the economic element) is a most significant variable in Pareto's estimation. The point is, however, that the influence of the interests is but one chain or sequence of effects among several; to Pareto, it is a part — indeed an important part — but not the whole. Ideas (derivations included), among other social phenomena, are a partial function of conditions in which economic interests and forces are important components. But the residues, the derivations, and the combination of social heterogeneity and class circulation also influence economic interests and forces. "Economic determinism," wrote Pareto,

"... was a notable forward step for social science, bringing out as it did the contingent character of certain phenomena, such as morals and religion, which many people regarded and still regard as proclaiming absolute verities. Undoubtedly, moreover, it contains an element of truth in that it takes account of the interdependence of economic and other social factors. Its error lies in representing that interdependence as a relation of cause and effect" (Sec. 829).

Again, it is "the error of substituting the part for the whole and disregarding the other" interdependencies or mutual dependencies (Sec. 2206; *cf.* 1586, 2146, 2205, 2207). The rule of interdependence applied to this question is simply this: "... sentiments *depend* on economic conditions, just as economic conditions *depend* on sentiments; and ... there are similar correlations among the other elements" (Sec. 2097, *cf.* Amoroso, 1938, p. 12). Economic determinism, then, is oversimplified one-way causation; and it was

20

one of Pareto's objectives to demonstrate that such was not the case. That he stressed certain elements (such as interests and the residues) as primary variables is hardly economic determinism as that theory or concept is usually employed. It is rather the specification of several important *interdependent* variables (Aron, 1970, p. 181).

There is one interesting respect in which economic determinism appears to be present in Pareto's work, though this may be but a vestige of styles of thought used by him in his economic analysis, as in the *Manuale* (Ricci, 1933, pp. 16 - 17; Pareto, in Gherity, 1965, p. 384). Whereas, for example, Toynbee later was to examine the moving social disequilibrium, as it were, in terms of challenge and response (and there are suggestions of this in Pareto's *Treatise*), Pareto generally conceived of and specified equilibrium in terms of the "contrast" of or interplay between *tastes* and *obstacles* (or constraints, or "ties") (Schumpeter, 1951, p. 125). The obstacles include limitations of cost (dependent upon technology) and limitations upon the individual imposed through social control forces, but basically the obstacles derive from scarcity of resources and opportunities. (Amoroso, 1938, pp. 5 - 6) In this sense — that is, in the sense of Robbinsian scarcity — there is an independent *economic* "force" on an abstract level. But such a view is conventional with economists who are not economic determinists (except as non-economists might infer from the usual preoccupation of orthodox economists with "economic" factors). In this respect, Pareto not only was conventional, but also took as one of his major themes the point that tastes (that is, the interests) were but one of several major interdependent elements. One might add, incidentally, that if Pareto errs it is not (or not so much) on the side of making his model too restrictive; rather it is in leaving it somewhat loosely constructed. But this is to say only that it is a general model and an approximate, probing one at that.

# *Part one:*

# The Three Dimensions of Policy

The objective of Part One is to establish the three major dimensions or sets of variables of policy — knowledge, psychology, and power — as they were understood by Pareto and developed in his general sociology in the *Treatise*. They will be discussed in the order just given and only sufficiently to establish their identity and general meaning in the Paretian system, although anticipation of later themes will be unavoidable. In Part Two, "The Making of Policy," the major Paretian themes will be developed through consideration of their interrelationship or interdependence.

# Chapter 2.

# Policy as a Function of Knowledge

Policy is a partial function of knowledge in that positions taken, ends defined, and means evaluated and employed, all *pro tanto* depend upon what is accepted as knowledge. Policy reflects what people believe. For that reason, if no other, what people believe is no less important than what people should believe. This is true on the individual and subgroup levels as well as on the more abstract level of social policy. Knowledge relates to several elements: the general cosmology of time and place; the particular attributed definition of a situation; the definitions of terms, concepts, and problems; the starting points, principles, or theorems used in drawing conclusions and making choices; and whatever is considered relevant (and/or conclusive) evidence for intuitive, inductive or deductive testing. Social policy, that is, society's effective policy choices producing the structure, conduct and performance of the economy, derives, *pro tanto*, from the interplay of different cosmologies, ideologies or theologies; different definitions of a problem or situation; different definitional tautologies; and, *inter alia*, different bodies of "knowledge." Furthermore, knowledge is essentially cognizance of reality and of values.

Epistemology is that branch of philosophy which inquires into the meaning of meaning, that is, into the different grounds of meaning and thus different connotations of meaningfulness as between different claimants to knowledge. Knowledge is accepted or rejected according to its credentials as knowledge, and epistemology is the considered quest as to the meaning of those credentials. Pareto began his *Treatise* with, grounded his sociology upon, and substantively developed his sociological analysis with a major epistemological differentiation. The fact of that distinction and its importance with respect to those uses establishes *knowledge* as a major variable for social equilibrium and, by extension, of policy in the Paretian system.

## 1. Logico-experimental and Non-logico-experimental Knowledge

Pareto was rather sophisticated concerning the incidence of "knowledge" in social equilibrium and the form of society, and, therefore, in socio-economic policy. He recognized that disputes may be settled in two ways: by argument, that is, by whatever is accepted (or what one side induces the other side to accept) as knowledge, and "by force of arms," (Sec. 594 n. 1) that is, by the use of power. (The question of differentiating the power that is argument or persuasion from the power that is arms will be discussed in chapter four.) He also was aware of the question as to who gains and who loses from a particular theory: "What advantage (or disadvantage) does the theory itself have for the person who puts it forward, and for the person who accepts it?"[1] (Sec. 14). Policy positions are seen as a function of the definition of one's interests, which is a function of differential awareness of one's own best interests (Sec. 2250). Pareto understood the policies ensnared in, obfuscated by, and sanctioned through the use of such words as *legitimate* and *criminal.* He also understood that prospective policy was a function of the continuing definition or connotation thereof (Secs. 2163, 2177). He realized that social reform (that is, policy with respect to continuity and change) was a partial function of what one considers knowledge to be, and in this respect he critically interpreted Walras (Sec. 1732 n. 2; and Pareto, 1910, pp. 138, 139; cf. Clerc, 1942, p. 588).

Pareto, it has already been seen, maintained that logico-experimental knowledge was one of the elements in social equilibrium (Timasheff, 1940, p. 149), but he also stressed the relative absence of data as a limitation upon logico-experimental decision-making, that is, decisions reached through the use of reason (Sec. 2143). Yet, above all, Pareto stressed that knowledge at any time was comprised not only of logico-experimental reasonings but also of non-logico-experimental understanding. As will be seen below, knowledge is a function of both scientific reason and emotion, and one's knowledge on any subject generally has components of both.[2] There is, acknowledgement, in effect, of what Dilthey called *verstehen* and of what Hayek referred to as the non-deliberative collective wisdom; as supplements in one way or another both supplement science. Even more significant is Pareto's insistence that most knowledge is essentially non-logico-experimental and that, therefore, most conduct is non-logical.

Before proceeding to Pareto's differentiation between logico-experimental and non-logico-experimental knowledge, several points should be made. These anticipate discussions in this and later chapters.

First, generally speaking, there are, two approaches to the relation of knowledge and social policy. The Platonic position is that knowledge is knowledge of the ideal, of what *should* be; this knowledge is derived from that which *is*. The Aristotelian position maintains that knowledge is knowledge of what *is* and therefore of what has status because it *is*. Platonism urges that knowledge is the ideal derived from existent reality, whereas Aristotelianism urges that the important knowledge is that of reality itself. In the context of the relation of knowledge and social policy, the former is a philosophy of potential reform, and the latter a philosophy of conservatism. Pareto, it will be seen, is essentially Aristotelian respecting knowledge and the relation of knowledge to social policy. His emphasis upon logico-experimental knowledge, or science, inherently stresses what *is* (versus what *ought* to be, insofar as this differs from what *is*). This is a conservative interpretation of science, an *ought*-tending interpretation of *is*, or what Muller (1938, p. 437) differentiates as *being* as opposed to *becoming*. The first point, then, is that Pareto's concept of science, *inter alia*, is status quo oriented. It is not the function of theory or science to create but rather to explain what exists. In the process, there is a tendency to legitimize the status quo since the theories which scientifically explain it tend to cast luster upon it.

Second, it is important to acknowledge Pareto's repeated and insistent theme that knowledge is different from and may be contrary to social utility. What is socially useful may not be (scientifically) true, and what is true may not be socially useful. This point and the next three are discussed in this chapter.

Third, closely related to the second theme are Pareto's theories of the role of derivations, the rationalization of non-logical conduct, and theories transcending experience.

Fourth, Pareto recognized the valuational character of science, notwithstanding the fact that science formally deals with matters of *is* and not *ought*.

27

Fifth, although Pareto rather denigrated the valuational process in society, that process is, as Parsons has shown, necessarily built into the Paretian analysis. The substance of this study will explicate the decision-making elements of that valuational process.

Sixth, the major Paretian theme of the psychological foundations of knowledge will be developed in chapter five.

Seventh, Pareto's notions concerning knowledge as relating to power play and to social control are discussed in chapters four and six, respectively.

Eighth, and finally, Pareto's conservative posture with respect to social change is developed in chapter seven.

To return to the main argument, social equilibrium or policy is a partial function of knowledge, that is, of whatever people accept as knowledge as a basis for effective choice. Pareto urged that there are two theoretically distinct types of knowledge, at least as pure types, the *logico-experimental* and *non-logico-experimental*. Together with his differentiation between logical and non-logical conduct and his insistence upon the predominance of the non-logical in human affairs, this distinction is at the heart of his substantive contribution to sociological theory.

Pareto's category of logico-experimental knowledge is in the tradition of empiricism, positivism, science, logical-empiricism, and operationalism.[3] According to Pareto, that part of human knowledge is logico-experimental which results from attempts to discover empirical uniformities through tests establishing the conformability of those uniformities with the world of experience (Secs. 86, 1403, and *passim*).

Logico-experimental knowledge relates to what can be experienced (Secs. 18, 29, 546, 593, 617, 977, 1665, 2001, and pp.1922–1924) and its status as empiric knowledge is relative, contingent,[4] and probabilistic (Sec. 1924), with general but not absolute principles on an "as if" basis. It is a blend of deduction and induction,[5] but its distinctive characteristic is that it relates to experiential and therefore experimental reality. It thus relates to what is[6] rather than to what might be, and it is in a state of continual development. The process is one of making successive and contingent approximations as to the nature of the uniformities empirically discovered and tested (*Treatise*, p. 1925).

Non-logico-experimental knowledge, on the other hand, relates to things lying in whole or in part outside the world of experience and, therefore, experiment (Sec. 1923). Its conclusions concern and/or are offered as the *a priori*,[7] certain, absolute, necessary,[8] and immutable, although they vary from writer to writer.[9] Non-logico-experimental statements tend to blend non-verifiable statements of fact and of value; to invoke higher principles (Sec. 531); be dogmatic, exclusivist, and absolutist (Secs. 408, 1420); use "indeterminate words and defective reasonings" (Sec. 408; cf. Secs. 493, 606n.1, 609 - 610, 872, 1086, 1469, 1786); to deal with metaphysical entities (Secs. 62, 2540) and essences;[10] ascribe objective existence to both arguments and the pseudo-objects of emotions (Secs. 1429, 1689); and, thus, be generally beyond the world of experience[11] and proof.[12] In general, the non-logico-experimental is the world of the metaphysical (Sec. 62), theological, and ideological (Secs. 378, 404ff, 408, 1086, 1538; and 613, 1793, 1794). In a word, it is the world of "theories transcending experience" (Treatise, chapter 4). Compared with the empirical confirmation test of the logico-experimental (Sec. 565), the non-logico-experimental is mere assertion,[13] and requires the direct support of faith or conviction.[14]

Pareto urged that logico-experimental knowledge is merely different from and not demonstrably intrinsically or epistemologically superior to non-logico-experimental knowledge.[15] But he carried his argument two steps further. First, he maintained that knowledge as it is found in society is a blend of both types and that the non-logico-experimental predominates in that blend. The logico-experimental is a relevant but nevertheless minor element in the social equilibrium. The first five chapters of the Treatise, indeed, the Treatise as a whole, is a probing demonstration of the extent and roles of the non-logical in thought and behavior in human society. It was Pareto's forte to puncture the complacently believed pseudo-knowledge of the non-logico-experimental world. Second, sociology (and the social "sciences" generally) had been primarily non-logico-experimental.[16] Pareto argued that sociology should and Paretian sociology would endeavor to substitute careful observation and analysis, that is, reason, for emotion, empiricism for a priorism, and logico-experimental for non-logico-experimental truth (Sec. 1405; cf. Bousquet, 1928, p. 17). Pareto firmly believed that his treatment of sociology in the Treatise was purely logico-experimental. The reader is reminded of this numerous times, a manifestation perhaps of Pareto's anxiety on the matter. However, many writers have concluded that the Treatise is, by Pareto's own standards, non-logico-experimental.[17]

Pareto argued, then, that social equilibrium was a partial function of knowledge of reality and that knowledge was a blend of both logico-experimental and non-logico-experimental knowledge with the latter predominating. In connection with this, Pareto made two basic distinctions which he applied throughout the *Treatise*. First, he differentiated between *objective* and *subjective* aspects of the study of phenomena. According to Pareto, the *objective* aspect is "without reference to the person who" believes certain alleged knowledge thereof "or to the person who assents to it" (Sec. 13). It concerns the phenomenon "as it is in reality" (Sec. 149). The *subjective* aspect concerns that phenomenon "with reference" (Sec. 13) to the knowing persons, that is to say, as the phenomenon "presents itself to the mind of this or that human being" (Sec. 149; *cf.* Henderson, 1937, p. 98). Thus, logico-experimental knowledge or truth relates to that which is objectively confirmable through experience or experiment, as contrasted with that which is purely or substantially subjective. Pareto pointed out, moreover, that notwithstanding the juxtaposition and dichotomy embodied in the differentiation (and the names given), "In reality both are subjective, for all human knowledge is subjective. They are to be distinguished not so much by any difference in nature as in view of the greater or lesser fund of factual knowledge that we ourselves have."[18]

Second, Pareto differentiated between *real* and *virtual* movements. A movement is defined by Pareto as a "transition from one state to another." A *real* movement is one which the sociologist would expect to occur on the basis of given conditions: "if we assume conditions and active influences as given, the various successive states of the group are determined. Such movements are called *real* in mechanics, and may be so called in sociology." On the other hand, *virtual* movements are those arising from an injected change of one or more of the conditions: "If, ... we assume as suppressed ... some condition in a sociological group, ... the sociological group will attain states other than those it really attains [that is, other than that or those it would have attained if left unchanged]."[19] Knowledge, argued Pareto, is a blend of both types, that is, a blend of what is and of what might be (Sec. 521); but he held that sociology properly should persevere to attain essentially knowledge of real movements. Several aspects of this will be discussed below, particularly in chapter seven.

Logico-experimental-knowledge is both objective and concerned with real movements, that is, with what is, at least in principle. Non-logico-experimental knowledge deals with the subjective or non-experiential and/or is subjective in procedure and is further non-operational or non-experiential insofar as it is concerned with virtual movements.

## 2. Logical and Non-logical Conduct

Given the differentiation between logico-experimental and non-logico-experimental knowledge, Pareto made a somewhat parallel distinction between *logical* and *non-logical* conduct. As Timasheff stresses, Pareto's basic substantive theorem, once again, is that of "the predominance of nonlogical action in social life."[20] The *Treatise* is an exploration of the enormous incidence, extent, and significance of non-logical conduct, just as it is with respect to non-logico-experimental reasoning and belief. And just as knowledge is a blend of logico-experimental and non-logico-experimental, so also did Pareto argue that conduct is a blend of logical and non-logical actions (Secs. 273, 2143, 2146; *cf.* Parsons, 1936, pp. 247, 261). Moreover, actions are intrinsically neither logical nor non-logical (Borkenau, 1936, p. 92).

Pareto's distinction between logical and non-logical conduct has been found confusing by some but the thrust of his analysis remains reasonably clear. Pareto defined *logical conduct* as "actions that logically conjoin means to ends not only from the standpoint of the subject performing them, but from the standpoint of other persons who have a more extensive knowledge — in other words, to actions that are logical both subjectively and objectively in the sense just explained. Other actions we shall call non-logical (by no means the same as 'illogical')" (Sec. 150). Pareto thus defined logical conduct in terms of the efficacy of means to ends, as that conduct which is logical with respect to means and ends relationships from both objective and subjective aspects. It will be noted that the definitional scope is that of the conjoining of means to ends. On the next page, Pareto specified that logical actions are those in which "The objective end and the subjective purpose are identical." Non-logical actions are those in which "The objective end differs from the subjective purpose."[21] In other words, logical conduct involves actions that both subjectively and, particularly, objectively may be said to lead to the attainment of the end sought. Several pages later Pareto further specified that "Non-logical actions originate chiefly in definite psychic states, sentiments, subconscious feelings, and the like" (Sec. 161).

The scope of non-logical conduct is coextensive with human

31

action: Pareto gathered examples and evidence from almost every nook and cranny of activity with which he was familiar. More specifically, he found elements of non-logical conduct (in terms of means being not objectively related to the achievement of ends) and, of course, belief in the use of or reliance upon magic, superstition, oracles, omens, wishful thinking, and fantasy. The scope of the non-logical extended to include custom, habit, folkways, mores, morals, religion, taboos, law (Secs.256, 400, 466, 809, and *passim*; *cf.* Timasheff, 1940, pp. 143ff), sense of duty, imitation, and thus a good deal of the basic stuff of life, to wit, culture in general.[22] Non-logical conduct has developed spontaneously according to Pareto, but it also has been manufactured (manifest function), although he doubts that the manipulative or manufactured portion is significant (Secs. 313, 1003 - 1007, 1122, 1124). This is a position which conflicts somewhat with the scope and importance he placed on manipulation in general. The conflict partially may be reconciled through recognition of his point that manipulation is a function of position, power play, and psychic states and is entered into largely as a matter of course, although the deliberate manipulation is present; see *infra*. Logical conduct includes most notably economic activity, but as already has been pointed out, there is in such activity the non-logical conduct element of tastes which, for economics, "are taken as data of fact" (Sec. 2079).

Pareto was understandably ambivalent as to the relative *desirable* importance of logical and non-logical conduct and the beliefs related thereto. On the one hand, a Hayekian received collective wisdom is acknowledged and extolled ("a stupid individual instinctively following beaten paths that have been counselled by long experience may be a blessing to his country") (Sec. 1397n.2; *cf.* Roll, 1956, p. 410). On the other, the primary thrust of the *Treatise* itself, indeed, its very *raison d'etre*, is the superimposition of logico-experimental analysis upon non-logical conduct and non-logico-experimental thought.[23] As Livingston seconded in his introductory editorial note to the English-language edition, Pareto supported "the methods by which the rational state of mind can be cultivated in the face of the countless pitfalls that environment, sentiments, the struggle for life, strew in our way" (*Treatise*, Vol. I, p. vi). Nonetheless, Pareto attempted to demonstrate objectively two propositions: logico-experimental truth (and thus logical conduct) differed from social utility, and simply because beliefs or conduct lacked a logical or objective basis did not mean that they necessarily had no social utility, a theme which will be examined at length later in this chapter. Indeed, the rise of reason over emotion (at least as a tendency) was seen by Pareto as but a phase in history (Sec. 2393; *cf.* chapter seven, *infra*). Some commentators have been unable to stomach the Paretian (and Freudian) emphasis upon the existence and pervasiveness of the non-logical (or non-rational). Some have been unable to accept without flinching the proposition that non-logical behavior and belief may have a social function whether or not they are dignified by the term *utility*.

Talcott Parsons has been one of the most penetrating analysts of Pareto's distinction between logical and non-logical conduct (particularly with respect to the problem of values, which is discussed below).[24] According to Parsons, non-logical conduct is, in Pareto's system, a genuine residual category (Parsons, 1936, pp. 248, 261), but it is ambiguous because it contains recourse to objective and subjective, means and ends, and empiric and non-empiric information. There is no need to examine Parsons' analysis in detail. As he and others have pointed out, Pareto tended to define logical conduct in terms of the objective efficacy of means to ends and to define non-logical conduct in terms of its subjective or psychological source or character.[25] To MacPherson, it seems that on the one hand there is the efficacy of means and, on the other, the absence of reasoning (MacPherson, 1937, pp. 459 - 461 ). To Timasheff (as to Parsons), the one is objective and the other is subjective (Timasheff, 1957, pp. 160 - 161). To Croce, the one is utilitarian and coherent; and the other is moralistic and incoherent (Croce, 1935, p. 12). To Ginsberg, logical conduct is both the efficacy of means *and* the maximization of utility (Ginsberg, 1936, pp. 223, 225, 228).

In general, the confusion may be held to derive from the fact that Pareto used a basic dichotomy formulated in several ways and tended to substitute equivalent parts of different formulations for each other: logico-experimental and non-logico-experimental knowledge, objective and subjective aspects of belief, and logical and non-logical conduct. In Pareto's view, logical conduct was paralleled by logico-experimental knowledge and the objective aspect, that is, by reason; non-logical conduct was paralleled by non-logico-experimental knowledge and the subjective aspect, that is, by emotion. The really significant problem, the problem of values, is discussed below, following a necessary examination of the problem of utility.

## 3. Derivations as Pseudo-Knowledge

Given Pareto's emphasis upon the predominance of non-logico-experimental knowledge and non-logical conduct, it is imperative to examine the nature of what, according to Pareto, most if not all people accept as knowledge most of the time but which is, by logico-experimental standards, only pseudo-knowledge. Approximately one-third of the pages of the *Treatise* — six of thirteen chapters — were devoted by Pareto to an identification, classification, and analysis of the *derivations*. In another forty percent of the *Treatise* — three chapters, two of which are over three hundred pages each — Pareto developed the role of the derivations in social equilibrium as one of the four key elements therein. (The others were interests, residues, and the combination of social heterogeneity and class circulation.) If, as Pareto in effect may be said to argue, policy is a partial function of knowledge, and if logico-experimental knowledge is a small part of what either is or passes for knowledge, then it follows that policy is, *pro tanto*, a substantial function of pseudo-knowledge. This is of no minor importance for Pareto's theory of policy.

In Pareto's analysis, *derivations* are the rationalizations (Robinson) or myths (Sorel) of a non-logico-experimental nature that are essentially metaphysical and *a prioristic* assertions, allegations, and speculations which have no foundation (or possibility of foundation) in fact. They are the substance, according to Pareto, of superstition, weather-magic, prayer, theology, morality, law, natural law, ideology, political formulas (such as the greatest good for the greatest number), and the like.[26] They are or use indeterminate words or expressions which correspond to nothing actual, which define unknowns by unknowns, and which combine definitions with unproven theses. In sum, they are the imaginary principles found in ethical and all *a prioristic* theories and myths and to which prescriptive and objective existence is ascribed. Derivations function to make the relative, normative, and contingent appear as absolute, given, and required; in effect, they comprise ostensible *is* statements which are in reality either *meaningless* or *ought* statements (Sec. 253). They exist in the forms most generally prevalent, that is, the concepts most reputable or honorific, in the particular society and age in which they circulate (Secs. 217, 454). They exist because of a felt need for logical or pseudological explanation, a human compulsion for the transcendental or absolute and belief in the existence of the absolute, and a belief that men ought to act rationally (Secs. 265, 579, 613, 616, 1397, 1400). Non-logical conduct, because of the foregoing, thus tends to result in pseudo-logical propositions using explanatory-justificatory theories, words, concepts, symbols, ideas, ideologies, and beliefs, all of a non-logico-experimental character but accepted as settled "fact" nonetheless.

Derivations are the myths, fictions, and arguments, with all their attendant casuistry, which are universally accepted as part of the national, cultural, economic, and religious heritage, as well as the rationalizing "truths" of reformers. Insofar as they are accepted as knowledge, consciously or unconsciously, they serve as a framework for policy decision and thereby help structure social policy. That is to say, rationalizing derivations function as argument in the game of policy. Moreover, through the structure of language, the use of particular words, ideas, symbols, and ideologies, derivations yield for man a definition or structure of reality, constrain alternatives, and establish plausible, presumptive, acceptable, and/or relevant grounds of decision.

Derivations as knowledge are perhaps most appropriately connoted by their function, which is not to indicate objective or confirmable truth, but rather to provide rationalization, justification, explanation, and demonstration that will substitute as belief for truth. Where logico-experimental truth is impossible, or at least nonexistent, derivations are the surrogate for truth. The basic character of derivations is their functioning to legitimize positions and conduct in terms of fictions, words, myths, symbols, principles, mysteries, and the like, to which are ascribed, in one way or another, objective existence, and which are acted upon as if they were true in a logico-experimental sense. It is one of Pareto's major themes that derivations function to mask and justify non-logical conduct by using pseudo-logic and pseudo-knowledge to make the non-logical appear logical and reasonable; in other words, they "give a flavour of rationality to conduct that is really the result of feeling and impulse."[27]

Table I summarizes Pareto's classification of derivations (Sec. 845). It will be observed that they are grouped in four classes, comprising arguments that are essentially (a) assertions, (b) appeals to or invocations of authority, (c) allegations of accord with an honorific or acceptable benchmark, and (d) proofs involving the manipulation of words. Each attempts in its own way and for those people to whom it is meaningful, that is, by whom it is used or accepted, to "explain, justify, demonstrate" (Sec. 845), in a word

TABLE I

Classification of Derivations

| Class I: | | Assertion |
|---|---|---|
| I. | a. | Assertions of facts, experimental or imaginary |
| I. | b. | Assertions of sentiments |
| I. | c. | Mixtures of fact and sentiment |
| Class II: | | Authority |
| II. | a. | Of one individual or a number of individuals |
| II. | b. | Of tradition, usages, and customs |
| II. | c. | Of divine beings, or personifications |
| Class III: | | Accords with Sentiments or Principles |
| III. | a. | Accord with sentiments |
| III. | b. | Accord with individual interest |
| III. | c. | Accord with collective interest |
| III. | d. | Accord with juridical entities |
| III. | e. | Accord with metaphysical entities |
| III. | f. | Accord with supernatural entities |
| Class IV: | | Verbal Proofs |
| IV. | a. | Indefinite terms designating real things; indefinite things corresponding to terms |
| IV. | b. | Terms designating things and arousing incidental sentiments, or incidental sentiments determining choice of terms |
| IV. | c. | Terms with numbers of meanings, and different things designated by single terms |
| IV. | d. | Metaphors, allegories, analogies |
| IV. | e. | Vague, indefinite terms corresponding to nothing concrete |

(Adopted from sec. 1419 of *Treatise*.)

to persuade (Secs. 445, 454). The persuasion is not only of others but also, and in a profound sense, of oneself.

Although to believers they are fact, to the social scientist, according to Pareto, they are pseudo-knowledge functioning to sanction and legitimize; they are rationalizations accepted as fact, a category of human artifact which may be simply labelled legitimations (Secs.445, 641, 809, 811, 1383, 1695, 1920, 2187, 2553). They are justification *a posteriori*,[29] but because man has a need to know (Sec. 1086), and also because the significance of ideas lies in the conduct or policy choices made by those who believe in and are thereby conditioned by ideas (Secs. 541, 1103, 1682), derivations are prospectively influential, albeit (as will be seen in Part Two) within constraints. Much of what is accepted as knowledge, then, is essentially merely *argument*. It is argument which is exaggerated (Sec.1389 and *passim*), propounded and accepted as definitive (Sec. 75) and which tends to assume the very point argued (Secs. 407, 1420ff, 2147, 2570-2571), but which if acted upon may be self-realizing and is in any event always in the center of the stage. One of Pareto's distinctive theorems, as will be seen shortly, relates to the functional significance of propositions formally meaningless.

Consider, Pareto argued, terms like these:

| justice | human | must | private property |
| duty | highest good | equitable | capitalism |
| sanctity | welfare | rights | humanity |
| absolute | legitimate | science | liberty |
| good | moral | democracy | truth |
| progress | socialism | proper | prosperity |
| solidarity | natural law | experience | honest |

which are "terms that do indeed arouse indefinite sentiments but otherwise correspond to nothing real" (Sec. 1551). Such terms elicit built-in responses and legitimate whatever is symbolized by them in the particular time and place (Secs. 960, 1337, 1551; *cf.* Timasheff, 1940, p. 145). They have nothing to conform to in the real world, yet it is always assumed that there is "something there" and objective existence is ascribed to them (Secs. 109, 382, 506, 639, 965, 969, 1069, 1071, 1424, 1547, 1551, 1576, 1689, 1765, 2572, and pp. 1927, 1928), whereas they are to the logico-experimental analyst purely subjective (Secs. 439, 969, 1042, 1081, 1161, 1210, 1739, 2147n.6) and ambiguous (Secs. 427, 439, 506, 815 - 816, 1042, 1775n.1, 1797ff, 2147n.6). They are accepted and "palmed off not as subjective but as objective entities" (Sec. 1576), whereas actually they "are all names that designate nothing more than indistinct and incoherent sentiments" (Sec. 1513). Indeed, "The majority of the words in ordinary usage correspond in their formation to 'non-logical' actions" (Sec. 883; *cf.* p. 1927).

What is true of certain terms is also true of language as a whole. Pareto understood very well that much of the stuff of life is comprised of words and symbols and that social organization and policy are *pro tanto* conditioned by the view of the world inculcated and ingrained by language (Sec. 2005; *cf.* Muller, 1938,

p. 427; *cf.* Perry, 1935, p. 102 and sec. 2273 and p. 1928). "Language," wrote Pareto, "is a very effective instrument for lending continuity to such groups and for personifying them; and the mere bestowal of a name on a sum of abstractions is often sufficient to transform it into an objective individuality" (Sec. 1071; *cf.* 688 - 689, 2147). Give an abstraction a name, a symbol, or a myth, and it will function to influence and legitimize policy as if it were an objective and pre-existent phenomenon, no matter how much coating and sophistry is necessary (Secs. 383n.1, 523, 1400, 2273). Definitions prejudge and build in policy solutions and positions (Secs. 371ff) and, like the concept of utility in economics (Sec. 2110), are essentially normative; a writer tends to "make his readers accept a definition that will help him to establish his thesis" (Sec. 383). So too do symbols (Sec. 960 and p. 1927), fictions (Secs. 229, 241, 834), and casuistries (Sec. 815 - 816, 834n.1, 1800ff, 1822, 1919ff), that is, concept and word manipulation in general, function to provide acceptable definitions of reality and, thereby, bases for both social equilibrium and policy. Unknowns are defined by unknowns (Secs. 425 - 426); question-begging concepts are elaborated upon and ostensibly specified by other question-begging concepts (Sec. 2163); and policy dialogue is an infinite regression of pseudo-objectified abstractions (Secs. 425, 2147, 2167, 2192).

"All these definitions and others of their kind present the following characteristics: 1. They use indeterminate words, which serve to arouse certain sentiments, but which do not correspond to anything exact. 2. They define unknowns by unknowns. 3. They combine definitions with theses unproved. 4. Their purpose, in substance, is to arouse the hearer's sentiments as far as possible in order to lead him to a pre-established conviction" (Sec. 442).

Policy is also in part a function of ideology or cosmology, including "what the plain man understands by 'virtue'," (Sec. 260; *cf.* 1397n.2) all considered as pseudo-knowledge. As Pareto pointed out, citing his friend Sorel, "... if a social doctrine (it would be more exact to say the sentiments manifested by a social doctrine) is to have any influence, it has to take the form of a 'myth'."[30] Myths, principles (Secs. 1797ff, 1822), and the like, all derivations, ambiguous as they are, thus give what is typically accepted as unchallenged "factual" substance — legitimation — to what is proper and virtuous in any society and to the definition of reality that epitomizes that society. Myths function as knowledge more or less as the aphorism of their subject. That there is obscurantism and mystery (Secs. 1347, 1524, 1566, 1567) involved serves to make the derivation more attractive and binding, that is, to some, more believable.

Derivations pass as knowledge, then, and do so in a manner that reflects something of what Freud called a belief in the omnipotence of thought, namely, according to Pareto, that "words seem to possess some mysterious power over things" (Sec. 182; cf. 227, 950, 1732n.2, 2096n.1; Larrabee, 1935, p. 515; and Brinton, 1954, p. 650). If such knowledge, for example, the invocations of weather-magic or politics, were indeed knowledge, what power would man have! (Secs. 182, 296n.2, 1501 - 1502.) "Belief in magic belongs to all ages and all peoples. Interpretations are the servants," wrote Pareto, "not the masters, of the thing" (Sec. 212).

Derivations as legitimations involve the invocation of authority, whether in the form of what is usually meant by appeal to authority or in the form of the other three classes of derivations. They are as elastic as a rubber band (Sec. 1689). Whether or not in the form of assertions of natural law, "they all arise in a desire to give a semblance of absoluteness and objectivity to what is relative and subjective" (Sec. 447). What makes derivations knowledge is their compelling authoritativeness, and what makes them so authoritative is that they are stated absolutely. They tend

"... to assume absolute forms or at least the appearance of concrete reality, ... in virtue of the practical advantage of not allowing a doubt of any kind to lodge in the mind of the person who is to be persuaded, and of utilizing, for that purpose, the force which absoluteness, or at least the presumed reality, confers upon principles" (Sec. 1878; cf. 407, 1695, 1868, 2144, 2155, 2197).

Men, "must show that their doctrine has merits other than that of satisfying their own particular natures, and so bend every effort to show its universality" (Bongiorno, 1930, pp. 362 - 363). Derivations thus necessarily use "simple principles that overstep realities and aim at goals that lie beyond them, sometimes far far beyond" (Sec. 1772). Derivations are, generally, then, metaphysical legitimations absolutely formulated. Policy, the "purposes of persuasion, ... arousing sentiments and urging people along a given line of conduct," has a place for derivations because "the human mind requires the ideal and the real in varying dosage" (Sec. 2159). Derivations provide the absolutely legitimizing comfort and security of knowledge.

Policy, in sum, is a function of belief: belief in what is logico-experimentally true, and belief in what is a non-logico-experimental surrogate for such truth. Thus policy is, *pro tanto*, a function of what men believe or come to or are induced to believe, whether objective or subjective, whether logico-experimental knowledge or the legitimations and arguments called by Pareto "derivations." These latter are, in any society, functional with respect to the organization of society and the eliciting and channeling of activity (Secs. 371ff. *cf.* Parsons, 1937, pp. 272, 275 - 276; and Schumpeter, 1951, p. 139). Policy is a partial function of the definition of reality, and derivations operate to define reality. In chapter five it will be seen how derivations are energizers in a process from which issue both social equilibrium and policy. Here it need only be established that derivations are energizers substantially because they are accepted as given, taken for granted, presumed as fact, that is, they constitute pseudo-knowledge as a basis of policy.

### 4. Utility as a Property of the Social System

One of the major themes of this study is that, in the Paretian model, society is a system of power, a process for the determination and operation of "knowledge," and a process of the interplay of psychic states, all existing simultaneously and all commingling. These are sufficiently fundamental to be called "properties" of society, although it appears preferable to refer to them as dimensions of policy (embodying what Pareto called elements of social equilibrium). Pareto did, however, refer to *utility* as a property of the social system.[31] So considered, utility has components reduceable to knowledge, psychology, and power. At this point, again anticipating certain ideas to be developed more fully later, it will be useful to consider utility as it relates to knowledge. What may be called *knowledge of utility* in relation to social policy was a most important and frequently reiterated topic for Pareto. From the previous discussion, it is clear that to Pareto not only logico-experimental truth but also non-logico-experimental derivations have considerable social utility.

This section will examine, first, the general subject of utility as a property of the social system and, second, the Paretian theme which differentiated between and refused to equate truth and social utility. Pareto's related concern about the potential danger from public discussion of certain topics also will be investigated.

Pareto differentiated between several aspects of utility: that for the individual; that of and for the community; and the heterogeneity of utility as between individuals (abstracting from the problem of the heterogeneity of utility between communities). Pareto's most general schema is outlined by him as follows (Sec. 2115):

a) Utility to the Individual
    a—1. Direct
    a—2. Indirect, resulting from the fact that the individual is part of a community
    a—3. Utility to an individual, as related to the utilities to others

b) Utility to a Given Community
    b—1. Direct utility to communities, considered apart from other communities
    b—2. Indirect utility, arising by reaction from other communities
    b—3. Utility to one community as related to the utilities to other communities

Thus, utility is complex since all of these considerations (and still others) are relevant (Secs. 2111ff, 2148). It is also vague, because consideration of utility in any context is a function of the norm used (Secs. 2111, 2129, 2143). Accordingly, his definition, if that it be, of utility is a highly formal one, stated in terms of indices of realization in the approximation of a maximum *given* the norm involved (Sec. 2111; *cf.* Homans and Curtis, 1934, pp. 280, 284).

Pareto's basic distinction is between utility *of* and *for*, which will be examined in a moment. It should be made clear first, however, that what is basically involved is the question, as Lopreato (1965, p. 13) well expressed it, of "utility for whom?" As Lopreato (1965, pp. 4, 15 - 16) also stressed, what is involved is the distinction between manifest and latent function. In Schneider's terminology, the issue is the role of the principles of indirection and ignorance (Schneider, 1962, pp. 493 - 497 and *passim*).

In Schneider's analysis, *indirection* involves the achievement or realization of ends through activity subjectively addressed to other intermediate goals; *ignorance* connotes the situation in which latent functions are the consequences of behavior subjectively directed to the realization of more proximate goals, where the latent function is achieved unintentionally and therefore unknowingly (at least by some). As will be seen shortly, one of Pareto's most distinctive themes is that social utility (read, limitedly but not totally inaccurately, "function") may result from — less despite and more because of — the non-logico-experimental status of derivations (Secs. 167, 311, 1152).

As is discussed in chapter three, Pareto also argued the principle of manipulating the residues by the derivations. This is a quite explicit and important theme reducing to the latent function produced indirectly through the role of beliefs (and to manifest function to at least some of the manipulators) (Sec. 1855). Pareto stated the principle of indirection quite clearly, when he maintained that theoretical discussions are not "very serviceable directly for modifying [conduct]; indirectly they may be effective for modifying [psychic states]. But to attain that objective, appeal must be made to sentiments rather than to logic and the results of experience" (Sec. 168; *cf.* 160, 1772, and *passim*).

The principle of ignorance is also present; indeed, one could argue that the role of non-logical action is equivalent to the sum of the principles of ignorance and indirection. Having already argued "that ritual practices intensified sentiments (non-logical actions) and that such sentiments were in turn sources of morality" (Sec. 361), Pareto later argued in a different context but to a relevant effect that "it will be just as well if the doctrine here stated be not very generally known to the masses who are to be influenced, for the artifice, to be fully efficient, has to remain concealed" (Sec. 2440; *cf.* 1749; also *cf.* Schumpeter, 1951, p. 140, and Ginsberg, 1936, p. 222). As will be seen below in no small detail, the elevation of latent to manifest function is also a part of Pareto's analysis (Sec. 1382n.4).

Belief, conduct, and policy thus may be examined in terms of personal considerations of utility, with personally elected norms and in terms of the latent function contributed by such belief, conduct, and policy for society. But remembering, first, that individuals are heterogeneous and, second, that social utility, whether in terms of latent function or not, also requires election of norms, the following questions properly arise: "Utility for whom?" "Utility, by whose norms?" "Which norms?"

Pareto's analysis of utility proceeded to differentiate between utility *of* and *for* a community. Just as it is possible to discuss the utility *of* an individual, that is, "the utility which the individual enjoys under given circumstances" (Sec. 2122), Pareto maintained that one can identify the utility *of* a community as if it were a collective unit. As Parsons points out, Pareto's concept of utility *of* a community is a version of the sociologistic theorem, enabling Pareto to consider utility as a property of the social system as a unit (Parsons, 1937, pp. 248, 297; and 1951, p. 331, *cf.* Homans and Curtis, 1934, p. 278). As one might expect, the utility *of* a community is specified in terms of prestige and military power (Sec. 2134). The utility *for* a community, on the other hand, relates to the utility of a given policy, and so forth, for its members; given the class structure and heterogeneous nature of society, it involves an internal distributive problem.

With respect to utility *of* the community *vis-a-vis* utility *for* the community, Pareto maintained that the population policy promotive of military power and thereby of utility *of* the community may differ from that population policy which promotes the utility *for* this or that group within the community (and perforce the population as a whole).

> "Take, for instance, the matter of population increase. If we think of the utility *of* the community as regards prestige and military power, we will find it advisable to increase population to the fairly high limit beyond which the nation would be impoverished and its stock decay. But if we think of the maximum of utility *for* the community, we find a limit that is much lower. Then we have to see in what proportions the various social classes profit by the increase in prestige and military power, and in what different proportion they pay for it with their particular sacrifices" (Sec. 2134).

Furthermore, "precisely because they cannot be compared, since they are heterogeneous quantities, no maximum ophelimity *of* the community exists; whereas a maximum ophelimity *for* the community can exist, since it is determined independently of any comparison between the ophelimities of different individuals."[3][2] Hence utility *of* and *for* tends to be an objective/subjective differentiation, at least in principle, although utility *for* is subjective in terms of the choice of norms used, and utility *of* an individual is subjective in terms of personal norms.

Distinguishing between economic ophelimity and sociological utility, Pareto argued thus:

"In pure economics a community cannot be regarded as a person. In sociology it can be considered, if not as a person, at least as a unit. There is no such thing as the ophelimity of a community; but a community utility can roughly be assumed. So in pure economics there is no danger of mistaking the maximum of ophelimity *for* a community for a non-existent maximum of ophelimity *of* a community. In sociology, instead, we must stand watchfully on guard against confusing the maximum of utility *for* a community with the maximum of utility *of* a community, since they both are there" (Sec. 2133).

With respect to utility *for* a community, then, Pareto lays down as principles of government policy "that a government ought to stop at the point beyond which no 'advantage' would accrue to the community as a whole, that it ought not to inflict 'useless' sufferings on the public as a whole or in part, that it ought to benefit the community as far as possible without sacrificing the 'ideals' it has in view 'for the public good,' that it ought to make efforts 'proportionate' to purposes and not demand burdensome sacrifices for slight gains" (Sec. 2132).

Pareto was aware that the use of such terms as "advantage," "useless," and the rest made the entire analysis only formal. The question of specific content was left up to the policy process, including the play of derivations and residues as well as power. But this is the genesis of Pareto optimum, within the limits imposed by the status quo distribution of property, personal ability, residues, and so on, with no necessary unique optimum. As Pareto expressed it, when the community can adopt a policy procuring greater benefits for all individuals, it should pursue it as long as it is advantageous to all, and, "... where that is no longer possible, ... it is necessary, as regards the advisability of stopping there or going on, to resort to other considerations foreign to economics — to decide on grounds of ethics, social utility, or something else, which individuals it is advisable to benefit, which to sacrifice" (Sec. 2129). That is, it is necessary to go beyond the Pareto optimum, or, dynamically, redetermine Pareto optimum through a change in the limits and/or existing norms.

Pareto later gave the following example:

"Let us imagine a community so situated that a strict choice has to be made between a very wealthy community with large inequalities in income among its members and a poor community with approximately equal incomes. A policy of maximum utility *of* the community may lead to the first state, a policy of maximum utility *for* the community to the second. We say, *may*, because results will depend upon the coefficients that are used in making the heterogeneous utilities of the various social classes homogeneous. The admirer of the 'superman' will assign a coefficient of approximately zero to the utility of the lower classes, and get a point of equilibrium very close to a state where large inequalities prevail. The lover of equality will assign a high coefficient to the utility of the lower classes and get a point of equilibrium very close to the equalitarian condition. There is no criterion save sentiment for choosing between the one and the other" (Sec. 2135).[33]

Social equilibrium and socio-economic policy (internally considered) involve contemplation of utility *for* a community. Even abstracting from the operation of the market *per se*, the market operates within an institutional framework which, *inter alia*, structures the distribution of income. Norms are necessary with which to choose one institutional arrangement over another, at the margin of institutional change. Utility *for* the community involves the problems of the subjectivity and normativeness of individual utility; the heterogeneity of utility as between individuals; the juxtaposition of utility *for* the community with utility *of* the community; intertemporal equilibrium;[34] the requirement of rules or norms with which to compare or weigh interpersonal utilities (that is, "to decide ... which individuals ... to benefit, which to sacrifice") (Sec. 2129); and the absence of objective rules by which to decide between norms ("there is ... no criterion but sentiment for choosing between the one and the other.")[35] (Sec. 2135, *cf.* 2151). All such knowledge is hard to come by. The situation is further complicated because, "Even in cases where the utility of the individual does not stand in conflict with the utility of the community, the points of maximum of the one do not ordinarily coincide with the points of maximum of the other" (Sec. 2138). These issues are at the heart of socio-economic policy and every theory of policy must somehow come to grips with them.

But Pareto's theme, given the importance of norms, returns to the significance of psychic states:

"We are to conclude ... not that problems simultaneously considering a number of heterogeneous utilities cannot be solved, but that in order to discuss them some hypothesis which will render them commensurate has to be assumed. And when, as is most often the case, that is not done, discussion of such problems is idle and inconclusive, being merely a play of derivations cloaking certain sentiments — and those sentiments we should alone consider, without worrying very much about the garb they wear" (Sec. 2137).

Finally, as several writers have pointed out, the utility *of* a community requires an *end*, the social determination of which is tied up with the ends embodied in rules with which to select between norms for the maximization of the utility *for* a community.[36] Society is a process of evolving such ends, rules, and norms, both personal and social. In Pareto's view, that process involves derivations, residues (sentiments), and power play.


## 5. Truth versus Social Utility

It has already been developed that, to Pareto, society's effective corpus of "knowledge" included both logico-experimental truth and non-logico-experimental belief, and that social equilibrium or policy, to the extent that it was a function of knowledge, was a function of both kinds of knowledge. Pareto went a step further. He argued, first, that just because logico-experimental truth was objective, society was not assured that its role would be beneficial. Second, simply because non-logico-experimental belief might have no foundation in objective fact did not mean that it would be necessarily harmful or of no benefit to society. In sum, Pareto argued the necessity of differentiating between truth and social utility, "that the experimental 'truth' of certain theories is one thing and their social 'utility' quite another, and that the two things are not only not one and the same but may, and often do, stand in flat contradiction" (Sec. 843). "A theory that is experimentally true may be now advantageous, now detrimental, to society; and the same applies to a theory that is experimentally false" (Sec. 249) The theme is stated over and over again, each time in conjunction with another theme but always to the same relevant effect.[37]

46

"The accord of a doctrine, or theory, with facts is one thing; and the social importance of that doctrine, or theory, quite another. The former may amount to zero, the latter be very great; but the social significance does not prove the scientific accord, just as the scientific accord does not prove the social significance" (Sec. 1682).

The intrinsic value of such satires may be zero when viewed from the experimental standpoint, whereas their polemical value may be great. Those two things we must always keep distinct (Sec. 311).

... the cause is to be sought not so much in the value of the arguments, which is exactly zero, as in the strength of the sentiments that they disguise" (Sec. 598).

Pareto very early in the *Treatise* established the differentiation between truth and social utility. He did so by enumerating four classes of cases "of frequent occurrence in social matters."

"a) Propositions in accord with experience that are asserted and accepted because of their accord with sentiments, the latter being now beneficial, now detrimental, to individuals or society

b) Propositions in accord with experience that are rejected because they are not in accord with sentiments, and which, if accepted, would be detrimental to society

c) Propositions not in accord with experience that are asserted and accepted because of their accord with sentiments, the latter being beneficial, oftentimes exceedingly so, to individuals or society

d) Propositions not in accord with experience that are asserted and accepted because of their accord with sentiments, and which are beneficial to certain individuals, detrimental to others, and now beneficial, now detrimental, to society" (Sec. 14).

Pareto's elaborate, detailed, and seemingly endless documentation of the prevalence of the non-logico-experimental and non-logical, covering hundreds of pages, also enabled him to argue that such predominance was strong evidence that social utility derived, in the sense of latent function (Lopreato, 1965, pp. 15 - 16), from scientifically meaningless and absurd non-logico-experimental reasonings and beliefs and the non-logical conduct related thereto. Those "who are disposed to consider nothing but logical conduct, regarding the non-logical as originating in absurd prejudices and

47

calculated to do nothing but harm to society," and "those who will consider a doctrine only from the standpoint of its accord with experience and declare that any other way of regarding it is absurd, fatuous, harmful" (Sec. 1679), are, according to Pareto, both incorrect.

"Consider," he suggested repeatedly, "the example of religion: ...

the social importance of religion lies not at all in the logical value of its dogmas, its principles, its theology, but rather in the non-logical actions that it promotes (Sec. 365).

It is therefore a serious mistake to measure the social value of a religion strictly by the logical or rational value of its theology (Sec. 167).

Nothing can be more mistaken than to evaluate the influence of a given religion by its theology. ... It would be erroneous to the same degree to appraise the social value of a morality by the theoretical statement of it (Sec. 466).

The belief that certain abstract entities exist independently of experience, and are not products of a partially arbitrary abstraction, is so self-evident, and so deeply rooted in the minds of most human beings, that the non-logical sentiment underlying it must be a very powerful one indeed. ... Moreover, since the belief has gone hand in hand with the progress of human societies, we are justified in surmising that however false it may be experimentally, it may play a role of some practical advantage in social life" (Sec.579; cf. 336, 928, 1386, and Livingston's comment in 999n.1).

Truth is different, then, from social utility. What is important is the policy consequences or significance of ideas. Knowledge, moreover, not only interacts with sentiments, but also is a question of power. The result is an ambiguous social "utility:"

"As regards logical and non-logical conduct there are differences between individual human beings, or, taking things in the mass, between social classes, and differences also in the degrees of utility that theories experimentally true or experimentally false have for individuals or classes. And the same applies to the sentiments that are expressed through non-logical conduct (Sec.249; cf. 1509, 1896ff).

48

Speaking, then, in general and very roughly, disregarding possible and in fact numerous exceptions, one may say that it is advantageous to a society that, at least in the minds of the majority of individuals not belonging to the ruling class, [the problem, 'What manner of viewing facts is most desirable for individuals, society, and so on'] should be answered in the sense that facts should be viewed not as they are in reality, but as they are transfigured in the light of ideals.[38]

It should now be increasingly apparent how difficult it is to separate one of Pareto's themes from the others. His theory of knowledge in relation to policy is necessarily intertwined with his theory of psychic states, that is, of the sentiments operating through the residues, and with his theory of power, including the circulation of the elite. Thus far, all that the present author has intended to establish is the Paretian theory of knowledge in relation to social policy and some of its involvements. The following chapters will elaborate upon the dimensions of psychology and power and the interrelations between the three dimensions.

Pareto was so imbued with the distinction between truth and social utility, particularly insofar as social control is concerned (see chapter six, *infra*), that he was solicitous lest the public airing of certain ideas be dangerous to society, to social utility, or to public order. Indeed, he was very much concerned, if not preoccupied, with the problem of authority (see chapter eight, *infra*). Well he might have been. As Muller, one of the most discriminating commentators on the *Treatise*, has pointed out, "The chief value of Pareto, in fact, lies in his ruthless, devastating analysis of all such pretensions — of all the modernistic versions of hoary fallacy that parade as realistic or scientific, as the latest thing in absolute truth."[39] Not only modernistic pretensions were attacked; Pareto was equally ruthless with the received divinities and superstitions as he was with those newly created. As Bousquet remarked, Pareto, with his "nihilistic attitude," developed theories which very readily could be "dangerous" (Bousquet, 1928, pp. 39, 40).

Thus, in the *Treatise* Pareto expressed anxiety that wide readership of his work might produce harm:

"... my sole interest is the quest for social uniformities, social laws. I am here reporting on the results of my quest, since I hold that in view of the restricted number of readers such a study can have and in view of the scientific training that may be taken for granted in them, such a report can do no harm. I should refrain from doing so if I could reasonably imagine that these volumes were to be at all generally read (Sec. 86. *cf.* Larrabee, 1935, p. 506; Henderson, 1937, p. 5; and DeVoto, 1933a, p. 546).

Yet almost every major theme developed in the *Treatise* necessitated that Pareto risk endangering society: *inter alia*, the predominance of non-logical conduct; the exposure of cherished beliefs as psychological rationalizations and wishful thinking; the nature of society as both a class and a manipulative system, including his theory of the elite; and so on. Thus, Pareto openly discussed and criticized the hypocrisy of sex mores (Secs. 208ff, 366, 1010, 1368n.5, 1330n.2, 1336, 1372, 1382, 1387); exposed non-logico-experimental reasonings as deception and self-deception; openly examined manipulation — cunning and force — by the ruling class and by pretenders thereto of all stripes; criticized the doctrine of papal infallibility (Sec. 585n.1); recognized the prejudicial element incorporated in the labels *criminal* and *heretic* (Secs. 207 - 211); exposed persecutions for "impiety" (Secs. 240, 318, 618); advocated the open discussion of church dogma (Secs. 1127n.1, 1454n.1), and ideology (Sec. 2175); recognized that the majority of men are passive consumers of derivations (Secs. 1415, 1580n.1, 1737, 2342); recognized the public hypocrisy of public figures: "All that we have been saying is a matter of common knowledge, and, in private, no one playing any part in public life or in high finance is so naive as to deny it; but in public those same leaders try to look shocked and hypocritically say that such talk is bosh."[40]
He also recognized the extensive practice of deception and pretence in human society:

"In very truth one good way to defend a thesis would be to suppress knowledge of the facts that tend to demolish it (Sec 1975n.1; *cf.* 2235n.2).

Many religious organizations make a practice of saying nothing of occurrences that might occasion scandal (Sec. 1749n.3).

... it is to a certain extent beneficial to believe that observance of the norms prevailing in a community is always advantageous

50

to individual and community, and that that belief should be neither doubted nor controverted (Sec. 2001).

Even the person seeking the method of teaching history best calculated to achieve the greatest possible social benefits must believe, or pretend to believe, that there is but one solution" (Sec. 1583; *cf.* 2341).[41]

Pareto's preference for openness on matters of religion recollects the similar posture of John Stuart Mill (*cf.* Samuels, 1966, pp. 90 - 91 and *passim*). Pareto also paralleled Trower's acknowledgement of the conservative frame of mind of agriculturalists (Samuels, 1966, p. 53). Quoting Cato the Elder, "... they who till the soil do not cherish evil thoughts," Pareto pointed out that "that is an indirect way of saying that residues present in farmers are different from the residues present in other citizens. Cato's last phrase implies a faint perception that country people are less prone to innovations ..." (Sec. 1726).

All in all, Pareto proceeded to open many "a breach in the ethical and *a priori* theories that have been explaining ... by imaginary principles" (Sec. 346). He defended the unveiling of nonsense: "But scientific problems are solved by facts, not by the holy horror of the few, the many, the all" (Sec. 379). He thus criticized the argument of setting a bad example (Sec. 299n.1); defended his exposure of the composition of religions (Sec.393); minimized any adverse effect of his analysis on religion ("To study such modes of expression in no way effects the things that are expressed.") (Sec. 941); and generally abstracted from possible dangers ("We are not passing judgment of any kind on the effects, whether socially beneficial or otherwise, of such disaccord, nor on the effects beneficial or otherwise of its being generally known or unknown to the public at large.") (Sec. 1824n.1; *cf.* 1975). Indeed, at one point he maintained that, "Fools of the breed that forgathers in societies for the improvement of morals may consider the publication of such lines a crime as serious as murder or burglary; but that cannot possibly be admitted from the standpoint of social utility" (Sec. 186 n.1; *cf.* 2147).

Still he was aware that "The trial of Socrates is merely the best known of a series of prosecutions that took place about that time and which indicate a popular reaction against unbelief in the intellectual classes" (Sec. 2345n.8). However, it was Pareto's view that "the foundations of non-logical conduct on which society rests" would not be demolished by open discussion itself. Rather, Platonic doctrines "are themselves one of the effects of the social disintegration; and that is why the condemnation of Socrates was a useless thing and therefore stupid, wicked, and criminal, just as the condemnation of any man for expressing opinions deemed heretical by the people about him has been and continues to be useless and therefore stupid, wicked, and criminal" (Sec. 2348; *cf.* 299n.1).

Pareto's main defense of his efforts involving open discussion took the form of a defense of freedom of thought invoking an interesting comparison between violations of "material" norms (private crimes) and violations of "intellectual" norms. Pareto condoned repression of violations of material norms when committed by individuals but not, or less so, when they are collective acts of attempted social reform.

> "Considering violations of material conformities among modern civilized peoples, we see that, in general, the use of violence in repressing them is the more readily condoned in proportion as the violation can be regarded as an individual anomaly designed to attain some individual advantage, and the less readily condoned in proportion as the violation appears as a collective act aiming at some collective advantage, and especially if its apparent design be to replace general norms prevailing with certain other general norms"[42] Sec. 2176).

When it came to violations of intellectual norms, although he was reticent with respect to the large numbers case, Pareto upheld violations by the one or the few.

> "... it will be apparent that — especially as regards violations by small numbers of individuals — many are the cases where violations of intellectual norms by individuals or by a few individuals prove advantageous, few the cases where violations of norms of a material order prove beneficial. For that reason, the implications of the formula ... whereby violations of norms of a material order should be the more vigorously suppressed, the more exclusively they are the work of individuals, the less so, the more they are the work of groups, do not in many cases take us too far astray from the maximum of social utility, as they would do if the formula were applied to violations of norms of an intellectual order. That, substantially, is the chief argument

52

that can be advanced in favor of what is called "freedom of thought" (Sec.2196).

Thus, although he obviously was sensitive to the charge that his writing might be dangerous and subversive, Pareto ultimately defended his open discussion of potentially dangerous themes on two grounds. First, if the themes were indeed dangerous, the danger would not derive from the open discussion but from otherwise existing conditions of disintegration. Second, writing as an individual there was little chance that he might subvert the status quo. Pareto was concerned that he might do harm, but his apparent defense was based upon his solitude and individuality, both of which he maintained at Celigny.


## 6. The Problem of Values

Up to this point the Paretian theory of knowledge in relation to social policy has been considered primarily in terms of knowledge of *reality*. The question arises, however, as to the place of knowledge of *values* in the Paretian system. The problem of the knowledge and role of values in the *Treatise* is an excellent example of one of the most difficult and enervating problems of interpretation in the history of ideas, namely the one problem which arises when a writer denigrates and disparages something which of necessity and/or in actuality is nevertheless present in one form or another in his work. That which is denied a formal place is, in fact, given a place however much that place is outside the explicit intent and consciousness of the writer.

Such was the case in the *Treatise*. As has already been seen, Pareto wrote derisively of the vagueness and unreality of valuational or ethical propositions. Words like *justice*, *good*, *moral*, and the rest, "are all names that designate nothing more than indistinct and incoherent sentiments" (Sec. 1513; *cf.* 1161, 1859, 2145 and *passim*; and see Tufts, 1935, p. 64). Such terms, moreover, do not correspond to any objective or concrete reality. Indeed, like the terms of aesthetics, they only embody attempts to make objective what is really subjective (Secs.1429, 1689 and *passim*). It is as if values were signs of weakness or of feminity. Values are a function of the imagination and accordingly are the products and manifestations of the sentiments. They are important to the social scientist only as pointers to the sentiments, that is, not substantively but functionally. Ethics and values are part of metaphysics, and Pareto's science of society would have as little to do with metaphysics as possible.

For this explicit denigration of values and valuational process Pareto has been severely criticized by some writers. McDougall wrote that "It is indeed one of Pareto's avowed purposes to construct his system of sociology without recognizing the reality of purposive activity of any kind; a purpose for which he is duly praised by the eulogists." McDougall added that "one main source" of Pareto's "confusion is failure clearly to distinguish the provinces of valuation (which properly belong to philosophy) from the provinces of science or the natural sciences." As a result, Pareto "fulminates and gibes against valuing activities of every kind" (McDougall, 1935, pp. 37, 50). Ginsberg considered that, aside from the proposition that norms are a function of the sentiments, Pareto made no attempt to deal with valuational problems, limiting the role of reason to "linking means and ends appropriately" (Ginsberg, 1936, p. 228; *cf.* 226, 227). (Ginsberg also remarked that "The notion of progress is never mentioned by [Pareto] without bitter derision. But it will be noticed that, though according to him there can be no reliable criteria of progress, he does not hesitate to speak of decadence which requires criteria of the same kind" (Ginsberg, 1936, p. 244).[43])

On the other hand, some writers have found no small amount of both explicit and implicit treatment of values in the *Treatise* (beyond intrusion of Pareto's own valuational positions and judgments, as pointed out by Ginsberg in the excerpt quoted above). Muller, maintaining that "Ultimately life is, for both the individual and society, an experiment in values," argues that the *Treatise* "throws a steady, often brilliant light upon the terms of this experiment, the possibilities of experience; ..."[44] Barzun noted Pareto's emphasis upon the importance of problems of choice resolved independently of science (Barzun, 1958, p. 218; *cf.* Perry, 1935, p. 98). The most significant commentaries in this regard, however, have been made by Tufts and Parsons. The main points made by Tufts are these. First, Pareto disparaged ethics by reducing ethical propositions to non-logico-experimental beliefs which are a function of sentiments and which have no correspondence with concrete reality. Second, the interplay between ideals constituted, in the Paretian system, a value-clarification process, such that "there seems to be no good reason on Pareto's own premises for a contemptuous attitude toward the ethical theorist

54

who finds his task in criticizing ideals with a view of deciding more wisely which are the better." Third, nevertheless, Pareto's insistence on the vagueness and unreality of ethics, coupled with his stress on the importance of the non-logical, means that "For the solution or even the understanding of our pressing problems of social ethics Pareto offers little" (Tufts, 1935, p. 77; *cf.* pp. 64, 69 - 71, 76).

Talcott Parsons' use of the *Treatise* in his *Structure of Social Action* already has been acknowledged. Parsons' comments will be summarized very generally.[45] The social system includes value elements (ends) and a valuational process. Some ends, those of logical conduct, are given by the interests although ultimately these also are non-logical. Non-logical conduct includes both *un*scientific (non-logical) and *non*-scientific (normative) elements; therefore ends are normative and coexist with conditional non-subjective and non-normative elements as well as non-logical elements. While ends are generally indeterminate, non-logico-experimental, and a function of the sentiments, ends are important in the Paretian system because action is choice involving the formulation and comparison of values, value systems, and value chains, albeit in a separation of intermediate and ultimate ends sectors. The sharing of integrated or common ends is important to social order. The valuation process, among other things, functions to integrate the ultimate ends of individual action systems into a common system of ultimate ends which functions to hold the system together (on the question of social control, see chapter six, *infra*). There are valuational elements in both the residues and derivations. For example, some of the residues are or include statements of the ends of action (Parsons, 1937, p. 227 and *passim*). Ends are embodied in the working rules (at least partially as a function of the valuational process) (Parsons, 1936, pp. 256, 260). There is an energizing function attributed to ideals. The valuational process includes not only the ends of individual action systems but also consideration of the "end which a society should pursue."[46] In general, ends are non-logical, and logical action is intermediate to ends. Pareto's "theory of the residues instead of being a means of minimizing the role of values in history is thus an affirmation of it."[47]

Pareto, then, denigrated values, norms, and ends whenever they are substantively discussed. Yet he tended to invoke the relevance of operation of values, norms, and ends as variables, albeit indeterminate and non-objective, in the process of social equilibrium or policy making. This may be interpreted either as an emphasis upon the limited ability of science to resolve problems of policy (choice), or as an emphasis upon the subjectivity and therefore futility of discussions of value, or both. Similarly, Pareto's (and Freud's) emphasis upon the role of the emotions in human action may be interpreted either as antirationalism (that is, an indication of the poor chances man has for developing and using his intel-, lect), or as a diagnostic statement of the barriers or problems to more rational (objective) policy making, or both. With respect to substantive values, Pareto's position is certainly one of relativism (in terms of sentiments, circumstances, power play, knowledge, and so forth). Capitalism is a religion, socialism is a religion, and so on, and the derivations used by religions should not be taken at face value but, rather, functionally. The world knows no objective values, but values are instrumental in the choices embodied in action. Life is a process of value exploration, clarification, confrontation, and selection for both individuals and groups. Values comprise an element in social equilibrium not specified yet nevertheless invoked by Pareto, an element conspicuous in logical action and implicit or inherent in non-logical action. Society is a valuational process in addition to whatever else it may be.

With respect, then, to the problem of the knowledge of values in the Paretian system, this author would suggest what is listed below. It should be understood that Pareto never systematically nor completely examined the problem of values and ends as functional in the social system, either as such or in his own model.

(a) The residues, as will be seen more completely in the next chapter, embody not only psychic states but also positions equivalent to or surrogates for values, norms, and ends with respect to fundamental problems of policy.

(b) Derivations cover for or mask, and in any event certainly include, *ought* statements, including the objectification of the subjective and valuational, which, simply because they are identified as derivations, does not negate their status in value systems.

(c) As will be seen in the next chapter, the derivations, through their differential impact upon this or that residue and therefore upon this or that sentiment, can influence (by weakening or disengaging, or, alternately, by strengthening) the various sentiments and therefore social equilibrium and policy.

(d) The concept of utility (and social utility), as already examined, is pregnant with built-in valuation (whether deliberative, presumptive, or deceptive).

56

(e) The market operates within an institutional and non-institutional framework — including non-logico-experimental belief, non-logical conduct, and derivations — which encompasses valuational elements and those forces exogenous to the individual that govern behavior, for example, through their influence on demand curves and policy positions.

(f) While the socialization process can be specified, interpreted, and analyzed in terms of the integration of psychic states, it also may be comprehended as a value-integration process (whether along Parsons' lines or not).

(g) Non-logical conduct embodies both emotions and values.

(h) As Pareto makes quite explicit, as seen above, there is a necessity to resort to ethics or politics to solve problems going beyond Pareto optimum, for example, the restructuring of participation in the economic system. This means, *inter alia*, that Pareto optimum statically used takes for granted existing norms, in itself a valuational proposition or position.

(i) Values, norms, and ends are indeed embodied in the working rules, although usually or at least frequently in such a way as to function indirectly (as developed above).

(j) Pareto, even beyond what has already been indicated, functionally embodied norms, values, and ends in general in his differentiations between objective and subjective and between real and virtual movements. In both cases, Pareto recognized an is/ought categorization.

(k) Pareto had a significant place for ideals in his system.

(l) As Parsons pointed out and developed, there is at least minimum evidence to support the notion that society does functionally require and/or develop social goals.

In sum, the *Treatise* has values, norms, and ends as non-logico-experimental instruments functioning with respect to the making of choices, both individual and effective social choices. These values, norms, and ends can be examined by the social scientist not necessarily for intrinsic "truth", but functionally, in the process of social equilibrium or policy making.

The foregoing propositions fall into three categories. Evidence for one group has already been presented. Evidence for another will be developed below. The third is comprised of those which have not yet been examined at all or only insofar as they relate to the problem of values. These latter will now be examined.

With respect to the distinction between real and virtual movements, Pareto's general or typical formulation was in terms of a differentiation between what *is* and what *might be*. But virtual movements frequently were identified by him as *ought* propositions. Thus, "Real movements are always considered independently of virtual movements — the study of what is kept distinct from the study of what ought to be (ought to be, if a given purpose is to be realized)" (Sec. 1925; *cf.* 371 - 372, 483, 518, 520, 2262, 2301n.1, 2317, 2411). Where Pareto considered virtual movements *in extenso*, as means to attain a given end, the analysis presumed and included an end (Secs. 1825 - 1895).

So also with the distinction between objective and subjective. In addition to the subjective aspect of what is nominally objective, the subjective was understood and portrayed by him as the normative or ought element in any situation (Secs. 1429, 1573, 1781).

With respect to the subjective aspect of what is nominally objective, Pareto indicated that he comprehended a valuational element in science in general and in economics in particular. In all science, he recognized there was intrusion of metaphysical elements (Secs. 1682, 1683 and *passim*). Moreover, theories reflected sentiments, non-logical beliefs, prevailing prejudices and opinions, and so forth (Secs. 12, 13, 523ff. 617, and *passim*). While science is progressive in character through the test of experience (Secs. 593, 617, and *passim*), the *is* character of the subject of science, that is, the assumption of the status quo, is valuational (Secs. 365, 2022). Definitions are normative in character (Secs. 119, 371, 1532). Science can serve the function of legitimation just as the derivations (Secs. 453, 1307ff). Knowledge, even scientific knowledge, is influenced by the socialization process (Sec. 1043). Not only is logico-experimental knowledge a function of the psychic posture of what will be seen below as Class I Residues (Secs. 2340, 2392), but also one's position in terms of the antinomy of realism and nominalism is a function of differential residues (Sec. 1651). Economics, particularly classical political economy, but even the more formal system of Pareto's day,[48] was partly sermonizing.

Political economy has hitherto been a practical discipline designed to influence human conduct in one direction or another. It could hardly be expected, therefore, to avoid addressing sentiments and in fact it has not done so. All along economists have given us systems of ethics supplemented in varying degrees with narrations of facts and elaborations of the logical implications of facts (Sec. 77).

The science of the classical economists, to describe it briefly, applied itself, in part at least, to the examination not only of what was but also of what ought to be, to a greater or lesser extent, substituting sermonizing for the objective study of facts (Sec. 2016; *cf.* 2017ff, 2147).

With respect to the ends embodied in ideals, ideals are essentially non-logico-experimental "systems of ethics, metaphysics, and theology" (Sec. 2158). It is the social scientist who studies ideals and myths "extrinsically only, as objective facts," and not as something to be substantively believed. Ideals, argued Pareto, are functional, however, because they stimulate conduct along and toward desired goals. They are useful "for purposes of persuasion, for arousing sentiments and urging people along a given line of conduct," and they are useful "because the human mind requires the ideal and the real in varying dosage" (Sec. 2159). Indeed, "if a social doctrine ... is to have any influence, it has to take the form of a 'myth' " (Sec. 1868). Insofar as the ideal is the valuational element in derivations, it is of functional significance. Yet Pareto also argued that ideals are "imaginary objectives" which satisfy "the human desire for logical, or pseudo-logical, ratiocination," but which "can do little or nothing in the way of determining conduct" (Sec. 1871). This touches on the relationship of the derivations to the residues (and thence to the sentiments), which will be examined below.

Suffice it to say here that Pareto also stipulated that so long as the actual goal, "for its part, is concrete and real," (Sec. 1870; *cf.* 151) an imaginary and even impractical ideal goal may serve as an energizer impelling action and conduct toward the realizable goal (Sec. 1870). "To state the matter" to the individual in terms of the actual goal "would amount to little in the way of rousing him to action. It is wiser, therefore," wrote Pareto, "to put before his eyes" the ideal goal, "located at quite a distance from" the actual goal, at a point, "where he would enjoy an enormous, though altogether fantastic, utility ..." The individual is thereby "forced to keep to the curve" of action and ends up at the actual goal "whither, however, he might never have gone had he not been stimulated by a tangential impulse along the line" of action (Sec.1869; *cf* 1772, 1799, 1866, 1879, 2184, 2274, and *passim*).

The values and ends embodied in more or less mythical and mythicized ideals thus have, in the Paretian system, functional significance, along with the other modes in which knowledge of values is instrumental in Pareto's model. This notwithstanding the fact that Pareto explicitly denigrated and derided substantive belief in non-logico-experimental derivations, including values.

# Chapter 3.

# Policy as a Function of Psychology

The main thrust of the *Treatise* is indicated by Pareto's diligent attention to the identification and classification of the residues and by his use of the residues in analyzing social equilibrium. Pareto's central arguments here are twofold. First, both behavior and belief are a function of complex, personal motivational-psychological complexes. Second, as a consequence social equilibrium is a function of the distribution and interplay of these psychic states. All behavior and belief, and particularly non-logico-experimental belief and non-logical conduct, ultimately reflect particular residues, or combinations of residues, which themselves are manifestations of sentiments. As will be seen in great detail in the remaining chapters, the thrust of Pareto's analysis is that social equilibrium (here, policy) is a function of knowledge, psychology, and power, with psychology predominating. The theme that pervaded Pareto's *Manuale*, *Systemes Socialistes*, and *Treatise* is, as Wicksteed (1933, p. 816) expressed it in his review of the *Manuale*, "a *psychology of choice.*" Social equilibrium (including economic equilibrium and policy) is a matter of the building up of effective social choices which are psychologically grounded. Livingston translated the *Trattato* under the title, "The Mind and Society" because, as he expressed it, "it illumines the whole relation of thought to conduct, and of thought to sentiment, and the relation of the individual in all his mental processes to the society in which he lives" (*Treatise*, Vol. I, p. vi).

Pareto's argument and analysis is clear, and the history of psychology, psychoanalysis, and social psychology, as well as sociology, certainly has not detracted from its general correctness. But the substance of Pareto's analysis, seminal as it was in a sense, was nonetheless ambiguous, ill-defined, and awkwardly structured. It has been pointed out, for example, that the residues are admixtures of values and psychological states, an unfortunate combination, albeit one difficult to avoid. The first subsection of this chapter will examine the general character of the residues as the primary element in Pareto's view that social equilibrium is a function of psychology. Later subsections will examine the particular residues identified by Pareto and will interpret the Paretian theory of social equilibrium as a function of psychology. With respect to terminology, this author will use the terms *residues* and *sentiments* when referring to Pareto's usual use thereof; the term *psychic state* (or *psychic posture*) will refer to the basic motivational-psychological posture of the individual, the intention being to include therein both the residues and sentiments.

## 1. Policy as a Function of Psychology

In a paragraph worth quoting at length because he evidently took great pains to avoid being misunderstood, Pareto wrote:

"Returning to the matter of our modes of expression, we must further note that since sentiments are manifested by residues we shall often, for the sake of brevity, use the word 'residues' as including the sentiments that they manifest. So we shall say, simply, that residues are among the elements which determine the social equilibrium, a statement that must be translated and understood as meaning that "the sentiments manifested by residues are among the elements which stand toward the social equilibrium in a relationship of reciprocal determination." But that statement too is elliptical and has again to be translated. Let us beware of ascribing any objective existence to our residues or even to sentiments. What we observe in reality is a group of human beings in a mental condition indicated by what we call sentiments. Our proposition must, therefore, be translated in the following terms: "The mental states that are indicated by the sentiments expressed in residues are among the elements that stand in a relation of reciprocal determination with the social equilibrium." But if we would express ourselves in a language altogether exact, that is still not enough. What in the world are those "mental states" or, if one will, those "psychic conditions?" They are abstractions. And what underlies the abstractions? So we are obliged to say: "The actions of human beings are among the elements that stand in a relationship of reciprocal determination with the social equilibrium. Among such actions are certain manifestations that we designate by the term 'residues' and which are closely correlated with other acts so that once we know the residues we may, under certain circumstances, know the actions. Therefore we shall say that residues are among the elements that stand in a relation of reciprocal determination with the social equilibrium." It is well enough to say all that once, just to fix with strict exactness the meaning of the terms we use; but it would be useless, tiresome, and altogether pedantic to be forever talking with such prolixity. That is why we replace the proposition just stated with its shorter original form: "Residues are among the elements that determine the social equilibrium" (Sec. 1690; *cf.* 875).

From the paragraph just quoted and from other passages it is evident in the *Treatise* that Pareto was highly anxious concerning the subject with which he was working, a subject, it must be remembered, which he concluded was *the* predominant element in social equilibrium. Social equilibrium, he believed, was a function of the interaction between the existing array of sentiments, and the residues were but manifestations of these sentiments. But what were the residues, and what were the sentiments? Pareto, to the dismay of his supporters, to the delight of his critics, and obtrusively to all, failed to provide unambiguous definitions of the concepts *residues* and *sentiments*. He gave no definition of the particular residues at all. He wrote almost nothing on the processes whereby the sentiments are manifested in the residues (Northrup, 1959, p. 271; Muller, 1938, p. 430). Much of what Pareto wrote on these matters is nonoperational, metaphysical (Moore, 1935 - 1936, p. 299), incomplete, and ambiguous.[1] Yet Pareto was not alone in enduring the trials and anxieties of understanding the psychological dimension of human behavior and belief.

Essentially the *residues* are behavior postures from and through which individuals face the world of physical and social reality. The *sentiments* are underlying subconscious psychological drives or instincts, or the impulses emanating from the process and structure of personality development. Thus what is meant by *psychic state* is the behavioral posture derived from and thereby manifesting those subconscious psychic forces. These are hardly unambiguous definitions. As a matter of fact, they are not intended as definitions, but as indicators of the structure of forces that Pareto envisioned and chose to use. Caution must be invoked: Pareto did not examine the subconscious; indeed, it is an engaging question as to just how much Pareto knew of contemporary developments in psychology, including psychoanalytic theory. There is no analysis of the sentiments or the forces comprising the subconscious. Pareto argued simply that there are sentiments and that they are manifest in residues, which he then proceeded to classify and use.

Together the residues and the sentiments indicate for the student of Pareto the psychic posture, which in the main characterizes this or that individual's style of conduct, belief, and life. The sentiments are not operational; the residues are manifestations of the sentiments but, the *Treatise* indicates no way of correlating them, so the sentiments remained unexplored. Behavior and belief are a function of the residues, which in turn are a function of the sentiments. This is the substance of Pareto's argument and the theorem he invoked to explain various facets of social equilibrium. This type of reasoning tended to involve Pareto in the tautology of behavior and drives (Barnes, 1948, p. 562), but he arrived at that juncture through emphasizing the importance of the psychic element. Not only is the tautology a potential trap for any psychological analysis, but also Pareto was particularly ill-equipped to inquire deeply into personality and motivation development. He could only assume and assert, for that is what it amounted to, the existence of psychological foundations of behavior. Moreover, the residues, the result of his attempt to deal with the psychological foundations in accordance with his precepts on logico-experimental knowledge, also were admixtures of psychic and valuational components.

Pareto's identification, classification, and use of the residues was a brilliant effort, although awkwardly established and formulated. The most significant point to be appreciated, in this author's view, is that Pareto's analysis in the *Treatise* was not a *psychology*; rather, it was a *sociology*. It was a sociology which argued the sociological importance of psychology and which attempted to delineate certain psychic postures as key independent variables in social equilibrium (Millikan, 1936, p. 328; Hughes, 1958, p. 262; Parsons, 1937, p. 385; Berger, 1967, pp. 273 - 274). There was in the *Treatise* no analysis of personality or motivation formation; no analysis of the unconscious and its mechanisms and processes; and no analysis of the connection between the foregoing and immediate behavior. The classification of the residues was not a function of, nor did it follow, basic psychological forces (Tufts, 1935, p. 67). Rather, the classification is functionally viable not only as a pointer to psychic phenomena *per se* and to built-in values but as an embodiment of the basic social problems of freedom and control and of continuity and change. Pareto left "the study of drives, urges, impulses, libidos and the id to the professional psychologist" (Brinton, 1954, p. 643). Indeed, "With the origin, nature, and mechanism of the psychic states to which the Residues correspond he has no concern whatever. He begins where the psychic states which produce the Residues issue in society" (DeVoto, 1933b, p. 573). Attention to the residues fitted in well with Pareto's methodological position, however inadequate his analysis and classification of them. Pareto could not have justified analysis of the non-operational (non-objective) sentiments, and he had to remain content with discussion of the ostensibly objective behavioral residues.

The title of the original English translation of the *Treatise*, "The Mind and Society," was quite suitable. As Creedy (1936, p. 179) suggested, "Pareto has, without knowing it, given an impressive proof of Cooley's theorem that mind and society are the obverse and reverse of the same thing, that which is in the individual mind being written out large in society, and that which is in society being reflected in the mind of the individual."[2] In Pareto's view, however, psychology was the independent and society the dependent variable. Yet the Paretian system was a multi-variable one of simultaneous and mutual (or reciprocal) interaction and determination, which gives rise to the relative impact of other forces on individual psychology (Muller, 1938, p. 430). The main implication of the latter point, that the residues were manipulable although not fundamentally changeable with respect to any given individual, will have to await later study in chapter five. A preliminary point, germane at this juncture, will now be examined.

According to Pareto, in any situation, the residues (read, psychic states) were the constant or invariant elements, and the derivations were the variable and secondary elements. Varying derivations alternately could mask the non-logical conduct issuing from the same psychic state. Given a belief, once the derivational element is identified, there remains the constant residue whose fruition the derivation was or represented. When Pareto referred to the residues as the constant or invariable element and to the derivation as variable, what he meant was not that the residues were, once given, constant for all time, that the psychic state was fixed, but that they were always present.

The ambiguity of the terms *constant* and *invariable* has led to no small amount of difficulty in understanding the *Treatise*.

What Pareto's analysis involved is not constant residues but constantly present residues, that is, residues as an ever-present factor. The crucial point is that the individual personality is in reality a complex psychic phenomenon comprised of all the residues with now one and now another stronger and predominant. In other words, the individual motivational complex was comprised of at least several tendencies of variable and varying strength. This interpretation allows for the functional role attributed by Pareto to the derivations. Derivations manipulate the sentiments through the residues, something which could not happen if the residues, or the sentiments, or the two combined, were actually invariant. The dynamic interaction that characterizes Pareto's model is possible only because, given the array of residues in an individual, the individual is, within constraints, malleable. Now one and now another residue may be strengthened (or disengaged or weakened) or, as it were, put in motion through the expression it is given by the derivations which are directed to the person. Pareto wanted to and did stress the importance of the residues and the strength of residues comprising any person's psychic character, but the important fact remains that the person's psychic character is composed of many residues, each of which may be stimulated or brought into play by this or that derivation and thus made more or less relevant or operative with respect to any particular social, or policy, situation.[3]

If psychic character was truly given and constant (non-malleable), or not so heterogeneous that it could be strengthened or weakened at one margin or another, then the derivations would be superfluous and not at all an element in social equilibrium. Pareto's position is that they are secondary — it is the residues that are primary — in importance, but that the derivations are instrumental to the strengthening or weakening in the calling into play of one or the other residues. A person's array of residues constitutes or governs his receptivity to various derivations, but varying derivations could give expression to one or another residue and thereby influence social equilibrium. The derivations exist because of the residues; and the derivations function to stimulate the residues, which stimulation is possible because of the psychic need for derivations, with now one and now another residue being so stimulated.

With the foregoing in mind, it may be reiterated that Pareto maintained several points. First, the positions of individuals in their daily affairs, including both economic activity and affairs of state, were governed by their psychological postures, that is, the residues. Second, the residues manifest underlying sentiments. Third, both non-logical conduct and derivations were profoundly a product of the subjective sentiments, performing psychological roles or serving psychological needs. Fourth, the sentiments governed what people needed, expected, and sought in social and personal life. Finally, social equilibrium or policy was a function of the interplay and interaction between sentiments manifest in residues, that is, of psychic postures.

## 2. Psychic States: The Residues

The human personality is comprised of an admixture of psychic propensities, of several diverse constituent feelings, such that the self is a complex set of drives of varying intensity. These psychic postures, ultimately said by Pareto to reduce to the sentiments, are elucidated by him in terms of classes of residues. Individual psyches are composed of differing proportions of these residues, and the proportions may vary over time and certainly vary between individuals. Pareto considered that the most important characteristic of individuals with respect to social equilibrium is their distinctive personal bundle of residues. The residues, unfortunately, according to Pareto himself, "usually wanting in definiteness, in exact delimitation" (Sec. 870), are the components of personality and motivation. They are alternatives generally only in that one may be stronger or weaker, not present or absent; there are marginal variations. Each individual has presumably at least a little of each residue in his psychic makeup. The crucial point for the analysis of social equilibrium, however, is that individuals manifest the residues in different proportions. It should be added that the same residue, as between individuals, may be directed to different objects or objectives.

*The Residues*

Pareto enumerated and described six classes of residues:[4]

I. Instinct for Combinations
II. Group-Persistences (Persistence of Aggregates)
III. Need of Expressing Sentiments by External Acts (Activity, Self-expression)
IV. Residues Connected with Sociality
V. Integrity of the Individual and his Appurtenances
VI. The Sex Residue

The foregoing are but the names of the several classes. The complete classification for each one is presented below in connection with the discussion of the relevant class, which discussion is conducted along the lines explicitly developed by Pareto.

### (I) *Instinct for Combinations*

The first of his two main classes of residues, the so-called Instinct for Combinations, Pareto specified as that element in the human psyche which issues in behavior tending "to combine certain things with certain other things" (Sec. 889), that is, to rearrange, to change status quo positions, to create in a new manner or way. "The instinct for combinations," he wrote, "is among the major forces determining the social equilibrium" (Sec. 896); it "is intensely powerful in the human species and has probably been, as it still remains, one of the important factors in civilization" (Sec. 889). The present class of residues embodies the propensity to innovate through the recombination or restructuring of existing things, with the substance of the things chosen for new combina tions generally if not always non- or extra-psychologically determined (although the attachment itself is a psychological phenomenon). The Class I residues also include an "impulse to combine residues;" a "hunger for logical developments," "the need people feel for covering their non-logical conduct with a varnish of logic;" and "faith in the efficacy of combinations" (Secs. 969, 972, 975, 976). The complete classification follows:

*I. Instinct for Combinations*
Ia. Generic combinations
Ib. Combinations of similars or opposites
    i. Generic likeness or oppositeness
    ii. Unusual things and exceptional occurrences
    iii. Objects and occurrences inspiring awe or terror
    iv. Felicitous state associated with good things; infelicitous state, with bad

v. Assimilation: physical consumption of substances to get effects of associable, and more rarely of opposite, character

Ic. Mysterious workings of certain things; mysterious effects of certain acts
    i. Mysterious operations in general
    ii. Mysterious linkings of names and things
Id. Need for combining residues
Ie. Need for logical developments
If. Faith in the efficacy of combinations

A detailed examination of Pareto's examples would reveal a heterogeneous collection of "combinations," but the general thrust of the class is clearly to identify a psychic impulse to combine, to rearrange, to make over, or to create, even in the absence of logico-experimental bases. As Pareto argued, "if it sometimes manifests itself in ridiculous and absurd ways, that fact detracts no whit from its importance" (Sec. 896). It should not need reiteration that Pareto made no effort to inquire into what psychological forces and mechanisms were at work in personality and motivation development which would issue in this (or any other) residue.

## (II) *Group-Persistences (Persistence of Aggregates)*

According to Pareto the second great class of residues involves the tendency to consolidate and perpetuate or make permanent existing arrangements, combinations, relations, beliefs, and the like, including "society" and "humanity" (Secs. 1052ff). It is the propensity to continue that which has become important, to maintain existing arrangements, and/or to allow only those changes which come through or within existing arrangements. It is roughly equated by Pareto to mechanical inertia: "it tends to resist the movement imparted by other instincts" (Sec. 992; *cf.* 1001). Whereas the Class I residues tend to disequilibrate, the Class II residues tend to maintain equilibrium or to maintain existing combinations intact. Carrying "the analysis a step further," Pareto maintained that residues of Class I may "become permanent under pressure of residues of Class II," (Sec. 995), by which he meant the attribution of permanency to new combinations upon their effectuation. It is instructive that Pareto envisioned Class II residues as contributing to both cohesion and order, that is, to the maintenance of the group (Secs. 1037, 1047, 1071, and *passim*). Pareto also included here the "persistence of abstractions"

69

(theologies and systems of metaphysics) (Sec. 1066), but also the "need of new abstractions" (Secs. 1086 - 1088). He saw the new not only facilitating continuity by replacing the old (thereby strengthening and revitalizing the underlying residue) but also by their very existence reflecting the continued strength of the residue. His viewpoint was, thus, a case of innovations functionally promotive of permanence or persistence. The thrust of the Class II residues is a psychic need for persistence of important arrangements, for continuity. The residues included therein follow.

*II. Group Persistence (Persistence of Aggregates)*
IIa. Persistence of relations between a person and other persons and places
    i. Relationships of family and kindred groups
    ii. Relations with places
    iii. Relationships of social class
IIb. Persistence of relations between the living and the dead
IIc. Persistence of relations between a dead person and the things that belonged to him in life
IId. Persistence of abstractions
IIe. Persistence of uniformities
IIf. Sentiments transformed into objective realities
IIg. Personifications
IIh. Need of new abstractions

Once again, Pareto included under this heading a heterogeneous collection of examples and subclassifications, the ostensible general character of which is their exemplification of a tendency to persist, the opposite of the tendency to innovate. In retrospect it may be suggested that what the classifications of the various residues really indicate is the material with which Pareto worked and which he arranged in support and elucidation of the psychic-state components he distilled from them in the aggregate.

(III) *Need of Expressing Sentiments by External Acts (Activity, Self-expression)*
The third class of residues involves a psychic "need for action" (Sec. 1089). Elaborating, Pareto wrote:

> "The acts in which sentiments express themselves reinforce such sentiments and may even arouse them in individuals who were without them. It is a well known psychological fact that if an emotion finds expression in a certain physical attitude, an indi-

70

vidual putting himself in that attitude may come to feel the corresponding emotion. The residues of this class, accordingly, stand conjoined with emotions, sentiments, and passions in a complex concatenation of actions and reactions" (Sec. 1091).

The first sentence quoted nicely indicates Pareto's awareness of the dynamics of personality and motivation formation, as summarized above. The remainder of the quotation indicates some confusion. Pareto never fully systematized his model of the subconscious, for example, the respective places and functions of emotions, sentiments, passions, inclinations, and so forth, perhaps to his credit. But there also is indicated a need for expression issuing in action.

Pareto enumerated only two subclassifications:

IIIa. Need of 'doing something' expressing itself in combinations

IIIb. Religious ecstasies

The former, a "demand for action," "gives rise to occult, magical, and religious rites" (Sec. 1093). When the sentiment involved rises "in intensity to the point of exaltation, exhilaration, delirium" (Sec. 1094), the latter residue is involved. The difference, wrote Pareto, was "merely quantitative" (Sec. 1094).

Although this class of residues seems to overlap one or more of the other classes, Pareto here evidenced his perceptive insight into the need for action. He recognized the need for a release, "escaping, in a word, from a state of passive abstraction" (Sec. 1090), the need to reinforce and reassure sagging ego, authority, and status.

(IV) *Residues Connected with Sociality*

The fourth class of residues relates to components of psychic states concerned with life in society and the necessity for discipline. With regard to the latter Pareto was ambiguous (not that he was so clear in respect to the former):

"This class is made up of residues connected with life in society. Disciplinary residues might also be grouped here, if one agrees that the sentiments corresponding to them are strengthened by living in society. In that direction, it has been observed that with the exception of the cat all domestic animals when at liberty live in groups. On the other hand society is impossible

71

without some sort of discipline, and therefore the social structure and the disciplinary structure necessarily have certain points of contact" (Sec. 1113).

Pareto quite obviously was aware of the necessity of social control in society[5] (see chapter six, *infra*) and he apparently was at least somewhat aware that participants (power players) in the social process are at the same time agents of social control. Yet there is no separate category of "disciplinary residues," although, perhaps, Pareto's discussion indicated germinal insight into the forces of the superego. Below is Pareto's classification of the Class IV residues.

*IV. Residues Connected with Sociality*
IVa. Particular societies
IVb. Need of uniformity
    i. Voluntary conformity on the part of the individual
    ii. Uniformity enforced upon others
    iii. Neophobia
IVc. Pity and cruelty
    i. Self-pity extended to others
    ii. Instinctive repugnance to suffering
    iii. Reasoned repugnance to useless sufferings
IVd. Self-sacrifice for the good of others
    i. Risking one's life
    ii. Sharing one's property with others
IVe. Sentiments of social ranking; hierarchy
    i. Sentiments of superiors
    ii. Sentiments of inferiors
    iii. Need of group approbation
IVf. Asceticism

The class of residues in question deals, *inter alia*, with a need for association; a need for uniformity, expressed in social control (repression of individual variations, persecution of heretics),[6] imitation, fashion, and the like (Secs. 1117 - 1119); and "a sentiment of hostility to innovations that are calculated to disturb uniformities."[7] With respect to the latter, Pareto wrote "It is interesting that many individuals who suffer from neophobias in some departments of life may look with favour upon anything new in some other direction, say in politics or religion, and for the simple reason that it is new" (Sec. 1132). He has noted another manifestation of the complexity of psychic states. In this connection he wrote: "One might also consider the opposite of neophobia — eagerness for innovations; but one may doubt whether that be a sentiment by itself and not rather a product merely of the instincts for combinations and, in our time, also of sentiments of adoration for the god of Progress" (Sec. 1132). Here he mentions another manifestation of overlap and ambiguity, as well as expresses his own feelings.

The Class IV residues, however, did enable Pareto to deal with manifestations of the process whereby individuals identify with others; approve and disapprove of the conduct of others; project one's own feelings to others; differentiate oneself from others; develop and practice altruism and asceticism; and develop phobias and sufferings which "are perversions of the instinct of sociality" (Sec. 1206). Once again, Pareto offered almost nothing by way of psychological analysis, engaging primarily, if not entirely, in description of the events, conducts, beliefs, and feelings which suggested to him the residues of sociality.

(V) *Integrity of the Individual and his Appurtenances*
Of the fifth class of residues, Pareto stated:

"This class is in a sense the complement of Class IV (sociality). To defend one's own things and strive to increase their quantity are two operations that frequently merge. So defense of integrity and development of personality are two operations that may differ little or even be one and the same. The sum of sentiments called interests is of the same nature as the sentiments to which the residues of the present variety correspond; hence sentiments of 'interest' ought strictly to be put in it. But they are of such great intrinsic importance in the social equilibrium that they are best considered apart from residues" (Sec. 1207).

The psychological process of identity-formation is recognized by Pareto as being a process of both socialization and individuation, a process of developing both outwardly and inwardly, a process with both sociological and psychological dimensions. Generally speaking, the Class V residues relate to the process of developing and maintaining individual identity and self esteem. The residues comprising Class V are as follows:

V. *Integrity of the Individual and his Appurtenances*
Va. Sentiments of resistance to alterations in the social equilibrium

73

Vb. Sentiments of equality in inferiors
Vc. Restoration of integrity by acts pertaining to the individual whose integrity has been impaired
  i. Real subjects
  ii. Imaginary or abstract subjects
Vd. Restoration of integrity by acts pertaining to the offender (vengeance, 'getting even')
  i. Real offender
  ii. Imaginary or abstract offender

Quite perceptively Pareto understood that the individuals identity tends to be challenged by real and imagined changes in the status quo:

"The equilibrium may be one actually existing, or an ideal equilibrium desired by the individual. But whether real or imaginary, if it is altered, or thought of as altered, the individual suffers, even if he is not directly affected by the alteration, and sometimes, though rarely, even if he gains by it (Sec. 1208).

The forces (or sentiments) that come into play when the social equilibrium is disturbed are nearly always perceived by the individual members of that society under some special form. Needless to say, they, as individuals, know nothing about any forces, nothing about any equilibrium. Those are just names which we, as scientists, apply to what is going on. They are conscious of an unpleasant disturbance — it may sometimes be painful, and very painful indeed — of their integrity as it was when the state of equilibrium was still being maintained."[8]

Moreover, Pareto understood the sensitivity of people to threats to their real or imagined identity (security) and the magnification of anxiety disproportionate to the objective importance of the thing feared: "So the sentiment that inspires resistance to alterations of equilibrium places alterations in insignificant matters on a par with alterations in very important matters, ..." (Sec. 1212). There is "... a sentiment of revulsion against anything disturbing to the social equilibrium as it has existed and is accepted by the individual."[9]

It is evident here that Pareto saw social equilibrium as a function not only of psychic states in general but also of the process whereby individuals define their status, identity, and security in terms of this or that facet of the status quo (Sec. 2471). This is evident not only in Class Va., "Sentiments of resistance to alterations in the social equilibrium," but also in Class Vb., "sentiments of equality in inferiors," which is, according to Pareto, "often a defense of integrity on the part of an individual belonging to a lower class and a means of lifting him to a higher" (Sec. 1220).

Also involved are some psychic defenses relating to what Pareto called "restoration of integrity." These are connected in part to identity formation (or purification), to the overcoming of feelings of inferiority, guilt, and helplessness (Secs. 1229 - 1311, e.g. 1298) and to the psychic mechanism from which intense hatred springs forth.

"In general terms, hatred arises from a desire to repel an attack on one's integrity. Vigorous conviction is an element in integrity, and that explains the violence of theological hatreds. Hatred wanes when faith wanes, or when the individual no longer considers the faith an essential part of his personality. ... Oftentimes any change in the existing state of things is deemed an offense and is repelled by attachment to tradition -- neophobia" (Sec. 1313).

Social equilibrium is thus a function of behavior and belief. It ultimately reduces to subconscious attempts on the part of individuals to establish and maintain (or define and defend) the integrity of their identity and of that with which the individual identifies.

(VI) *The Sex Residue*
The final residue examined by Pareto concerns sex. It is identified in such a way as to confirm the view that Pareto's general analysis was intended only as a first approximation, that it was not written as a complete statement of man's psychological equipment (Sec. 1396n.1). In addition, Pareto inquired into sex not in terms of physical appetite but only "in so far as it influences theories, modes of thinking — as a residue. In general terms, the sex residue and the sentiments in which it originates figure in huge numbers of phenomena, but they are often dissembled, especially among modern peoples" (Sec.1324, *cf.* 852).

In his discussion of the Class VI residue, which alone of the classes was given no subclassifications, Pareto referred to "people who preach virtue as a way of lingering, in their thoughts, on sex matters" (Sec. 852), and to brains "fermenting with prurience" (Sec. 1375). This is indeed interesting from a writer who spends seventy-eight pages discussing sexual taboos, erotic literature, libertinism, worship of sex organs, birth control, sexual behavior of priests and nuns, chastity, prostitution, and so on. But Pareto's direct concern and confrontation with sex serves to throw in relief his main theme, namely, that of the phenomenon of *displacement.* Sexual energies are inhibited and are transferred to other interests, and sexual neuroses may yield anxious behavior in other fields of conduct (*cf.* Ginsberg, 1936, p. 236, and Borkenau, 1936, p. 39; *cf.* Ascoli, 1936, p. 85). For "displacement," Pareto used "dissembled" (as above):

"But that instinct is often enough logicalized and dissembled under guise of asceticism ... (Sec. 852).

All such things go to show how at all times thoughts of sex crowd into the human mind. Certain it is that forced chastity, especially when it is scrupulously observed, tends to introduce amorous sentiments into situations where there is, and can be, no question of erotic relations. That is already apparent, in germ, in the extreme fondness of a little girl for her doll, an animal, her friends, and sometimes, though she may be unaware of it, for her parents. The fact can be proved, for when the girl marries or comes into contact with a man in some way or other, such forms of affection either disappear or diminish in intensity" (Sec. 1356).

Pareto not only recognized the sexual element in psychology and motivation but also had a theory of infantile sexuality. His theory was perhaps different from Freud's, inasmuch as Pareto's was more in terms of displacement and less, if at all, in terms of stages. Pareto found the sex residue "... in the piety of a certain French pastor who, out of loathing for pornography, goes to a show to measure the length of the ballet dancers' skirts and the precise amount of ankle and thigh they leave exposed" (Sec. 1372; *cf.* 1719). He found it in puritanism: "Our puritans also fight immorality, at times in such ways as to make one's mouth water for sin. I say nothing of those who under pretext of educating the young to chastity write books to impart all the details of the sexual act" (Sec. 1388). The sex residue also existed in "... the petticoated sex-reformers of our day who for sheer love of purity cannot get their minds off prostitution" (Sec. 1390).

Moreover, he discerns the germ of another ego defense mechanism: "Veneration and hatred for a given thing may likewise be forms of a religion which has that thing for its object of worship. ... It is also a trite remark that the men who most malign women are the ones who can least do without them" (Sec. 1357).

Pareto was highly perceptive and sophisticated, then, in recognizing that, with respect to social equilibrium and aside from physical sex itself, the general effect of the sex residue is to intensify other residues.[10] Through displacement it seeks in other areas of life (for example, economic and political activity) for substitutive gratification of the energies originating in sexual drives but which otherwise are unable to find expression.[11]

## 3. Interpretation

Pareto's theory is that social equilibrium is a function of psychology. As in the case of his theory of knowledge, it will be seen that Pareto's discussion dealt with fundamental problems of policy. But precisely because these fundamental problems are difficult and complex, interpretation itself is difficult. Moreover, Pareto's discussions pale before then and now contemporary psychological and psychoanalytical studies and theories. His use of the residues is very suggestive, so much so that it is difficult to do them justice in short summarization. Pareto had, nonetheless, a profound knack for revealing feelings masquerading as facts.

At this point it should be indicated that Pareto, apparently for purposes of convenience, abstracted from later thorough and independent analysis of the last four classes of residues (III through VI). He considered that the effect of their operation was sufficiently akin to that of the Class II residues that he could take account of them as if they were Class II residues (Secs. 2415, 2471; cf. Homans and Curtis, 1934, p. 119). Without implication concerning the merits of such an accounting — the reduction to a pair of polar psychic stances is certainly oversimplification — the procedure here will have to be the same as that of Pareto himself.

With respect, then, to Pareto's two main residues, it is possible to differentiate between two different psychic states or attitudinal postures. These may be called *patrism* and *matrism*, characterizing here the dominance of Class II or Class I residues, respectively. Accordingly, matrism would connote permissiveness with respect to received norms and behavioral patterns (or group persistences); permissiveness with respect to variation and innovation; disinter-

77

estedness with respect to power; absence of religious sentiments; looseness of morality; and the like. Patrism would connote prescriptiveness with respect to received norms, behavioral patterns, and the status quo generally; religious fundamentalism or fanaticism; moral strictness; interest in the acquisition of power; authoritativeness with respect to received social control authorities; adoration of the routine and conventional; and the like.[1][2] It is difficult to further clarify these concepts. They are psychological postures, but each is in its own way both compliant, aggressive, and withdrawn. Pareto's general point was that every individual's psychic posture is comprised of both Class I and Class II residues, with proportions varying between individuals. But his most distinctive point was that individuals tend to be predominantly of one psychic type or the other. (The terms *patrist* and *matrist* were not used by Pareto.) In addition, Pareto's cyclical theory of history was one of alternating periods of prescriptiveness and permissiveness, or faith and skepticism (Secs. 1680 - 1681, 2341ff, and *passim*), as will be developed in chapter seven, *infra*. In general, it will be noticed that patrism and matrism involve positions psychological in character with respect to continuity and change and to freedom and control.

Individuals demonstrating predominance of Class I residues were thought by Pareto to be permissive with respect to authority and innovational in temperament; individuals manifesting Class II residues were prescriptive and routinist. (In passing, it may be noted that there was contained in Pareto's model the germ of Perlman's theory of the labor movement. Entrepreneurs are rich in Class I residues and are opportunity conscious, while workers are wealthy in Class II residues and are security conscious (Secs. 2187, 2232). Interestingly, also, saving was held to be a function of Class II residues (Secs. 2228 - 2233), that is, a passive function of psychic reaction to income — not unlike Smith and Keynes — and explicitly not a function of interest rates (Sec. 2232n.1). Workers and *rentiers* are psychologically akin). Individuals were recognized to be both permissive and prescriptive, albeit toward different objects, but predominantly one or the other. Pareto's discussion and model is complicated further by inclusion of differential postures toward power, conniving or scheming, the use of force, humanitarianism (permissiveness but a Class II residue, albeit among the weakest) (Sec. 2475; *cf.* 1716, 2471 and *passim*), the masses, and the status quo institutional framework. Thus, the patrist mentality is essentially authoritarian, elitist, for the status quo, willing to use force, and Aristotelian with respect to knowledge in relation to social policy. As the history of psychology suggests, the construction of psychic types on such a level is difficult. Still, Pareto's model has a clear patrist-matrist thrust and was quite perceptive.

Much more meaningful and useful, however, although still complicated and difficult to work with, is an interpretation of the Class I and Class II residues in terms of continuity and change. As should already be evident, it is quite easy to interpret the two classes in terms of progressivism and conservatism, respectively. Perhaps the great majority of commentators on the *Treatise* thus have interpreted the two as being change-orientated and change-resistent postures.[13] There is much to be said for this view, for there can be little if any question that the main thrust of Pareto's analysis in this regard was that liberal and conservative positions with respect to the question of change are essentially psychic (or psychological) postures *per se*. As such they are tied up with the socialization, individuation, and identity-creation processes of personality and motivation development.

Social equilibrium and policy in the Paretian system were a function of the interaction of psychological states generally differentiated in terms of marginal urges and resistences to change. Social equilibrium and policy are a function of the distribution or proportion of Class I and Class II residues within and between the two major classes of society and as such are psychological in character. As will be seen in more detail below, Pareto went further and specified that it is "desirable ... that combination-instincts should predominate in leaders and the instincts of group-persistence in subordinates" (Sec. 2427; *cf.* 2454, 2457ff; and *cf.* Bongiorno, 1930, pp. 367, 369). Pareto's analysis of the residues does incorporate consideration of the forces and values implicit in the problem of continuity and change.

The evidence for such a continuity-change interpretation derives from Pareto's own formulation of the two residues in question and also from his use thereof as interpretive and explanatory propositions. For example, Pareto differentiated between Athenian and Roman psychic states (on a psycho-cultural level) in terms of continuity and change (Secs. 220ff). He also differentiated between Athens (too many Class I residues) and Sparta (too many Class II residues) using the same dichotomy (Sec. 2419). Consider also, for example, the following:

"The chief utility of the sentiments of group-persistence is the resistence they offer to harmful inclinations of individual interest and to the impetuous sweep of passions. Their chief drawback is that they inspire a conduct that is logically consistent with them but detrimental to society. To perform their first, their conservative, function such sentiments have to be very strong. When they lose their vigor to any considerable extent they are unable to resist powerful interests and aggressive passions, and vent themselves in effects of the second sort only — those which are detrimental to society" (Sec. 2420).

Quite aside from the judgment required as to when a particular effect may be said to fall in one or the other category, it is clear that the Class II residue was seen by Pareto as a conservative posture functioning with respect to continuity. It is also clear that the operation of the Class II residue embodied social control functions. "We are interested, however, in distinguishing individuals who aimed at undermining group-persistences, at substituting logical for non-logical conduct, at deifying Reason, from individuals who defended group-persistences, stood by tradition, were therefore favourable to non-logical conduct and burned no incense to the goddess Reason" (Sec. 2346).

At roughly the same point, Pareto maintained that "impiety" in the sense of guilty behavior or attitudes toward the gods, the dead, one's parents, and/or country "designates an offense against the principal group-persistences" (Sec. 2345n.8). Again, quoting one of his sources describing a particular third party: "A lover of the unusual, eager for anything new, he was prone, as men of such temperaments are, to fomenting heresies and dissensions" (Sec. 2381n.1). Once again it is obvious that postures with respect to continuity and change involve the problem of order regarding freedom and control.

Pareto's main use, however, of the two classes of residues was in the development of two major personality types, the Speculators and the *Rentiers*, who became archetypal figures in his analysis of history and social equilibrium.

"*Entrepreneurs* as a class are recruited from individuals in whom the combination-instincts indispensable to success in enterprise are highly developed. Individuals in whom the Class II residues predominate remain among the mere owners of savings. *Entrepreneurs* are in general, therefore, adventurous souls, hungry for novelty in the economic as well as in the social field, and not at all alarmed at change, expecting as they do to take advantage of it. The mere savers, instead, are often quiet, timorous souls sitting at all times with their ears cocked in apprehension, like rabbits, and hoping little and fearing much from any change, for well they know of bitter experience that they will be called upon to foot the bill for it. The inclination to an adventurous and extravagant life, like the inclination to a quiet and thrifty life, is in great part a matter of instinct and only to a very slight extent a matter of reasoned design (Sec. 2232).

In the speculator group Class I residues predominate, in the *rentier* group, Class II residues (Sec. 2235).

*Rentiers* are, in general, secretive, cautious, timid souls, mistrustful of all adventure, not only of dangerous ventures but of such as have any remotest semblance of not being altogether safe. ... Speculators, on the other hand, are usually expansive personalities, ready to take up with anything new, eager for economic activity. They rejoice in dangerous economic ventures and are on the watch for them (Sec. 2313).

The S group is primarily responsible for change, for economic and social progress. The R group, instead, is a powerful element in stability, and in many cases counteracts the dangers attending the adventurous capers of the S's. A society in which R's almost exclusively predominate remains stationary and as it were, crystallized. A society in which S's predominate lacks stability, lives in a state of shaky equilibrium that may be upset by a slight accident from within or from without" (Sec. 2235, *cf.* 2139).

The resolution of the problem of continuity and change is thus a function of the distribution of psychological postures of risk assumption and risk avoidance. In Pareto's system this means the distribution of Class I and Class II residues and the objects to which they become attached, with the instrumentation and values of continuity and change (the elemental question, which change?) hanging in the balance.

But it is too simple to reduce the Class I residues to change and the Class II residues to continuity, though Pareto's precise formulation is ultimately ambiguous. The concepts *change* and *continuity* are, for one thing, too encompassing, quite aside from the fact that speculators are not in favor of and *rentiers* not opposed to all change. As Pareto himself pointed out by way of explicit qualification, some changes are conservative:

"Members of the R group must not be mistaken for "conservatives," nor members of the S group for "progressives," innovators, revolutionaries. They may have points in common with such, but there is no identity. There are evolutions, revolutions, innovations, that the R's support, especially movements tending to restore to the ruling classes certain residues of group-persistence that had been banished by the S's. A revolution may be made against the S's ..." (Sec. 2235).

As a number of writers have pointed out, including Faris (1936, p. 665), De Voto (1933b, pp. 575 - 576), and Hughes (1958, p. 269), the meaning of the two psychic components summarized as Class I and Class II residues is not only complex but also is ambiguous. Several points appear crucial. First, acts in and of themselves do not necessarily connote change or continuity; their meaning is contextual or circumstantial, as well as either real or imagined. Second, change connoting change or departure from what otherwise would have been the case reduces to continuity if what otherwise would have been the case is (another) change. This is a matter of judgment, probability, and circumstances. Third, change under the aegis of Class I residues may be forward looking, whereas change under aegis of Class II residues may be backward looking. The differentiation, however, depends at least in part on what substance is attributed to backward and forward respectively, which is also circumstantial in character. (Specifically, it in part relates to the heterogeneity of the forces and factors comprising any particular status quo). Fourth, Pareto's analysis differentiated between *form* and *substance* and allowed, *inter alia*, for both continuity in form and change in substance and for change in form and continuity in substance. Fifth, Pareto's Class II residues are not simply aversion to change, although a particular individual dominated by Class II residues may be so predisposed. In the usual case, Class II residues involve aversion to change otherwise than through accepted or traditional channels or forms. Much depends on what becomes accepted as traditional through psychic identification. Sixth, and most important, Class I and Class II residues connote psychic postures, which means, in the Paretian system, non-logical conduct. This is to say that there are subconscious mechanisms and processes, one of whose results is the attachment

82

of the individual to this or that pattern or object involving now change and now continuity as the individual identifies and defends his ego. The attachment derives, as a general rule, not from anything intrinsic in the pattern or object but from a more or less random process of psychological involvement. People are not simply for or against change; rather they are for or against change and continuity as the particular changes and continuities have psychic meaning for them individually and subconsciously, or as the particular events have psychic meaning for them as continuity or change. Every individual wants to continue what is important to him.

The weight of Pareto's analysis resides in the general proposition that positions with respect to continuity and change derive from psychic postures, however difficult it is to further specify the Paretian model. Given the significance of the residues as delineations of components of psychic states, this means that Pareto examined the resolution of the problem of continuity and change in terms of psychology, however little psychological analysis and model-building was undertaken in the *Treatise*. What appear as innovational and conservative positions are, according to Pareto, a function of underlying psychic forces, that is, the sentiments, together with more or less random attachments to objects of identity-creation, with attachment itself a psychic phenomenon. The analysis of the residues was in part at least an attempt to come to grips with this issue.

There are actually several key and interrelated points to be made. First, Pareto argued the psychological character of the problem of continuity and change. He argued that positions with respect to continuity and change were psychological in character. His analysis of the resolution of the problem of continuity and change was essentially psychological. Pareto's analysis in the *Treatise*, therefore, was a psychological theory of the problem of continuity and change. Second, and somewhat conversely, Pareto incorporated in his analysis of the residues elements of the problem of continuity and change. The residues are identified by Pareto in a manner that encompasses continuity and change forces. That is to say, the central part of Pareto's theory of continuity and change is contained in his analysis of the residues. Third, by inference Pareto included in his psychological analysis the values of continuity and change, albeit not as values *per se* but as valuational elements in the guise of the residues. Behavior is important to Pareto not because it is a function of rational (logical) value analysis and choice but because it is a function of psychic states (that is, non-logical); yet, as Parsons has shown, the functioning of the residues instrumentally embodies values.

In addition, Pareto's description of the residues also included consideration and inclusion of facets of the problem of freedom and control. First, as already has been pointed out, the operation of the forces of both continuity and change, particularly or most dramatically the former, embodies social control functions. Second, the operation of the Class II, IV and V residues includes social control elements (as indicated in the foregoing discussions). As Henderson pointed out, some of the residues of these classes "constitute, so to speak, the mortar that binds the society together, ... and thus essential to the survival of the society" (Henderson, 1937, p. 55). Third, the thrust of Pareto's discussion with respect to freedom and control is parallel to that of continuity and change: both freedom and control have a psychological or subjective character; elements of freedom and control as well as valuational elements relating to them are included in the residues; psychic states are partially analyzed in terms of freedom and control; and freedom and control is parallel to that of continuity and change: both forces of socialization, individuation, and identity-creation in individual personality-motivation development.

It can be argued, then, that Pareto's analysis of the residues included consideration of elements and values both of the problem of freedom and control and of the problem of continuity and change. His analysis suggests the complex psychological and analytical character of these problems and of the interrelationships between them. The reduction of the residues of Classes III through VI to Class II suggests the conservative character of the problem of freedom and control when applied to the problem of continuity and change in the Paretian theory of policy. Pareto's analysis also suggests the impact of the identity-security process in psychological development on the strengthening of continuity as opposed to change. Finally, there is some suggestion that the problem of freedom and control may be specified in terms of continuity and change, that is, that the former may be defined in terms of the latter. Various aspects of the foregoing are developed below, particularly in chapters six and seven.

The intention of this chapter has been to establish the sense and context in which Pareto maintained that social equilibrium and policy were a function of psychology. The primary purpose of the concluding section of the chapter has been to show that elements of the problems of continuity and change and of freedom and control were included by Pareto in the residues as ostensibly non-valuational components. In conclusion it may be reiterated that Pareto's analysis of the residues was more a sociology than a psychology; that his analysis of the residues was ambiguous and unsatisfactory, however suggestive; that the problems of continuity and change and of freedom and control were fundamentally psychological in character; and that Pareto's analysis of psychic states incorporated elements both of freedom and control and of continuity and change. That Pareto's categories of residues are ambiguous and difficult to apply should not obscure the fundamental import of his work. Social equilibrium and policy are a partial but fundamental function of complex psychic states.

# Chapter 4.

# Policy as a Function of Power

It has thus far been seen that knowledge and psychology are two dimensions or sets of variables in the theory of socio-economic policy manifest in Pareto's *Treatise.* Insofar as they were most distinctively obtrusive to Pareto, they were seen as the ubiquity and predominance of non-logico-experimental reasonings and the grounding of choice in psychic states. These were the themes — the elements of social equilibrium — which Pareto explicitly attempted to examine and document as a contribution to general sociology and which, accordingly, he attended to in great detail in the *Treatise,* going beyond his earlier analysis of interests.

But still a third dimension or set of variables pervades the *Treatise,* a dimension of which Pareto was quite cognizant but which he apparently assumed or was convinced was so abundantly obvious that it did not require separate demonstration. This third dimension is *power.* Not enumerated as one of the elements in the social equilibrium, power was, nevertheless, the context in which the interplay of knowledge, psychic states, and so on took place. Pareto's analyses of social phenomena in terms of beliefs and residues were conducted in such a manner that arguments made in terms of one variable could and often would be restated in terms of power. In other words, the significance of derivations and residues was defined in terms of society seen as a system of power.

Pareto did not present a separate and systematic examination of the subject of power — as he did with derivations and residues, the chief components of knowledge and psychology, respectively. Consequently his general theory of power must be distilled from his discussions and analyses in the *Treatise.* The main themes of that general theory of power are, however, easily discerned: social equilibrium or policy is a partial function of power and power play; his is an elitist (ruling class) theory of the power structure; freedom and control are seen as the distribution of power in society; circulation of the elite is the redistribution of power in society and, thus, is one facet of the problem of continuity and change; there is an interplay of concentrations of power (aside from consideration of the elite and of government *per se*), including the practice of corruption; and power is exercised or administered through manipulation, through force and fraud (deception and manufactured consent). The central Paretian ideas establishing policy as a function of power will be developed in this chapter. Those relating to the interaction of power with knowledge and psychology and those relating to the problems of freedom and control and continuity and change will be developed in subsequent chapters.

## 1. Economy and Society as a System of Power

It was one of Pareto's central insights that society and economy, no less than polity, are *political* processes, that is to say, systems of power (Bobbio, 1956, p. 245). Although Pareto acknowledged the difficulties of defining and measuring such a complex concept as power (Secs. 2106 - 2107), he nevertheless argued that power in all its manifestations is a determinant or force through which problems of policy or choice are resolved. Rejecting abstract principles as merely "an expression of... individual sentiments," Pareto insisted that "as between the various social classes no principle of 'right' can be found to regulate the division of social advantage. The classes that have the greater strength, intelligence, ability, shrewdness, take the lion's share." Indeed, "It is not clear how any other principle or division could be logically established and even less clear how once they were established logically they could be enforced or applied in the concrete" (Sec. 1509). Society is a system of power. To the powerful go the fruits of the banquet and the spoils of combat. Jockeying for position takes many forms. These themes are central to Pareto's theory of power. For example, arguments and claims for "equality" were considered by Pareto to be merely "almost always... demands for privileges" (Sec. 1221). The demand, claim, or sentiment of equality "is related to the direct interests of individuals

88

who are bent on escaping certain inequalities not in their favor, and setting up new inequalities that will be in their favor, this latter being their chief concern" (Sec. 1227). Conduct, whether issuing from belief, interest, or sentiment, involves power play, and such play may be direct or indirect, and so on.[1]

Policy, or, in Pareto's terminology, social equilibrium, derives from power play and thereby from society as a system of power or as a system of mutual coercion. "If Smith is interfering with Jones, Jones calls it 'freedom' to escape from the interference. But if Jones in his turn gets control of Smith, he calls it 'freedom' to tighten the ropes. In both cases the term 'freedom' has the pleasantest associations for Jones" (Sec. 1554). What Jones wants, of course, is to escape the exposure he has had to the exercise of Smith's coercive powers — Smith's "freedom" — and to be able to subject Smith to his coercive power. It is substantially the case, argued Pareto, that "men holding power have, as a rule, a certain inclination to use that power to keep themselves in the saddle and to abuse it to secure personal gains and advantages, which they sometimes fail to distinguish clearly from party gains and advantages and almost always confuse with the gains and advantages of country" (Sec. 2267).

The process is one of conflict and mutual manipulation (Secs. 1498, 1524, 1748, 1755, 2262, and *passim*). Although there is a governing elite, and Pareto wrote of "the plutocracy that is the ruling power in civilized countries today" (Sec. 1755), democracy does afford many outlets for ambition (Sec. 1152; *cf.* 1775). But whether under one form of society (or government) (Sec. 2267) or another, the social process is one of conflict. Conflict has been universal, as between various cults (of religion, of reason) (Sec. 304, and *passim*), but, "In our times conflicts are chiefly economic" (Sec. 2187). Whether in terms of international relations or domestic policy, the conflict tends to be economic in character and involves mutual coercion: "In our day the foreign policies of the various countries are almost exclusively economic, and domestic policy comes down more than anything else to economic conflicts" (Sec. 2300).

So the social system is a process of power play; the policies that emerge are a function of power; and, insofar as the economy has become a dominant aspect of society, economic conflict and mutual economic coercion have become dominant. Thus a policy of laissez-faire, that is, the "norms of free competition," means "that the working-man and the capitalist should be left to fight out the problem of division between themselves" (Sec. 2147). But, of course, coercive power is partially a function of the law (Sec. 2188), so that government itself is an object of capture in order to secure, protect, and enhance coercive advantages (Sec. 2262, and *passim*).

Moreover, the corporate system is itself a system of mutual coercion. Pareto argued not only that democratic regimes "might be defined as a sort of feudalism that is primarily economic" (Sec. 2259; *cf.* 2558), but also that "The trusts in the United States today correspond exactly to the Roman latifundia,..." (Sec. 2355). The protective tariff is an instrument of coercion by businessmen (Sec. 2327, and *passim*). Politicians and labor leaders, in establishing their own feudalism, have their own devices (Sec. 1714; *cf.* 2484n.1), so also with physicians (Sec. 2154n.1). The industrial economy, both domestically and internationally, is a system of exploitation through the application of coercive powers (Secs. 2225, 2235). Income distribution thus is a function of power play: "As regards employers of labour,... many of them are 'speculators' who hope to make up for their losses in a strike through government aid and at the expense of consumer or taxpayer. Their quarrels with strikers are quarrels between accomplices over the division of the loot" (Sec. 2187).

As already indicated, law, including constitutional law, is an instrument to secure and enhance a desired distribution of dominance and submission (Timasheff, 1940, p. 149), of freedoms and of exposures to the freedom of others, and of opportunities to capture income. Moreover, as Lopreato has stressed, Pareto not only establishes the universality of conflict and of coercion (Lopreato, 1965, pp. 26, 27), but also "hypothesizes an interdependence and an integration of parts within a basic context of conflict of interests" (Lopreato, 1965, p. 32). He thus shared with Marx a view of "the role of conflict as an endogenous cause of social change and social reintegration" (Lopreato, 1965, p. 30). Pareto's theory of power envisions mutual coercion or struggle as a mover of society (B.B. Seligman, 1962, p. 393), and it is thus both a theory of freedom and control and a theory of continuity and change as well as a theory that policy is a function of power play.

As indicated above, Pareto nowhere systematically analyzed power as he did his approaches to knowledge and psychology. But his discussions of polity, economy, and theocracy — which pervade the *Treatise* — abound with power play.[2] Moreover, his references to power are usually in a context of analyses involving the

interrelations of power with psychology and knowledge. Consequently, the main related Paretian themes will be identified in
subsequent chapters.

Pervading these themes, however, are two further general elements of Pareto's theory of power, his theory of the ruling class
and his theory of manipulation. The former is well known and,
consequently, need receive but summary attention here. The latter
is less well appreciated: for Pareto, society was not only a system
of power but also, as such, was a process of mutual manipulation.
Indeed, the Paretian vision is that of a manipulative society.
Throughout his discussion run the questions: Whose norms?
Whose happiness and unhappiness? (Sec. 1898). Who is to be sacrificed? (Secs. 1810, 1884n.1, 2129, 2134, 2135).

## 2. Theory of the Ruling Class[3]

Just as society is a struggle for power, with the fruits accruing
to those with power, society is at the same time a structure of
power. The distinctive characteristic of that structure, according
to Pareto, is its division into ruling and subject classes. In his view,
society is governed by a ruling class, and history is largely the
history of that class (Sec. 1734). Indeed, "Every people is governed by an *elite*, by a chosen element in the population; and, in
all strictness it is the psychic state of that *elite* that we have been
examining" (Sec. 246). While it is unnecessary to go into a
thorough examination and critique, it may be pointed out that
Pareto's is one of the leading theories of a ruling class. It has many
of the ambiguities and difficulties characteristic, perhaps, of all
·such theories.

Near the end of a long chapter on the properties of residues and
derivations, Pareto took up the subject of the "heterogeneousness
of society and circulation among its various elements"
(Sec. 2025). "Whether certain theorists like it or not," he argued,
"the fact is that human society is not a homogeneous thing, that
individuals are physically, morally, and intellectually different"
(Sec. 2025). Individuals may be grouped into social classes, and
Pareto had his own system for ascertaining in principle just who is
and who is not in the "*elite*" (Secs. 2027ff). Yet his analysis is
qualified by the caveat "that the social classes are not entirely
distinct, even in countries where a caste system prevails" (Sec.
2025). Moreover, the analysis is further complicated by circulation

of the elite, especially the fact "that in modern civilized countries circulation among the various classes is exceedingly rapid" (Sec. 2025 ). The Paretian theory of the circulation of the elite has been a distinctive characteristic of his theory of the ruling class.

There are three central points of Pareto's elite theory. First, society is divided into classes. Second, society is governed by a ruling elite. Third, the membership of that elite is subject to change, but it rules whether society is ostensibly an aristocracy or a democracy and whether circulation is rapid or slow. There are "two strata in a population: (1) a lower stratum, the *non-elite*,...; then (2) a higher stratum, *the elite*, which is divided into two: (a) a governing *elite*; (b) a non-governing *elite*" (Sec. 2034). In other words, there is a ruling class in society, the powers of governance residing in the hands of a relative few within the ruling class:

> "...whether universal suffrage prevails or not, it is always an oligarchy that governs... (Sec. 2183).

> We need not linger on the fictions of 'popular representation' — poppycock grinds no flour. ...Ignoring exceptions, which are few in number and of short duration, one finds everywhere a governing class of relatively few individuals. ...(Sec. 2244).

> A governing class is present everywhere, even where there is a despot, but the forms under which it appears are widely variable. In absolute governments a sovereign occupies the stage alone. In so-called democratic governments it is the parliament. But behind the scenes in both cases there are always people who play a very important role in actual government (Sec. 2253).

> The governing class is not a homogeneous body. It too has a government — a smaller, choicer class (or else a leader, or committee) that effectively and practically exercises control" (sec. 2254).

The struggle for power, in part, takes the form of a struggle to control government as the *de ju,e* and formal decision making apparatus in society (Borkenau, 1936, p. 127). Who is sacrificed depends on who is successful in manoeuvering into a position of dominance (Secs. 2134 - 2135, and *passim*). Pareto's discussion is generally along the lines of what today would be called a zero-sum game. It is interesting that at one point he advanced a notion of both a positive-sum game and something resembling an invisible hand. In this latter view the interests of the governing class are seen "often" to coincide with the interests of the subject class, so that "in the end" the machinations of the governing class "may prove beneficial to the subject class"[4] (Sec. 2250). Out of this struggle for power comes the circulation of the elite:

> "Aristocracies do not last. Whatever the causes, it is an incontestable fact that after a certain length of time they pass away. History is a graveyard of aristocracies (Sec. 2053).

> They decay not in numbers only. They decay also in quality, in the sense that they lose their vigour, that there is a decline in the proportions of the residues which enabled them to win their power and hold it. The governing class is restored not only in numbers, but — and that is the more important thing — in quality, by families rising from the lower classes and bringing with them the vigour and the proportions of residues necessary for keeping themselves in power. It is also restored by the loss of its more degenerate members (Sec. 2054).

> Potent cause of disturbance in the equilibrium is the accumulation of superior elements in the lower classes and, conversely, of inferior elements in the higher classes (Sec. 2055).

> In virtue of class-circulation, the governing elite is always in a state of slow and continuous transformation" (Sec. 2056).

Although it is tempting to examine more thoroughly Pareto's theory of the ruling class and to compare and contrast it with that of others, such as Mosca's, such is not at all germane to the present purpose. Some of the details and, primarily, the subsidiary themes of class circulation (that is, circulation of the elite) will be examined in subsequent chapters. The relevant point here is that the ruling class is a more or less open-ended one and is itself an object of power play. Nonetheless, society is governed by a ruling class.

Pareto's theory of the elite is thus an integral part of his theory of power and his theories of freedom and control, and of continuity and change. At the heart of each, as Schumpeter and Spengler have both acknowledged, is the continuing process of selection whereby society in effect chooses its leaders:

> "Pareto's theory of 'class-circulation' is important for several reasons. It emphasizes the importance of social, economic, and

political circulation and selection, elements which have largely escaped the attention of modern economics. Second, Pareto's theory, while open to exception, serves to focus attention on two facts which commonly tend to be ignored: (a) the importance of the strategically situated decision- and rule making minority in the formation of social form and policy; (b) the sensitivity of this minority to numerical and qualitative change, and the consequent susceptibility of a social system to change (Spengler, 1944, p. 130).

[Pareto, like Taussig] was among those few economists who realize that the method by which a society chooses its leaders in what, for its particular structure, is the fundamental social function... is one of the most important things about a society, most important for its performance as well as for its fate" (Schumpeter, 1951, p. 217).

In this and in other respects Pareto's themes underscore, at least in retrospect, problems which have become major fields of inquiry in political sociology and in sociology proper.[5] In the theory of economic development, as an additional example, the importance of the leadership-selection process has become increasingly recognized. The main thrust of Pareto's analysis remains, however, that leadership-selection is part of the struggle for power, and in that respect and in many others policy is a function of power[6] (Wollheim, 1954, p. 573).


## 3. Power Play as Mutual Manipulation

In the vision of Pareto, society is a system of power, and the practice of power is manipulation. What is today more extensively interpreted in sociology as, generally speaking, interaction and roleplaying was to Pareto essentially a process of mutual manipulation. He did recognize some of the nonmanipulative facets of behavior but chose to concentrate on the manipulative.[7] At any rate, a major theme which may be distilled from the *Treatise* is that, society being a system of power, power play is mutual manipulation. The Paretian concept is that of the manipulative society.

Before proceeding to an examination of manipulation *per se*, several preliminary considerations should be examined which are

94

of particular relevance at this time. First, it should be recognized that, in Pareto's view, *aside from* consideration of the ruling elite and government itself, society and economy involve or may be reduced to an interplay between private concentrations of power. For power to be effective it is generally necessary that it be concentrated. These private power concentrates or modern fiefdoms may be in the form of trusts, corporations, unions, and so forth. It is the behavior and interaction of these concentrations of nominally private power which is of paramount importance in the formation of society's effective policies.[8]

From the analysis in the *Treatise*, therefore, the proposition can be inferred that there is a tendency in the modern industrial capitalist economy for power to be concentrated in private economic units. The result, perhaps, is something of a "dictatorship of the economically powerful" (Bogardus, 1955, p. 520), but certainly a regime of what has more recently been called "private government" (*cf.* Samuels, 1965, pp. 248 - 249). Pareto emphasized "the importance of the strategically situated decision- and rule-making minority in the formation of social form and policy" (Spengler, 1944, p. 130). He thereby not only acknowledged *de jure* or official government and the established political parties but also *de facto* governance and the leverage exercised by non-governmental institutions, for example, corporations, unions, and private associations of various kinds.

Closely related to this recognition of private government is an acknowledgement of the equivalent of what Max Weber called "political capitalism" (Gerth and Mills, 1946, pp. 66 - 67), a system in which profit opportunities accrue to those with political influence and prerogative. This being the case, power play is not confined to economic warfare between nominally private organizations; it extends to include competition between such units for the favors and largesse available through capturing the power of government. In such a manner private government comes to dominate or dictate the policies of official government (masquerading as the "public interest"). The absence of theoretical analysis of the subject by Pareto again compels reliance upon the examples serving as the basis for the conclusion. Thus, employers and unions are recognized to be in competition for control of government policy in order to structure the legal framework of the market to improve their respective opportunities for gain:

"Now employers who themselves enjoy economic protection manifest great indignation at strikers for trying to rid themselves of the competition of non-union workers. The rejoinder is never made that they are trying to keep others from doing what they are doing themselves, and that they fail to show how and why free competition is good for the workingman and bad for the employer of labour" (Sec. 2188).

Pareto has already been quoted as saying "that substantially, and whatever the form of government, men holding power have, as a rule, a certain inclination to use that power to keep themselves in the saddle, and to abuse it to secure personal gains and advantages, ..." To this, among other things, he adds: "The governing class sees to appropriating other people's property not only for its own use, but also to share with such members of the subject class as defend it and safeguard its rule ..." (Sec. 2267). With the A's connoting those in power and the B's those out of, but seeking power he remarks: "The B's, remember, are in no sense trying to prevent *everybody* from doing the things they complain of, but only the A's. Their object is not so much to change the social system as to turn it to their own advantage by unseating the A's and taking their places" (Sec. 2262). Thus, "In many national parliaments it is not difficult to perceive through the fog of political derivations the substance of private interests for which the given regime is maintained"[9] (Sec. 1713). Little wonder, then, that in his *Liberte Economique d'Italie* Pareto wrote, with respect to the use of force against demonstrations by the masses protesting poverty and hunger: "The pretext is the maintenance of social order, but the real end is the maintenance, the consolidation, and, if possible, the augmentation of the system of plunder" (Pareto, in *Vilfredo Pareto on Italy*, p. 476). The *Treatise* is, indeed, well sprinkled with allusions to what is essentially political capitalism.

One form which the foregoing takes is corruption, including the contrivance of artificial scarcity — real or imagined[10] — with corruption yielding the price which functions to overcome such scarcity. Such is the case with unbearable legislation in general (Sec. 2609; *cf.* 2153n.1); with fees charged by priests to procure dispensations from prohibitions imposed by them (Sec. 1697); and with suppressing a book in order to raise its price (Sec. 1749n.1). Another form, of course, is that of raiding the government treasury (Sec. 2300 and *passim*). Corruption is the tool of political capitalism whereby the ambitious may be successful, for example, "in obtaining licence to exploit less clever neighbors by political in-

fluence, customs, tariffs, or other favors of all sorts and kinds ..."
(Sec. 2300).

The compass of the Paretian view of the manipulative society includes not only the ruling class and government *per se* but also private concentrations of power and the phenomena of political capitalism and corruption. Moreover it included and generally was epitomized by the practice of *force* and *cunning*, synonyms for the latter of which are *fraud* and *manufactured consent*, including deception on the level of manifest function. Even moral reform was seen by Pareto as a weapon or instrument of power play, and he recognized it might backfire:

> "The attitudes of the various Popes towards the Franciscan movement were determined by a variety of causes. ... The Pope had to solve a problem that rulers are very frequently called upon to face: to find ways, through appropriate combinations and for the purpose of fighting their enemies, to avail themselves of the sentiments that might make new enemies for them or be of service to enemies who were already there. ... The Popes favoured the Franciscans to the farthest limits of orthodoxy. When the Franciscans overstepped those limits, they repressed them. The Popes were willing to use them as auxiliaries. They could not tolerate them as enemies. They were glad to use them against heretics, and against rich and powerful elements in the clergy who were disposed to assert their independence of the Holy See. Moral reform was a good weapon for fighting such churchmen. But reform had to stop at the point beyond which the Holy See itself would have been hurt. In the end this latter conception prevailed; for, as always happens, the pretended return to the Gospel ended in being only a mask for heresy. That indeed is the real reason why so many new admirers of St. Francis have come forward in our day. They are simply enemies of the Papacy and use praises of St. Francis as a weapon in their war" (Sec. 1810; on election reforms, see Sec. 1524).

The manipulative society is one in which people are *used* by other people for the latter's personal ends. Specifically, the masses generally are considered as being used for the economic and political ends of the elite. The governing class can continue in power only by the adroit use of force and cunning:

"... one finds everywhere a governing class of relatively few individuals that keeps itself in power partly by force and partly by the consent of the subject class, which is much more populous. The differences lie principally, as regards substance, in the relative proportions of force and consent; and as regards forms, in the manners in which the force is used and the consent obtained" (Sec. 2244; *cf.* Lopreato and Ness, 1966, p. 32, and Welk, 1938, p. 37n.).

As will be seen below, particularly in Part Two, Pareto hardly refrained from detailing the means of manipulation. The latter chapters of the *Treatise* are almost, as Larrabee remarked, a "handbook of mass manipulation" for potential use by the "politician, evangelist, and advertiser" (Larrabee, 1935, p. 513; *cf.* Clerc, 1942, p. 586). Pareto amply demonstrated his practical and theoretical belief in the fact and efficacy of force and fraud.

"Consent and force appear in all the course of history," he wrote, "as instruments of governing" (Sec. 2251). With respect to the latter of the two instruments, "All governments use force, and all assert that they are founded on reason" (Sec. 2183). Pareto's main argument is contained in the following passages.

"To ask whether or not force ought to be used in a society, whether the use of force is or is not beneficial, is to ask a question that has no meaning, for force is used by those who wish to preserve certain uniformities and by those who wish to overstep them; and the violence of the one stands in contrast and in conflict with the violence of the others. In truth, if a partisan of a governing class disavows the use of force, he means that he disavows the use of force by insurgents trying to escape from the norms of the given uniformity. On the other hand, if he says he approves of the use of force, what he really means is that he approves of the use of force by the public authority to constrain insurgents to conformity. Conversely, if a partisan of the subject class says he detests the use of force in society, what he really detests is the use of force by constituted authorities in forcing dissidents to conform; and if, instead, he lauds the use of force, he is thinking of the use of force by those who would break away from certain social uniformities. Nor is there any particular meaning in the question as to whether the use of violence to enforce existing uniformities is beneficial to society, or whether it is beneficial to use force in order to overstep them; for the various uniformities have to be distinguished to see which of them are beneficial and which deleterious to society. Nor, indeed, is that enough; for it is further necessary to determine whether the utility of the uniformity is great enough to offset the harm that will be done by using violence to enforce it, or whether detriment from the uniformity is great enough to overbalance the damage that will be caused by the use of force in subverting it; in which detriment and damage we must not forget to reckon the very serious drawback involved in the anarchy that results from any frequent use of violence to abolish existing uniformities, just as among the benefits and utilities of maintaining frankly injurious uniformities must be counted the strength and stability they lend to the social order. So, to solve the problem as to the use of force, it is not enough to solve the other problem as to the utility, in general, of certain types of social organization; it is essential also and chiefly to compute all the advantages and all the drawbacks, direct and indirect. Such a course leads to the solution of a scientific problem; but it may not be and oftentimes is not the course that leads to an increase in social utility. It is better, therefore, if it be followed only by people who are called upon to solve a scientific problem or, to some limited extent, by certain individuals belonging to the ruling class; whereas social utility is oftentimes best served if the members of the subject class, whose function it is not to lead but to act, accept one of the two theologies according to the case — either the theology that enjoins preservation of existing uniformities, or the theology that counsels change" (Secs. 2174 - 2175).

Pareto considered "what means a governing class has at its disposal in order to defend itself by eliminating individuals who might conceivably overthrow it as possessing superior talents of a type likely to be dangerous to its rule." He included in his classification of means (a) "the infliction of death;" (b) "persecution not carried as far as capital punishment: imprisonment, financial ruin, exclusion from public offices;" (c) "exile and ostracism;" and (d) "admission to membership in the governing class of any individual potentially dangerous to it, provided he consents to serve it" (Secs. 2477, 2478, 2479, 2481, 2482). Also recognized is the necessity of preventing discontented elements from the governing class becoming available to lead dissident groups from the subject class (Sec. 2502).

The main logic of Pareto's view of force as a means of power play led him to consider the case where the governing class "is inclining more and more in the direction of humanitarianism ... and ... is becoming less and less capable of using force and is so shirking the main duty of a ruling class" (Sec. 2191). As will be seen subsequently, Pareto upheld the exercise of violence by the official status quo, that is, legal violence, over extra-legal or illegal private violence. The former was considered by him to support existing social norms whereas the latter would overthrow status quo social norms (*cf.* Sec. 2189). Force not only is a means of defending the hegemony of the ruling class, and thereby the status quo, but also is proof of the virility of that class and therefore of its fitness to govern. To succeed, a ruling class or government admittedly needs more than force.[11] If it fails (is unable or unwilling) to use force, it should fail. "Since it failed in that function, it was salutary that its rule should give way to rule by others; and since, again, it was the resort to force that was wanting, it was in keeping with very general uniformities that there should be a swing to another extreme where force was used even more than was required. ... It was a good thing that power should pass into the hands of people who showed that they had the faith and the resolve requisite for the use of force" (Sec. 2191; *cf.* 2180 and *passim*). Pareto's analysis is manifestly complex. At certain points he favors the status quo, but at others he sides with the successful use of force.

Normative propositions are thus derived from functional possibilities as Pareto saw them. He elevated functional means to the level of approved necessities. As with social utility and the public interest, force is itself morally relative, and the specification of its use is subjective, but these facts did not keep him from extolling its functional role in the resolution both of freedom and control and of continuity and change. May the stronger win, or may the one willing to use violence win, for that is *prima facie* evidence for the need for violence and of the need to either replenish or reactivate (restore) a waning virility in the ruling class. It will be noticed that the transformation of functional possibilities into normative necessities is partially obscured by the dual use of the concept *uniformities*. In some instances the term connotes generalizations in the nature of scientific laws, for example, the functional use of violence; in others, it connotes status quo norms, that is, regularities which become the subject of social science but which exist because of custom, and so forth. Such transformation and dualism relates to Pareto's conservatism, which will be developed in chapter seven.

But the elite does not rule by force alone. Rather, both force and fraud are necessary, in business as well as in politics. Here, as will be elaborated in Part Two, is the place for derivations: concealing, rationalizing, masking, functioning to disengage dissent when necessary, to preclude dissent if possible, always creating consent and consensus in support of achieved or sought-after positions in the game of power play. Pareto quoted Polybius, Montesquieu, and Machiavelli (Secs. 313n.1, 314, 2534 - 2536) in support of the theme that religion was a function of deliberate artifice, a soporific if not opiate of the masses. Pareto also recognized the wide extent of pretence and deceit (Secs. 636, 1156, 1583, 1755, 1924 - 1925, 2146, 2274, and *passim*); the fiction and deception of majority rule when in fact government is by ruling class (Secs. 1857, 2183, 2244, 2259, 2268); the use of oracles and omens by rulers to persuade their followers (Secs. 2436, 2445); the practice of dissimulation (Sec. 1713n.4; *cf.* Amoroso, 1938, p. 17); the practice of imaginary ends (Secs. 1869ff, 1882, 1896); and the use of derivations to disguise, conceal, and shelter interests (Secs. 1713, 1884, 2268, 2553; *cf.* Schumpeter, 1951, p. 140). Several of these have already been discussed or acknowledged; others will be developed in chapter five, particularly in the sections on the interrelations of power and knowledge, and of power and psychology.

As Prezzolini wrote, "Politics means illusions; ..." (Prezzolini, 1943, p. 359), and both businessmen and politicians manipulate the objects of their power play through deception, as an instrument of cunning and as a substitute for force, in order to create or manufacture assent (Lopreato, 1965, pp. 23 - 31). As seen in chapter two, non-logico-experimental reasonings — derivations — have their social utility. Insofar as deception and cunning — fraud — deal with knowledge or pseudo-knowledge, such knowledge is at the service of power. Once again it is obvious how difficult it is to separate the main Paretian themes. It is necessary, in developing the dimensions of knowledge, psychology, and power, to touch on their interrelations. Suffice it to say here that policy is a function of power. Society is a system of power, with a ruling class, with private concentrations of power, and with all participants in the socio-politico-economic decision-making process engaging in mutual manipulation, ultimately using some variant(s) and combination(s) of force and fraud. Policy is a function of knowledge, psychology, and power, the interrelationships of which will now be examined. As has perhaps become quite apparent in this chapter, it will be increasingly difficult to separate Pareto the scientist from Pareto the counsellor.

# Part two:
# The Making of Policy

In the Paretian system, social equilibrium is a function of knowledge, psychology, power, and their interaction. The main relationship between knowledge and psychology is that the former is a function of the latter, that is, belief is a function of accord with sentiments. Yet beliefs — derivations — are tools of users upon subjects. The sentiments are manipulated by beliefs found to be in accord with the sentiments in order to abet the ends sought by the user. Knowledge is an instrument of power. In one sense, knowledge is power; in another and more fundamental sense, knowledge is in the service of power, a mode for the exercise of control. This Part will examine these primary interrelations between knowledge, psychology, and power as Pareto understood them; and also the resolution of the problems of freedom and control and of continuity and change in the Paretian system.

*Chapter 5.*

# Psychology, Knowledge, and Power

Social equilibrium is a function of physical, external, and internal variables. The main internal elements are interests, residues, derivations, social heterogeneity, and class circulation. Such a listing delineates the Paretian model in Paretian terms. In the context of the present study, the Paretian model is translated into the proposition that policy is a function of knowledge, psychology, and power. As already indicated, Pareto placed great emphasis upon the predominance of non-logico-experimental reasonings, non-logical conduct, and, thereby, the operation of psychic states (the sum of the sentiments and the residues). In short, he stressed the primary importance of psychology in the decision-making process. Still, the Paretian system is one of generalized equilibrium between interdependent elements or variables. The purpose of this chapter will be to specify the interrelations between psychology, knowledge, and power as they exist in the *Treatise*. Section one of chapter three discussed the emphasis placed by Pareto on the residues and the different treatment accorded the residues as functionally interdependent variables (with the other elements). These are sources of difficulty in interpretation. The first section below will specify the interrelations between knowledge and psychology, immediately after which the subject of the dynamics of psychic states will be more thoroughly examined. Subsequently, the interrelations between power and psychology and power and knowledge will be specified.

## 1. Knowledge and Psychology

In the Paretian system, policy is a partial function of knowledge. That is to say, decisions — including society's effective decisions concerning resource allocation and the structure of the economic decision-making process — are a function of what is or becomes accepted as the definition of reality in every aspect of life, however inaccurate, heterogeneous, incoherent, or inconsistent. Pareto emphasized that knowledge is comprised of both logico-experimental and non-logico-experimental reasonings, — of scientific truth and pseudo-knowledge (primarily the derivations). Moreover, non-logico-experimental knowledge predominates (as does non-logical conduct). Logico-experimental knowledge tends to prevail in the field of science (itself, however, inclusive of non-logico-experimental reasonings) and in the effectuation of interests. (Interests themselves are a function of tastes, that is, equivalent to the sentiments, and sentiments may interfere with the realization of felt interests.)

Policy is a partial function of knowledge, but knowledge exists, according to Pareto, in a particular relationship to psychology. The primary relationship between the two he sees as the fact that belief — as well as conduct — is a function of what accords with the sentiments. Throughout the *Treatise* runs the theme that such and such a proposition, whether logico-experimental or non-logico-experimental, is accepted only or primarily because it is consistent with, or is in accord with, the sentiments. A condition for the acceptance of a proposition as knowledge is that it satisfies a psychic need of the potential believer. What is accepted as knowledge is a function of its accord with one's sentiments: knowledge is the dependent variable *vis-à-vis* psychology. Belief is a function of what one wants, or is disposed, or is induced, to believe. Knowledge is not, or not only, the rationalization of interest and position; it is more fundamentally and more ubiquitously a rationalization of, and thereby a comfort to, one's psyche or psychic needs. Derivations ultimately perform this psychological function and are accepted only insofar as they are in accord with one's sentiments. The social utility of pseudo-knowledge (and there is social utility of logico-experimental knowledge in this respect, too) lies in its role in terms of personal psychology.

The theme that belief is a matter of what accords with sentiments pervades the *Treatise* (Secs. 14ff, 41 - 42, 78, 514, 779, and *passim*), and its manifestations, accordingly, are numerous. That a proposition is held as true "designates mere accord with certain sentiments, which carries with it the assent of the believer" (Sec. 1567). Truths merely voice the sentiments that support them (Sec. 1397n.2). Social equilibrium is a function of the interplay of sentiments operating through knowledge (Sec. 1586). Knowledge of utility and ophelimity is a function of the residues (Secs. 2148, 2151); so, too, the metaphysical postures of nominalism and realism are a function of the sentiments (Class I versus Class II residues) (Secs. 1651, 2368ff). Religion is psychological in its genesis and character, and functions, moreover, with respect to psychic needs (Secs. 616, 1073, 1081, 1854, 2345n.7; *cf.* Muller, 1938, p. 435; Amoroso, 1938, p. 20; and Hughes, 1958, pp. 80 - 81). Since the psyche requires security and assurance, one of the roles of the derivations — particularly the ethical derivations (knowledge of reality including therein knowledge of values) — is to "substitute *a priori* a single and qualitative solution for the multiple and quantitative solutions that experience furnishes *a posteriori*" (Sec. 2166n.1). In such a manner, values are built into the residues and operate through both logico- and non-logico-experimental reasonings. In such a manner, also, specific solutions to general problems — the problem of specificity which is an elemental question of policy — are grounded in the emotions.

Moreover, the form of society is not a function of deliberate reasoning. Contrary to the view (wishful thinking, according to Pareto) of those who over-intellectualize social forces, society is a world of non-logical, not logical, conduct (Henderson, 1937, pp.21, 27). It is built up non-deliberatively, in the main, through psychologically grounded knowledge and behavior. Behavior itself is a function of psychology, and the human psyche is primarily non-logical.

Argument and persuasion are generally directed not to scientific proof but to conviction, that is to say, to appeal not to accuracy but to sentiments. "... appeal must be made to sentiments rather than to logic and the results of experience. The situation may be stated, inexactly to be sure, because too absolutely, but nevertheless strikingly, by saying that in order to influence people thought has to be transformed into sentiment" (Sec. 168). Political economy is thus seen as a practical discipline designed or functioning to influence conduct through addressing sentiments (Secs. 77, 118). All argument involves derivations, and they are both derived from the residues and function to appeal to the sentiments.

A corollary to the theme that belief is a function of what

accords with the sentiments is embodied in Pareto's insistence that conduct (behavior) is a function of sentiments, not of belief. If anything, derivations are a function of, and function to rationalize, conduct. People act not because of their beliefs but because of their emotions, their beliefs themselves being a function of their emotions.

"... human beings are moved much more by sentiment than by thought" (Sec. 2146).

"The main error in the thinking of the plain man, as well as in metaphysical thinking, lies not only in an inversion of terms in the relationship between derivations and human conduct — the derivations being taken, in general, as the cause of the conduct, whereas really, the conduct is the cause of the derivation — but also in ascribing *objective existence* to derivations proper and to the residues in which they originate" (Sec. 1689; *cf.* 1690).

"Beliefs and conduct are not, to be sure, independent; but their correlation lies in their being, as it were, two branches of one same tree" (Sec. 166; *cf.* 176, 220, 1854, 1999, 2145, and *passim*).

Belief is a function of accord with sentiments. Conduct, rather than being a function of belief is also a function of the sentiments.

Before examining the role of derivations in the present context and as a prelude to consideration of the dynamics of psychic states, several points may be made in passing. First, not only that knowledge represented by theories, ideals, superstitions, and so forth, but also that knowledge embodied in words and language itself are a function of accordance with sentiments, and thereby both kinds operate because of and upon the sentiments. Words, according to Pareto, tend to be largely symbols for sentiments, mere reflections of sentiments (Secs. 431, 541, 960, 1042, 1210, 1508n.1, 2147, 2206). Words like *justice*, *nature*, and *welfare* "are all names that designate nothing more than indistinct and incoherent sentiments"[1] (Sec. 1513). Conversely, words are triggers, serving to bring into play the sentiments they elicit or arouse:

"... the thing is viewed in the light of the sentiments the name arouses, and it is to its advantage, therefore, to have a name that awakens favourable sentiments and to its disadvantage to have a name inspiring unfavourable sentiments" (Sec. 113).

With respect to arguments using and concerning the meaning of such words as *value* and *capital*,

"... since such arguments are primarily rhetorical, they are strictly dependent on words capable of arousing the sentiments that are useful in convincing people; and that is why literary economists very properly are so much concerned about words and much less about things" (Sec. 118).

Words thus function because of their accord with sentiments and may serve to obfuscate (Secs. 401, 2553) and legitimize (Secs. 401, 431, 1602 - 1603) as well as communicate. Communication in Pareto's system is a psychological (Sec. 883 and *passim*) as well as a political process, quite aside from simple conveyance of ideas.

The second point to be made in passing concerns the role of principles in society. Pareto maintained that principles function through their evocation of sentiments. Therein lies their social utility, whatever the fact or the possibility of their logico-experimental truth. This is predominantly the case in the social sciences and in politics generally, but it is also the case, albeit less so, in the physical sciences. Principles are surrogates for sentiments (Secs. 815, 1464); indeed, principles are sentiments, or the absolutist formulation of them (Secs. 798, 1464; *cf.* 306n.1, and Timasheff, 1957, pp. 140 - 141). With belief a function of accord with sentiments, the choice of principles by a politician will depend upon their expected acceptability to prospective constituents or voters (Sec. 502; *cf.* 809). Again, truth value is a secondary consideration, as are the notions that no principle is always beneficial and that principles are ever in conflict and require the necessity of choice.

Third, one of the foundations for Pareto's theme that belief is a function of accord with sentiments is embodied in the fifth residue included in Class I, a "hunger for logical developments" (Sec. 972). "This residue," wrote Pareto, "explains the need people feel for covering their non-logical conduct with a varnish of logic — a point we have already stressed time and again and at length" (Sec. 975; *cf.* 1397, 1400). Belief, a function of accord with sentiments, is necessary because of feelings of guilt or insecurity stemming from the nature of conduct, that is, the non-logical or non-rational character of much of life, namely, the sentiments. In addition, the need for logical development "also accounts for that element in social phenomena ... which constitutes the whole subject of derivations. The usual purpose of a derivation, in fact, is to satisfy with pseudo-logic the need of logic, of thinking, that the human being feels." At this point, Pareto wrote in a note: "We need dwell no further here on residues of this type because they are virtually the subject of this work as a whole" (Sec. 975, 975n).

The final point regards the matter of truth versus social utility. At one juncture Pareto referred to this issue as the conflict between *knowing* and *doing* (Sec. 1786). Given the ambiguity of social utility, it is nevertheless one of Pareto's ideas that social utility ultimately relates to or may be at least partially defined in terms of the functioning of sentiments. The basic notion is that belief, albeit false logico-experimentally, has social utility in the manipulative society. Beliefs both reflect and elicit sentiments.

"We are now witnessing the rise and dominance of the democratic religion, just as the men of the first centuries of our era witnessed the rise of the Christian religion and the beginnings of its dominion. The two phenomena present many profoundly significant analogies. To get at their substance we have to brush derivations aside and reach down to residues. The social value of both those two religions lies not in the least in their respective ideologies, but in the sentiments that they express"[2] (Sec. 1859).

As already suggested, much of the core of the interrelation between knowledge and psychology in the Paretian system has to do with the derivations: These are ostensibly knowledge but are a function of the residues. The proposition that what is accepted as knowledge depends upon the psyche thus throws in relief the element called derivations. They function to mask non-logico-experimental reasonings, to disguise them as logico-experimental, to make them appear rational. In so masking and in obscuring the nature of belief, the derivations legitimize the very sentiments which they disguise. So also with non-logical conduct. Derivations serve to rationalize conduct that is emotionally generated. Moreover, derivations rationalize for both the individual himself and others (self-deception and deception of others, both latent and manifest). The same residue may lead to or may be supported by different derivations (Sec. 1378); the same derivation may disguise different residues (Sec. 2169); when one derivation is destroyed, another will replace it (Millikan, 1936, p. 329); indeed, since the rationalization of non-logical conduct and belief is variable, any

110

suitable derivation will do (Sec. 616, *cf.* Henderson, 1937, p. 55, and Timasheff, 1957, p. 162). "These derivations, so utterly illogical and sometimes indeed so ridiculous, all lead up eventually to one same conclusion; ... they are merely the incidental element, the principal element lying in the sentiments and interests that gave rise to the conclusion which the derivations are an effort *a posteriori* to justify."[3] Since knowledge is a function of accord with sentiments, the role of argument (that is, derivations) is to persuade through appeal to the sentiments (Secs. 445, 514, 586, 596, 598, 1413, 2520; and *cf.* Pareto, in Hamilton, 1962, p. 46).

## 2. Dynamics of Psychic States

Belief is a function of the residues (which manifest sentiments, together comprising psychic states). Conduct, apparently and ostensibly a function of belief, is not so at all; it is itself a function of the residues. As indicated in Part One, the great thrust of the *Treatise* is the cardinal and ubiquitous importance of the residues (sentiments). Social equilibrium and policy are a function of psychology or psychic states, psychology and psychic states being the independent, and society the dependent, variable. Pareto devotes hundreds and hundreds of pages to a forceful refutation of over-intellectualization, to criticism of over-emphasizing argument *per se* (Sec. 1765, and *passim*). Arguments were, to Pareto, essentially rationalizing derivations, and their importance to the social scientist lies less in any logico-experimental truth value they may have and more in their service as pointers to underlying sentiments. In any social situation the phenomena are, *pro tanto*, comprised of variable derivations and the constant element, the residues.

But if the residues are given, how is it possible that the derivations work on the residues? Put somewhat differently, since, according to Pareto, the derivations reflect the sentiments, how is it possible that the derivations may manipulate the sentiments? On the surface, at least, the independence of the residues seems to conflict with the character of the manipulative society and the functioning of the derivations. The difficulty is compounded by the absence of a thorough and integrated statement on the subject in the *Treatise*. One forceful but incomplete expression competes with another.

There are many instances in the *Treatise* wherein Pareto minimized the malleability of the residues and thereby minimized — explicitly or implicitly — the impact of the derivations. When he began to theorize about the significance of pseudo-scientific theories, for example, he differentiated between the "substantial" part, "the expression of certain sentiments," — the residues, and the "contingent" part, — the explanatory derivations (Sec. 798). Pareto's typical comments ran to the effect that derivations "as we already know, do not, on the whole, exert any great influence" (Sec. 1753). He wrote "of the error of assigning too great an importance to derivations as regards determining the social equilibrium" and of reasoning "as though they functioned by themselves independently of residues" (Sec. 1965). Frequently going out of his way to minimize the impact of derivations on sentiments (Secs. 1841 - 1843), at one point he wrote that "Many people enjoy reading the pessimistic poems of Leopardi just as they enjoy listening to a well-written tragedy. But neither poem nor tragedy has much influence on their conduct" (Sec. 1999). Thus the influence of derivations upon major elements was said to be the "least important" of all chains of influence (Sec. 2206). Shortly thereafter Pareto maintained that the effectiveness of certain derivations "depends largely upon the pre-existing sentiments that they express, and only to a slight extent upon sentiments that they create" (Sec. 2191).

But what is the importance of the derivations with respect to the residues? What is their influence? What of the fact that there are sentiments which derivations may "create"?

The first steps in providing a meaningful answer in terms of the *Treatise* were taken in chapter three. There the issue was raised that, although Pareto made psychology the independent and society the dependent variable, his system was one of interdependence and mutual determination, so as to imply an impact of other forces upon psychology and thus the malleability and manipulability of the residues. It was suggested that Pareto's reference to the residues as the constant element was to be interpreted not as connoting fixity of psychic states, but rather the ubiquitous, constantly present, importance of the residues; that psychic states were complex and dynamic; that the residues (sentiments) comprising the psychic state of an individual were of variable strength; and that the derivations functioned to strengthen and weaken now one and then another, that is, different, residues. Psychology, in sum, was crucial to Pareto, but the psyche was the instrumental object of the derivations.

112

This interpretation will be examined in more detail in order to more fully understand and appreciate the interrelationships between power and knowledge and power and psychology. In so doing, the making of policy in the Paretian system will be seen as interrelation between power, knowledge, and psychology. It will be shown, first, that in the *Treatise* the residues are circumstantial in character; second, that they may be individually weakened and/or strengthened; and, third, that they are the intermediate objects of manipulation (intermediate *vis-à-vis* the ends served by the manipulation). It will be seen that psychic states *are* important, but not as invariant and given constraints. Rather, they are factors with and upon which power players (and selves) have to deal and work; they are given but malleable elements which may be used. Consider first the circumstantial character of the residues. Pareto not infrequently pointed to the dependence of both interests and sentiments upon other social forces, such that sentiments are at least in part recognized as being engendered by environment. Quite early in the *Treatise* he wrote of psychic states as being "in great part the product of individual interests (economic, political, and social), and of the circumstances under which people live" (Sec. 167). Accordingly they are subject to modification. Later he wrote of "changes in certain circumstances, which modify residues in certain individuals and then gradually in others"[4] (Sec.2003; *cf.* 2225, 2351; see also Timasheff, 1957, p. 161). He added that, "on the whole, sentiments tend to vary with occupation" (Sec. 1227); that "sentiments *depend* on economic conditions, just as economic conditions *depend* on sentiments" (Sec. 2097); and that so-called "strong" sentiments may, *inter alia*, be "stirred by a large number of pressures ..." (Sec. 1836). The best example is one used by Pareto himself: the impact of tariff protection stimulating Class I residues in both the governing class and in the country as a whole (Sec. 2215 and *passim.* Another example is war; *cf.* 2221ff).

His comments not only were a function of his model of general interdependence (Secs. 1731, 2060 - 2061, 2205ff), but also were a result of circumstances and derivations being explicitly considered capable of producing influences upon the residues, including the potential creation of or calling into play of new residues. Almost invariably his main point is the paramount importance of the residues in the social equilibrium, but the derivations are not without influence. At one point Pareto wrote that, "As we already know, with religions as with all other doctrines, social values depend to a very slight extent upon derivations and to a very large extent upon residues" (Sec. 1854). The "very slight extent" is given recognition elsewhere.

> "... we saw that residues were much more stable than derivations, and we were therefore able to regard them as in part "causes" of derivations, but without forgetting secondary effects of derivations, which sometimes, be it in subordinate ways, may be "causes" of residues" (Sec. 1732).

> "Secondary as the influence may be and at times very feeble, the derivations proper can never be absolutely without influence" (Sec. 1829).

> "But as a rule the effectiveness of such derivations depends largely upon the pre-existing sentiments that they express, and only to a slight extent upon sentiments that they create" (Sec. 2191).

This latter quotation is significant. In the Paretian system derivations largely work upon pre-existing residues, yet they also have a creative function. Indeed, with respect to certain beliefs and reasonings (having to do with faith in the efficacy of combinations), some "will in the long run engender in the minds of people a sentiment" supporting such belief, "and such a sentiment is virtually indistinguishable from a sentiment originating outside experience or pseudo-experimentally" (Sec.980), that is from one originating spontaneously within the psyche.

The crucial matter is not simply whether derivations can create totally new residues in the psyche of an individual, although, as will be seen in a moment, Pareto admits exactly that, the more important issue (because more extensive) is whether derivations can strengthen and/or weaken existing residues. Pareto's view is precisely that derivations can so strengthen and/or weaken, notwithstanding his persistent emphasis upon the importance of residues. The importance of residues in the manipulative society is that they must be taken into consideration and dealt with by potential manipulators, that is, by those who would strengthen or weaken this or that particular residue in this or that group of individuals for this or that end.

It was Pareto's view that derivations functioned to arouse, promote, intensify, stir, and generally strengthen certain sentiments (residues) *vis-à-vis* others which might be disengaged or allowed to remain passive. As already has been seen, for example, a "thing is viewed in the light of the sentiments the name arouses, and it is to its advantage, therefore, to have a name that awakens favourable sentiments and to its disadvantage to have a name inspiring unfavourable sentiments" (Sec. 113; *cf*. 1513, 2147). Since arguments are "primarily rhetorical, they are strictly dependent on words capable of arousing the sentiments that are useful in convincing people; and that is why literary economists very properly are so much concerned about words and much less about things" (Sec. 118). The basic notion of the selective arousing, intensifying, and stirring of particular sentiments is often reiterated:

> "Their purpose, in substance, is to arouse the hearer's sentiments as far as possible in order to lead him to a pre-established conviction" (Sec. 442).

> "If a person is trying to preach to people in order to steer them into paths that he considers best, he will condemn or praise such sentiments and the various expressions of them" (Sec. 1685; *cf*. 1555, 2268, 2440, and *passim*).

> "What from the logico-experimental standpoint, may be a mere war of words may, from the standpoint of doctrinal propaganda, be tremendously effective in view of the sentiments that are called into play" (Sec. 1636).

> "As we have over and again repeated, the persuasive force of such productions resides not in the derivations, but in the residues and interests that they call into play" (Sec. 1892).

The latter quotation nicely expresses the tactical significance of both derivations and residues, indicating the constant importance of the residues as such and also the evocative significance of the derivations with respect to particular residues. The basic theme, of the selective strengthening and/or weakening of particular residues, is repeated elsewhere. The "logic of sentiments" is indeed to arouse the sentiments through the manipulation of derivations (Sec. 514; *cf*. 480); derivations are used which are "calculated to stir emotions" (Sec. 1528); "ritual practices" intensify "sentiments (non-logical actions) and ... such sentiments were in turn sources of morality" (Sec. 361); and, "two contradictory derivations" may be "simultaneously used," serving "a desire to influence the sentiments of the persons listening to the derivation," one being effective with some, and another with others, the "sentiments upon which the derivations are designed to work" being different as between different individuals or groups (Sec. 1716). A specific example of the general theme concerns patriotism, a function of Class II residues.

"Everything ... becomes perfectly clear if one centres on intensities in Class II residues. Where those residues are strong and are kept stimulated by a prudent government that is skillful in taking advantage of them, a population willingly assumes the burdens of preparedness for war. Where they are weak or are weakened by a government that is concerned solely with certain material interests and does not look forward to the future, the population refuses to assume the burdens of national defense" (Sec. 2454).

Thus derivations selectively may give expression to specific pre-existing sentiments (Sec. 2192), and they may "sometimes intensify sentiments and interests and serve in certain cases as instruments of propaganda" (Sec. 2146). Socialism, for example, which has its own theology and derivations, has strengthened Class V residues "in people of the lower strata of society"[5] (Sec. 1858). The role of myths and ideals is also, for example, to arouse sentiments, rouse to action, and so on, by exaggeration and by appeal to and by activating particular residues. They serve to set in motion and strengthen selected sentiments (Secs. 1866ff, 1772, 1877ff).

"As we have seen in every page of these volumes ... the influence of practice upon theory is, in social matters, much greater than the influence of theories upon practice. It is the theories that make the adjustment to practice, and not practice the adjustment to theories. But that does not mean — and that fact too we have repeatedly stressed — that theories have no influence on practice. All that it means is that ordinarily the influence of theories upon practice is much weaker than the influence of practice upon theories — a quite different matter" (Sec. 2008).

The phrase omitted from the quotation just rendered indicates the ground of Pareto's concern: "and contrarily to ordinary opinion, especially the opinion of moralists, men of letters, and pseudo-scientists" (Sec. 2008). Contrary to what he perceived as general opinion, residues are the crucial element, and derivations are important only in regard to their effect upon the residues. That effect is precisely the point here. As Brinton has acknowledged, although Pareto minimized the role of derivations (as understood conventionally, that is, as themselves having a force), they play upon the residues, deactivating some and stimulating others, exercising their impact *through* the residues (Brinton, 1954, pp. 645, 648; *cf.* Amoroso 1938, p. 12; cp. Finer, 1966, p. 30).

In the same vein, a "theory is judged by the sentiment that creates it, and the accord therefore cannot be other than perfect, and the judgment other than favourable" (Sec. 581; *cf.* 1881n.1). But, as indicated earlier, derivations may even engender sentiments (and therefore non-logical conduct) hitherto absent (although perhaps dormant).

"Belief in the non-logical conduct was not imposed by logical device of the Church, of governments, or of anybody else. It was the non-logical conduct that forced acceptance of the logical theories as explanations of itself. That does not mean that such theories may not in their turn have stimulated the belief in the non-logical conduct, and even may have given rise to it in places where it had not existed previously" (Sec. 217).

"The acts in which sentiments express themselves reinforce such sentiments and may even arouse them in individuals who were without them. ... a complex concatenation of actions and reactions" (Sec. 1091).

Pareto was endeavoring in the *Treatise* to call attention to and emphasize the residues, whereas others limited themselves to the derivations alone. To Pareto, the residues were the crucial element in social equilibrium, and the derivations were important only through the residues. But that importance was still great in Pareto's system, for it is the capacity of the derivations to strengthen and/or weaken particular residues that enables manipulation. At one point Pareto denigrated attacks upon the manifestations of residues:

"... it is by no means certain that to suppress the manifestations of a sentiment is to destroy the sentiment itself" (Sec. 1842).

117

"A truly imposing mass of fact stands there to show the scant efficacy of trying to influence residues by attacking their manifestations or, what is worse, derivations inspired by them" (Sec. 1843).

Despite these comments, his main emphasis is that it is the residues themselves which may not be directly assaulted. Rather, their manifestations may be manipulated in order to weaken or strengthen particular residues:

"People who preach aim at modifying residues, but they never, or almost never, attain that end. They do, however, and with no great difficulty, attain another, which is modification in the manifestations of existing residues" (Sec. 2096n.1).

Sentiments or residues may be taken advantage of, thereby "giving ... manifestations, to be sure, such forms as ..." may please the manipulators (Sec. 1997). The users of derivations choose those which are capable of according with the particular sentiments they want to strengthen or call into play. They thus manipulate the residue (sentiment) by manipulating the appropriate belief. Pareto quoted Robert de Jouvenel approvingly:

"It is said that newspapers make public opinion. The reverse is no less true. A reader is quite ready to accept the opinion of his newspaper, but the newspaper chooses the opinion that it judges best fitted to please the reader. ... Luckily the questions on which the public voices its attitude are few in number. It may have very positive opinions but they are few. So long as those few are never shocked, one may guide one's readers where one wills in all others" (Sec. 1755n.1; cf. Amoroso, 1938, p. 16)

In choosing one rather than another derivation, the newspaper is able to engage one or disengage another sentiment and thus mobilize support for policies it wants to see realized. Given the psychic state of its readers (or what the editorialist thinks that psychic state to be), it appeals through appropriate derivations to the efficacious residues.

Given the circumstantial character of the residues and the malleability of the residues comprising an individual's psychic state, the analysis now may proceed to the subject of derivations as the intermediate instruments manipulating the residues, which residues are themselves the intermediate steps to the manipulators' ends (*cf.* Homans and Curtis, 1934, pp. 240ff, especially 244 - 245; MacPherson, 1937, p. 464; and cp. DeVoto, 1933b, p. 578). Derivations may be used to influence interests and sentiments (Sec. 1864). Literature, including literary political economy, functions to influence and to preach (Sec. 971). Derivations may serve as an opiate to reinforce the status quo. With *c* standing for derivations, Pareto says:

> "As a sum of pleasing fictions, *c* satisfies the desires, quiets the longings, of people who are eager to forget the misery and the ugliness of the real world and take refuge in the realms of the fanciful and the ideal, so disarming active enemies of existing conditions and maintaining the social complex, *s*, intact or without too great change" (Sec. 2553).

Social control also operates through the manipulation of sentiments to produce guilt feelings about the violation of group norms:

> "The power that precepts have in a given society at a given time lies chiefly in the fact that they are accepted by the majority of individuals comprising that society, and that individuals who violate them experience a sense of discomfort, find themselves ill at ease. Such precepts are merely an expression, and no very exact one, of the residues operating in that society" (Sec. 1918).

Both sides on any issue will appeal to the sentiments (Sec. 2570). The sentiments may be instrumentally exploited in order for the manipulator to make money (Sec. 1045). As already quoted, the intensity of Class II residues may be stimulated or weakened by government policy (Sec. 2454). In addition, the notion of "public needs" is itself a device whereby sentiments may be manipulated to support this or that use of government:

> "Practically, the doctrine of 'public needs' is useful to the governing class, or a class aspiring to power, as justifying its control and having it more readily accepted by the subject class. ... in such language the fact of the oppression that is being suffered ... is made less apparent" (Sec. 2272).

The general principle is repeatedly stated as a maxim of effective government:

"... the art of governing lies in manipulating residues, not in trying to change them" (Sec. 1805).

"... the art of government lies not in trying to change residues but in skillful manipulation of existing residues. ... in persecuting derivations in order to modify residues governments waste enormous amounts of energy, inflict untold sufferings on their subjects, compromise their own power, and achieve results of little account"[6] (Sec. 1748n.1).

"... the art of governing consists in knowing how to take advantage of the residues one finds ready to hand" (Sec. 1857).

"... the art of government lies in finding ways to take advantage of such sentiments, not in wasting one's energies in futile efforts to destroy them, the sole effect of the latter course very frequently being only to strengthen them. The person who is able to free himself from the blind dominion of his own sentiments is capable of utilizing the sentiments of other people for his own ends" (Sec. 1843).

"... the general rule that it is wiser and easier for a government to exploit existing residues than to modify them" (Sec. 1832).

The sentiments exist, then, to be used, manipulated, and exploited "as instrumentalities of government" (Sec. 1838; cf. 2247; and Henderson, 1937, p. 29; DeVoto, 1933b, p. 575; and Lopreato and Ness, 1966, p. 36). Psychic states being complex and malleable, they may be marshalled and directed along predetermined and manipulated lines. But manipulation — and manipulators — must ultimately deal with the residues, taking them as they find them and using them accordingly. To emphasize the derivations without attention to the residues they are to work upon or to not recognize the fact that they do work on the residues, is both incorrect and inept.

The thrust if not the essence of Pareto's analysis is displayed in a section entitled, "Influence of derivations on residues," in Chapter XI of the *Treatise*. Pareto began this section with the suggestion that the influence of derivations upon the residues is similar to the influence of the need for action (Class III residue) and of the need for logical development (Class Ie residue). Indeed, it is only because of the latter influence that "derivations have any perceptible effects in determining the social equilibrium." But,

> "A derivation which merely satisfies that hankering for logic which the human being feels, and which neither is transmuted into sentiments nor re-enforces sentiments, has slight if any effect on the social equilibrium. It is just a superfluity: it satisfies certain sentiments, and that is all. Briefly, but not in strict exactness, one may say that in order to influence society, theories have to be transmuted into sentiments, derivations into residues"[7] (Sec. 1746).

Pareto continued:

> "Generally speaking, a derivation is accepted not so much because it convinces anybody as because it expresses clearly ideas that people already have in a confused sort of way — this latter fact is usually the main element in the situation. Once the derivation is accepted it lends strength and aggressiveness to the corresponding sentiments, which now have found a way to express themselves" (Sec. 1747).

The elemental policy question is, then, who will elicit what policy by securing support from which sentiments by using or invoking which derivation? The game of policy is one of the interplay of sentiments called into action through derivations: "Sentiments therefore must be met with sentiments" (Sec. 1748). It is at this point that Pareto stated in a note that "the art of government lies not in trying to change residues but in skillful manipulation of existing residues" (Sec. 1748n.1). He cautions that manipulation of derivations may run astray, "so that the individual is stimulated to do the very thing one would dissuade him from doing" (Sec. 1749). Such perverseness must be precluded by wise tactics. Given, then, other criteria of the choice of an appropriate derivation ("Generally the cheapest verbal subterfuges are called into play — derivations based on authority, and the like. But that does not matter. More often than not it is the best way."),

> "The important thing is to have a derivation that is simple, and readily grasped by everybody, even the most ignorant people, and then to repeat it over and over and over again" (Sec. 1749; cf. 1772, and Aron, 1970, p. 161).

It is in this section that Pareto dealt with newspapers: "The influence exerted by great newspapers in our time is a good illustration," he wrote, "of the influence of derivations" that "... their power is great."

"It is all due to the art they have developed for working at residues through derivations. Speaking in general, the residues have to be there in the first place. That fact determines the limits of the newspaper's influence; it cannot go counter to sentiments: it can only use them for one purpose or another. [At this point the quotation from Robert de Jouvenel is inserted in a note.] By rare exception, and in a very long run, some new residues may be manufactured and one that has apparently died out be revived" (Sec. 1755).

This explains, wrote Pareto, why governments (parties in power) support opposition newspapers. First, the regime "makes sure that the newspaper it buys will hold its tongue at the right moment, that it will not rouse every sleeping dog, that it will steer its readers towards venting their spleen in ways less dangerous to the government than others." Second "there are ways of opposing certain measures, certain proposals for legislation, which may influence sentiments quite as favourably as the best defense, if not more so" (Sec. 1755). The power of newspapers is thus that they work at the residues through derivations, "fundamentally ... to exploit the sentiments of people who read newspapers" (Sec. 1760).

The section is concluded with the warning, also already quoted, against "assigning too great an importance to derivations as regards determining the social equilibrium ... and ... to reason as though they functioned by themselves independently of residues" (Sec. 1765). They do not so function; it is precisely because they do operate upon the residues that their policy significance is both enormous and practical. Pareto pointed out that writers like Rousseau and Voltaire "did not create the public sentiments of their day. The sentiments created the reputations of those writers." "... the seed that is sown bear fruit, or fails to bear fruit, according as it falls on congenial or uncongenial soil" (Sec. 1763). But it is the nature of psychic states that they are complex and malleable and that the right seed (to wit, the appropriate derivation) will take hold and elicit the desired result (to wit, the desired sentiment supporting the desired policy). If one sentiment or one

122

derivation will not work or suffice, there is another sentiment and another derivation which will. Derivations will work primarily but not exclusively if the subject is predisposed (Sec. 1543). However, the manipulator[8] has a complex and malleable psychic state as the object of his manipulation, and he should be able to find and use derivations which will work. As suggested in chapter three, the dynamic interaction that characterizes Pareto's model of social equilibrium or policy is possible only because, given the array of residues comprising the psychic state of any individual, the individual is, within constraints, malleable and manipulable. Now one and now another residue may be strengthened through the expression it is given by the derivations which are directed to the person,[9] and the residue thus made more or less operative with respect to any particular policy situation. It is because the residues vary in intensity and malleability that the derivations have a role in social equilibrium. Policy is a function of psychology, and knowledge is a function of what accords with the sentiments; but the sentiments are şo multifaceted that there is quite a variety of pseudo-knowledge which may be utilized to appeal to and thereby set into action particular sentiments (residues).

The same individual may be a conservative in one matter and a liberal in another, depending *inter alia* on his emotional involvements and commitments. These latter are a function of the derivations which have welded his psyche to one side on one issue and to another side on another. To use the Marshallian scissors' analogy, one's identity is a function of two blades, one, one's "raw" psyche, the other, the derivations to which one is exposed. That the emergent individual is complex is due to both the complexity of the "raw" psyche and the variety of the derivations to which he is exposed. The decision-making participant is an emergent product of personal psychic equipment and the derivations used by and upon him. Expressed differently, the Paretian analysis was a sociology (*cf.* Berger, 1965, pp. 273 - 274) which assumed the strategic participatory importance of individual psychology, and the Paretian world — the manipulative society — was a world of virtual movements, the most subtle of which involved the incremental but nevertheless strategic engagement and disengagement of components of psychic states.

On the basis of the foregoing the next sections of this chapter will sketch the remaining interrelations between power, psychology and knowledge as they were developed in the *Treatise*. In the remaining two chapters of Part Two, the Paretian analysis will be examined as it bears on the problems of freedom and control and of continuity and change.

## 3. Psychology and Power

It was seen in chapter four that, in Pareto's view, power was exercised and the game of power was played through force and cunning. The practice and implementation of force (which was something more than, although inclusive of, physical violence) was relatively slightly discussed in the *Treatise*. On the other hand cunning, fraud, deception, the evocation of consent or passive acquiescence, were widely treated, as should be evident from prior discussions and quotations. The *Treatise* is, indeed, something of a survey of man's practice of deception and self-deception. The point to be emphasized here, however, is that the influence of power in the manipulative society is partly through force and partly through cunning, with Pareto concentrating his analysis upon the latter.

The opportunity for cunning as a mode of power play derives from the fact that social equilibrium or policy is a function of psychology. Policy connotes choice; choice is in part a function of the sentiments, policy thus is *pro tanto* a function of the sentiments, and the sentiments are components of malleable complex psychic states, therefore, power players seeking to influence choices have the opportunity to work upon the sentiments. In other words, since, "human beings are moved much more by sentiment than by thought," that is, non-logico-experimental knowledge and non-logical conduct predominate, the opportunity is present for individuals who "are clever enough to take advantage of that circumstance to satisfy their own interests ..." (Sec. 2146; *cf.* Hook, 1935, p. 747).

When social policy involves or requires going beyond the limited conditions of Pareto optimum, it then is necessary "to decide on grounds of ethics, social utility, or something else, which individuals it is advisable to benefit, which to sacrifice" (Sec. 2129). But, for example, when social policy involves the problem of choosing between maximizing utility along Benthamite intensive or extensive margins, social policy is a function of ranking utilities as between lower and upper classes. Since ethical and utility valuations are partially a function of psychic states, "There is no criterion save sentiment for choosing between the one and the other"

124

(Sec. 2135). Choice is necessary, and values are instrumental in the process of selection, but it is Pareto's point that values and therefore choices are a partial function of the sentiments in effect built into the residues.

Since policy is a function of psychology, power uses psychology. The power player must work with the psychic states as he finds them (just as, it may be said, the monopolist or monopolistic competitor must work with the demand curve as he initially finds it). But the psychic states are malleable, and it is precisely the logic of manipulation through cunning to realign — engage and disengage — the residues so as to secure the desired policy. The fundamental interrelationship between power and psychology in the Paretian system is that psychology becomes the handmaiden of power. Given the predominance of non-logico-experimental reasoning and non-logical conduct,[10] "Sentiments therefore must be met with sentiments," (Sec. 1748) which is to say, sentiments must be led. Where the power player is endeavoring to lead along desired paths or to create desired convictions, power play is a matter of arousing the appropriate sentiments (Secs. 442, 490, 1685). Pareto emphasized that social equilibrium or policy is predominantly a function of psychology, but in the context of society as a system of power, and with psychology a matter of malleable complex psychic states, psychology is a function of power play.

But if psychology may be used *by* power, there is also in the Paretian system a psychic basis *of* power. It will be seen in the following chapter that the dynamics of the power structure, according to Pareto, involve a changing pattern or distribution of residues within and between classes. At this point the fundamental Paretian proposition — and a further relationship between power and psychology — may be indicated. Just as governing involves the manipulation of the sentiments, for example, the appeal to sentiments of patriotism in the masses in order to gain acceptance if not approval of the policies of the existing regime (Sec. 2254; *cf.* 2454), the *capacity to govern* is itself a product of the sentiments. More precisely, the psychic basis of power in the Paretian model lies in the requirement that there be a proper (although different) proportion of Class I and Class II residues in each of the two classes, the elite and subject classes.

Since social equilibrium is a function of the residues, it follows that the social optimum is a function of the optimum combination of residues. According to Pareto, "... a maximum of prosperity is yielded by a certain proportion between Class I and Class II residues, an excess in either proving alike harmful" (Sec. 2513). Combine the necessity for an optimum aggregate combination or proportion of residues with the elite theory of the power structure and there is

> "the advantage ... of having a community divided into two parts, the one in which knowledge prevails ruling and directing the other in which sentiments prevail, so that in the end, action is vigorous and wisely directed" (Sec. 1786).

Such an explanation should not obscure the fact that the ruling class is *not* ruling by virtue of its command over logico-experimental knowledge; rather, it, too, is dominated by sentiments. Pareto's primary point — notwithstanding a tendency to extol the rationality of the ruling class — is that of emphasizing "... how desirable it is that combination-instincts should predominate in leaders and the instincts of group-persistence in subordinates" (Sec. 2427; *cf.* 1853, 1932, 2250, 2274, 2439, 2463, and 2554). (It should be pointed out, however, that the psychological willingness to use logico-experimental knowledge as a basis of policy is a function of Class I residues.) In other words, there must be elements of both classes of residues in each social class but Class I residues should predominate in the ruling class and Class II in the subject class.

Moreover, "... it is not enough that a governing class possess Class I and Class II residues in the proper proportions; it is also necessary that proper use be made of them" (Sec. 2415; *cf.* 2191). With proper proportions between and within elite and subject classes, a nation will have a people possessing ability to innovate combined with ability to make proper use of novelties" (Sec. 2429). The rulers possess "Class I residues in abundance so that proper advantage could be taken of the residues in the masses" (Sec. 2454).

If this is the case, then, it is no wonder that Pareto considered that "it is better for the subject portion of the population to believe that there is an exact identity between the ethical value of a measure and its social utility" (Sec. 2274). By so believing they contribute, among other things, to a stability of the proper relationship between ruled and subject classes. Indeed,

> "It is advantageous to society that individuals not of the ruling classes should spontaneously accept, observe, respect, re-

vere, love, the precepts current in their society, prominent among them the precepts called — roughly, inadequately, to be sure — precepts of 'morality' and precepts of 'religion' — or we might better say of 'religions,' including under that term not only the group-persistences commonly so named, but many other groups of similar character" (Sec. 1932).

On the other hand, humanitarianism "is a specific trait of weak governments." It is "to be classed among the Class II residues; but ... it is among the weakest and least effective of them. It is a malady peculiar to spineless individuals who are richly endowed with certain Class I residues that they have dressed up in sentimental garb" (Sec. 2474). With democracy, humanitarianism is a result "of weakness in Class II residues, which are among the strongest forces inspiring human beings to self-sacrifice" (Sec. 2463).

Psychology is thus related to power in two ways. First, power play in part takes the form of manipulating the sentiments. Second, the power structure is in part a function of the distribution of residues. As power has use for psychology, psychology influences the power structure and power play. In particular, the capacity to govern — especially in matters of state but also in all other areas of life involving sub- and superordination — is a product of the sentiments, the sentiments of any particular power player and of those with whom he interacts. Power play is the *mutual* manipulation of sentiments.


## 4. Power and Knowledge

In the Paretian system social equilibrium is partially a function of knowledge, that is, of the view that people individually and collectively have of the world, of the possibilities for action, and, *inter alia*, of good and bad (approbation and disapprobation). Policy is partially a function of people's definition of reality (including values), a definition embodied in and to no small extent the product of the definitional meanings and connotations of words, theologies, ideologies, of reasonings in the broad Paretian sense, including, of course, myths. Pareto's theory of knowledge in relation to socio-economic policy was developed in chapter two, where, among other things, it was stressed that most people usually define reality in terms of derivations, or non-logico-experimental or pseudo-knowledge.

127

A basic interrelationship between power and knowledge in the Paretian system is that power play involves the mutual manipulation of definitions of reality. Alpha may want Beta to act and/or think in a certain way or along certain lines because it is to Alpha's advantage for Beta to do so. Because Beta's policy choices are in part a function of his (Beta's) definition of reality, Alpha will attempt to influence Beta's definition of reality in such a way and to the end that Beta will make choices of the variety preferred by Alpha. Insofar as policy is a function of the definition of reality, power players endeavor to manipulate that definition. A second interrelationship and one more subtle than the first, which is chicane and cunning already, is that, insofar as policy is a function of psychology and psychology is influenced by the derivations, power players endeavor to manipulate the definition of reality as an instrument through which to influence psychic states.

From what already has been developed in this study it must be clear that derivations — and logico-experimental science (Sec. 1683) — are means in the game of mutual manipulation from which issues social policy. The use of derivations, that is, cunning, is a substitute for force both logically and substantively (Secs. 1127n.4, 1952, 2192). Manipulation of the definition of reality is undertaken both in defense of and in promotion of interests and power positions, ultimately to make them appear legitimate and natural and thereby above challenge and disputation, if not discussion (Secs. 1066, 1081, 1689, 1695, 1883, 1884, 1892, 2147, 2182, 2184, 2210, 2272, and 2272n.1). Derivations, according to Pareto are essentially euphemisms for particular interests (Secs. 1221, 1222, 1883n.1, 2173, 2570n.1). They correspond to social forces, not unlike sentiments themselves (Sec. 1066); and they are used selectively by power players depending upon what terms and reasonings appear conducive to promote their desired goals through a propitious definition of reality (Secs. 401, 427, 1898). Moreover, derivations will be used to obscure as well as to precisely define reality (Sec.2272).

Coupled with Pareto's theory of the elite, the relation between power and knowledge comes to this:

"... the person in command needs rational combinations particularly, and the person who obeys needs more particularly an unreasoned rule independent of his scant knowledge" (Sec. 364; cf. 2250).

As expressed in the *Manuale*:

"Faith is the only powerful stimulant to human action, and therefore it is far from desirable, in the interests of society, that the majority of mankind, or even any large numbers, should handle social matters scientifically. Hence there is a conflict between the conditions of action and the conditions of knowledge, which furnishes a fresh proof of the lack of wisdom of the apostles of the universal and indiscriminate extension of knowledge" (Quoted in Wicksteed, 1933, p. 814; *cf.* Secs. 1786, 1932).

For example, humanitarianism in the masses makes them more docile and thereby facilitates the maintenance and exercise of power by the rulers (Moore, 1935 - 1936, p. 297).

Derivations may serve as an "opiate" even for the ruling class, "... an opiate to their already listless vigilance, and may [break] down their already feeble resistance" (Sec. 2200). But derivations generally function in this regard to mitigate the sorrows and quiet the longings of the potentially discontented and disaffected among the masses.

"The derivations may ... have availed to mitigate the sorrows of many people by inspiring hopes in a better future and inducing them to live, mentally, in a 'better' world than the experimental world" (Sec. 2345n.7; *cf.* 1081);

"And the A's use derivations to keep the B's quiet, telling them that 'all power comes from God', that it is a 'crime' to resort to violence, that there is no reason for using force to obtain what, if it is 'just', may be obtained by reason" (Sec. 2192).

"As a sum of pleasing fictions, [the derivation element] satisfies the desires, quiets the longings, of people who are eager to forget the misery and the ugliness of the real world and take refuge in the realms of the fanciful and the ideal, so disarming active enemies of existing conditions and maintaining the social complex ... intact or without too great change" (Sec. 2553).

But pseudo-knowledge is not just administered as an opiate, to disarm and disengage. The dogmas of religion are soporifics (Secs. 364 - 365), but usually there are "two theologies" of one kind or another, "one of which will glorify the immobility of one or

129

another uniformity, real or imaginary, the other of which will glorify movement, progress, in one direction or another" (Sec. 2173; *cf.* Lopreato, 1965, p. 26). In more general terms, knowledge as the definition of reality is manipulated to secure an accord between the goals of the manipulators and the understanding necessary, *pro tanto*, for the goals to materialize. Logico-experimental truth is eclipsed by social, and private, utility.

The significance of derivations as instruments of power in the manipulation of definitions of reality as the basis of policy is indirectly indicated in a discussion that runs throughout the *Treatise*. Yet nowhere is it systematically dealt with, and it is given somewhat different and ambivalent statements at one point and another. The discussion concerns the extent to which derivations are deliberately contrived by power players. What appears to be Pareto's basic position may be stated employing a distinction between use of and creation of derivations.

First, Pareto may be said to have differentiated between the deliberate and non-deliberate use of derivations. His view is that derivations are primarily used non-reflectively, but that power players, particularly those in the ruling class, tend to use them deliberatively without believing in them and generally knowing rather well that they are essentially useful myths.

Second, Pareto differentiated between the availability of ready-made derivations and the deliberate creation of new ones, his view being that the derivations in use at any time were primarily those found by current power players, but some were in use which were the result of deliberate contemporary artifice.

In both cases, it is to be emphasized, there is a necessity to differentiate between the governing class, which uses and may create derivations, and the subject class, which accepts and believes in them, at least as tendencies (Secs. 1853, 1932, and *passim*). In all cases, whether their use be deliberate or non-deliberate, whether they be the received myths or newly manufactured ones, the derivations function to define reality and thereby influence policy.

The foregoing interpretation of Pareto's position with respect to deliberate contrivance and use is evidenced in part by the numerous instances in which he minimizes but does not deny deliberateness of use and contrivance; the issue is not whether but to what extent. There are few conscious hypocrites; most people deceive themselves unconsciously: "Many people live satisfied with their own beliefs and are not in the least concerned with the problem of

130

reconciling them with logico-experimental science" (Sec. 2342; *cf.* Bongiorno, 1930. p. 362).

Differentiating between use and creation, he points to "the purposes to which [derivations] may be turned once they have become customary. Then it is natural enough that the shrewd should use them for their own ends just as they use any other force in society. The error lies in assuming that such forces have been invented by design. An example from our own time may bring out the point more clearly. There are plenty of rogues, surely, who make their profit out of spiritualism, but it would be absurd to imagine that spiritualism originated as a mere scheme of rogues" (Sec. 316). Non-deliberative use is primary, but deliberate use is made by the shrewd; although conscious creation is greatly minimized, there is some of it:

"Founders of religions are not shrewd hypocrites endeavoring surreptitiously to attain certain ends. The apostle, as a rule, is a man convinced of his own message — that, in fact, is an almost indispensable requisite if he is to win any following. So in cases where documents are lacking, to ascribe astute and knavish intentions to him carries one, in all probability, far from the truth" (Sec. 1124).

Again, deliberativeness is possible but minimized. So also with "many ideals ... that state rules of conduct." These "are, if not in form, in substance at least, given — are, that is, products of the thinker's society, in which he finds them ready-made, and not products of his theoretical meditation" (Sec. 1892).

Both deliberate use and contrivance not only are recognized, albeit minimized, but also at times are given prominence by Pareto.

"The schemer consciously aims at $m$ and preaches $T$; but the same thing is also done by many individuals who are in all good faith. Cynically selfish people are rare and downright hypocrites equally so. The majority of men merely desire to reconcile their own advantage with the residues of sociality (Class IV); realize their own happiness while seeming to strive for the happiness of others; cloak their self-seeking under mantles of religion, ethics, patriotism, humanitarianism, party loyalty, and so on; work for material satisfactions while seeming to be working only for ideals. In that way, furthermore, such men are able to win the support of people who are attracted by the beauty of the ideal, *T*, but who would be indifferently, if at all interested in the humble, earthly purpose, *m*. That is why they go rummaging about for theories adapted to the achievement of their purpose, and find them without difficulty; for the market is glutted with theories manufactured by theologians, moralists, social writers, and other people of the kind, who keep their counters covered with an article so greatly in demand, and so are able to attain their own advantage while seeming only to be in quest of the sublime" (Sec. 1884; *cf.* 2349).

Again, most people are passive, and there is a ready-made stock of derivations, but deliberate use and contrivance is the forte of the schemer and his lackies. "They know what they are driving at, and they are not unaware that all roads lead to Rome!" (Sec. 453). Indeed, "... the powerful, instead of saying simply that they want a thing, go to the trouble of devising sophistries to show that they 'have a right' to it: they imitate the wolf's palaver with the lamb" (Sec. 1689). In such a way the ancient generals were "ingenious enough to go and invent favourable omens outright — many of them, and such good ones that no one would have wished more or better" (Sec. 2436; *cf.* 2440). "Natural law is just a rubber band: the powerful can stretch it to whatever length they choose" (Sec. 1689). So, too, it is important "to have a derivation that is simple, and readily grasped by everybody, even the most ignorant people, and then to repeat it over and over and over again" (Sec. 1749). Throughout the *Treatise*, moreover, there are numerous instances of deliberate deceit and concealment recognized by Pareto, or what today would be cited as cases of manifest function (Secs. 401, 453, 1853, 1854ff, 2146, 2184, 2259, 2274, 2313n.2, 2440). Other examples, albeit often ambiguous, lie in the many newspaper editorials and columnists quoted by Pareto, who generally seem to deliberatively select the derivations most useful for their purpose (Sec. 1755; *cf.* 1755n.1)

Pareto stressed the ubiquity of belief in derivations, *ergo*, their non-deliberative appeal, the variety of ready-made derivations, and the positive but minimized role of deliberate manufacture of derivations. The manifest character of myths to the elite is evident and prescribed. Indeed, "myths in enormous numbers are manufactured" in matters of domestic as well as foreign policy (Sec. 2147). It would seem that derivations are generally used non-reflectively but are, perhaps in concentration, used deliberatively by the ruling class. Derivations are used insofar as they are already available, but new ones may be manufactured, again, by the active manipulators in the ruling class. Such use and manufacture is, after all, the essence of cunning. To the extent that the crucial variable is the sentiment or residue, having found a sentiment "ready-made in the masses at large, ... one after another [the manipulators] have taken advantage of it, giving its manifestations, to be sure, such forms as they pleased" (Sec. 1997).

In sum, the making of policy is partially the product of the manipulation of knowledge of the definition of the situation through the more or less systematic utilization of derivations. The latter involves both the deliberative and non-deliberative use of existing derivations and also the deliberate contrivance of new ones. Superimposing the elite theory of the power structure, the picture emerges of a scheming governing class manipulating the definition of the situation to suit its interest (Mannheim, p. 138; Bogardus, 1955, p. 509n.5), particularly the definition gullibly believed in by the subject class. The picture must be tempered, of course, as indicated above, by the fact that the ruling class is itself governed by its sentiments and by the derivations which define reality for it. But just as psychology is used by power, so also is knowledge. Truth and power-utility are two different things. Power play includes mutual manipulation of knowledge as a basis of policy; social equilibrium is partially a function of the knowledge upon which people act.

## 5. Psychology, Knowledge, and Power

The making of policy in the Paretian system thus far has been specified in terms of certain generalizations of interrelationships between pairs of knowledge, psychology, and power and concerning the character of psychic states. It has been stipulated that belief is a function of accordance with sentiments; that psychic states are malleable and complex; that the residues may be manipulated by derivations; that psychic states are manipulated by power players; that there is a psychic basis of power; and that knowledge is manipulated by power. What remains is to tie together the thread that connects these interrelationships. Knowledge is manipulated by power to work upon the sentiments as an alternative to the use of force.

*Given* that policy in a fundamental sense (according to Pareto)

133

is a function of psychic states, *given* that psychic states are complex and malleable, *given* that knowledge is a function of accord with sentiments, and *given* that the residues may be differentially stimulated by derivations, Pareto concluded that power players manipulate knowledge, including derivations, as a means of manipulating psychic states. Both by soporific and by stimulant, power uses knowledge or pseudo-knowledge to manipulate the mind. The manipulation of psyche by myth — the fundamental importance of psyche, but the instrumental or tactical significance of myth — in a society of power play is the grand theme of the *Treatise*.

In the Paretian model of social equilibrium or policy, the particular answers to questions involving specific content emerge from the interplay of power players, psyches, and derivations and from their interrelation and mutual manipulation. Problems of policy ultimately involve or reduce to specifics, and marginal choices must be made as to details, that is, specific choices for specific purposes (*cf.* Tufts, 1935; and Homans and Curtis, 1934, p. 19). The problem of specificity arises in many questions: "good for whom" (Sec. 439); solidarity on whose terms (Sec. 449 and *passim*); when is harm harmful to society (Sec. 1127 and *passim*); when is crime a crime (Sec. 2163); when is government "legitimate" (Sec. 1127; *cf.* 2166n.1); when follow one general principle and when another (Sec. 2147); what is "necessary for the good of society" in a particular situation (Sec. 2139); who determines "the facts as they are" (Sec. 2270); what is secondary and what is principal, and what is variable and what is constant (Sec. 2410); and, *inter alia*, whose natural law (Secs. 401, 402, 408). Pareto's general solution is that specification is a function of the operation of the decision-making process as it bears upon a particular situation, that is, of the results of the mutual manipulation of psyches by cunning (the use of derivations) and by force, as well as by chance (Sec. 2441).

Pareto nowhere presented in the *Treatise* anything like a complete statement of the interrelation of power, knowledge, and psychology. Nowhere, indeed, is there in the *Treatise* even a complete statement of a theory of power. Consider, however, the following four excerpts, selected essentially at random, as keys to Pareto's thinking on the subject:

1. Upon quoting from one of his sources "All human beings will want to share in material pleasures and replace one another

in the possession of power," Pareto interjected: "The history of that is what history is" (Sec. 2566n.3).

2. "The person who is able to free himself from the blind domination of his own sentiments is capable of utilizing the sentiments of other people for his own ends. If, instead, a person is prey to his own sentiments, he cannot have the knack of using the sentiments of others, and so shocks them to no purpose and fails to derive any advantage from them. The same may be said, in general, of the relations between the ruler and ruled. The statesman of the greatest service to himself and his party is the man who himself has no prejudices but knows how to profit by the prejudices of others (Sec. 1843). .

3. ... in any society persons who have the knack for praising people in power find ready admission to the governing class (Sec. 2211).

4. ... we see that, substantially, and whatever the form of government, men holding power have, as a rule a certain inclination to use that power to keep themselves in the saddle, and to abuse it to secure personal gains and advantages ... Wherefrom it follows that: 1. Individuals holding power behave in more or less the same way under the various systems of government. ... 2. Uses and abuses of power will be the greater, the more extensive the government's interference in private business. ... 3. The governing class sees to appropriating other people's property not only for its own use, but also to share with such members of the subject class as defend it and safe-guard its rule, whether by force or by fraud — the support the client lends to the patron. ..." (Sec. 2267).

Perhaps the best way of surveying in retrospect the Paretian theory of the making of policy through the interrelation of power, knowledge, and psychology is to present a rough catalog of what amounts to principles for the use of power in Pareto's manipulative society. This is perhaps the most characteristically Paretian course to take for two reasons. First, Pareto himself provided no systematic statement. Second, something of the thrust of Pareto's whole analysis is that such cannot be systematized but, rather, is an *ad hoc* sort of thing, albeit evidencing what he called uniformities. The following propositions, or normative principles for the use of power in the Paretian model, are adopted in sequence from

135

Chapter Eleven of the *Treatise*, "Properties of Residues and Derivations." They are by no means a complete handbook for manipulators, nor are they intended by the present author to be one (Borkenau, 1936, pp. 172 - 173). But they do roughly point to the meaning of the proposition that knowledge is manipulated by power to work upon the sentiments as an alternative to the use of force.

1. Contradictory derivations may be used to influence the particular sentiments of different persons to whom the derivations are addressed (Sec. 1716).
2. To influence society, translate theory into sentiments, derivations into residues (Sec. 1746).
3. Derivations are accepted if they accord with the sentiments, and function to strengthen and make aggressive the sentiment thereby expressed (Sec. 1747).
4. Sentiments and non-logical conduct are generally impervious to reason and logico-experimental demonstration, so that sentiments must be met with sentiments (Sec. 1748).
5. To spur men to action, use simple principles which overstep realities and aim at goals which lie beyond them (Sec. 1772).
6. Derivations serve as logical justifications for conduct that is really a function of sentiments (Sec. 1802).
7. The art of governing lies in manipulating existing residues, not in trying to change them[11] (Sec. 1805).
8. Derivations can be stretched to mean anything desired (Sec. 1815; *cf.* 1249).
9. The strong residues can be strengthened and the weak residues weakened by suppression (Sec. 1832).
10. Protect residues by protecting their associated derivations (Sec. 1832).
11. Just as the indifference of the manipulator is necessary, so is the ardent belief by the manipulated (Sec. 1853).
12. To promote continuity, promote religion (Secs. 1855, 1932).
13. If the sentiments manifested by a social doctrine are to have influence, the doctrine should take the form of a myth (Sec. 1868).
14. The role of ideals is as energizer, arouser, impellents (Sec. 1869).
15. The masses possess an unending alternation of theologies and metaphysical systems (Sec. 1881).

16. Aim at the real end, preach an imaginary end (Sec. 1884).
17. The masses pay little attention to the sources of rules but are satisfied so long as the rules exist and are accepted and obeyed (Sec. 1930).
18. Facts should be seen by the masses not as they are in reality but as transfigured in light of ideals (Sec. 1932).
19. Morality and religion should not be identified simply with one special morality and one special religion, to avoid giving to derivations an emphasis belonging only to the residues (Sec. 1932).
20. Talk of eternal justice but act as if she didn't exist (Sec. 1956).

With policy generally a function of power, knowledge, and psychology, it is somewhat more particularly, according to Pareto, a function of knowledge and psychology in the service of power. Power itself is a function of the distribution of residues, which in turn are subject to manipulation by the derivations. Policy making comprises and policy emerges from a system of general equilibrium, a system of marginal moves and marginal changes. This system is one in which all variables are manipulable; in which government, truth, social utility, and power, knowledge and psychology are all both independent and dependent variables; in which economic results (structure, conduct, and performance) are a product of decision-making, the pretensions of ostensibly absolutist derivations notwithstanding yet very much influenced thereby nonetheless.

*Chapter 6.*

# The Problem of Freedom
# and Control

## 1. Power and Social Control

The question of freedom or autonomy versus control is one of
the major problems, in a fundamental sense, with which any
theory of policy must be concerned and upon which any theory of
economic policy has much potential impact. Ultimately, the problem of freedom and control has to do with the structure of the
socio-economic decision-making process; for that and other reasons it is of profound social, theoretical, and personal importance.
It has to do with such questions as whose rights, whose exposure
to the freedom of others, whose capacity to coerce, and so on.

Although Pareto at one point directed attention to the necessity
for and benefits (echoed, as it were, throughout the *Treatise* with
respect to prosperity) following from a satisfactory reconciliation
of discipline and freedom (Sec. 242), there is no distinct or systematic treatment of the problem in the *Treatise*. Yet, if that work
involves a theory of social change, which it unquestionably does, it
also encompasses a theory of social control. Albeit almost completely implicit and undistilled, the problem of freedom and control is in several respects a major continuing subject in the *Treatise*. Such could hardly have been otherwise, given Pareto's scope
and purpose. Approached in a distinctively Paretian manner, the
problem of freedom and control is essentially that of the distribution of power in society.

Pareto dealt with the issue, in large part, through his discussion of the social system, his elite theory of the power structure, and his related theory of class circulation. At least with respect to Pareto's interpretation, analysis of power is substantially equivalent to analysis of the problem of freedom and control; the power structure generally may be interpreted as functioning as a system of social control. Pareto's references to order, social utility, and the like notwithstanding, there were no mysterious forces of social control akin to a *deus ex machina*. Rather, social control (including the non-deliberative forces of social control, which are themselves taken advantage of by active power players) was the result of power play by man himself. Law, at the same time that it served order as social control, was also an instrument of those who can use the state for private or party ends. So, too, with the church. It is an instrument of social control but also a power player, or a power player and thereby an instrument. Social control, then, was essentially the same thing as, or emerged from, power play, and Pareto's theory of power becomes a theory of social control.

Lopreato quite appropriately has concluded that Pareto's theory of social control necessarily included elements of both (using Dahrendorf's terminology as employed by Lopreato) *integration* and *coercion* (Lopreato, 1965, p. 23). As Lopreato pointed out (Lopreato, 1965, p. 25ff), Pareto stressed that both existed in society, and he synthesized them so as to include both the residues of sociality and the use of force. "Consensus, deception, and coercion appear, therefore, to be complementary forces in the cohesion of society." In the context of Pareto's view emphasizing the universality of coercion, Lopreato also concludes that Pareto considered "coercion as an inevitable process that makes consensus possible." In particular, "it is the relations between" ruling and governed classes "that to a large extent articulate the mode of social organization and the degree of social cohesion or disintegration in society" (Lopreato, 1965, pp. 28, 33). Indeed, "the basic forces of integration and consensus are also the ultimate causes of conflict and coercion"[8] (Lopreato, 1965, p. 27; *cf.* Schumpeter, 1951, p. 139).

Social control thus issues from power play; or, the two are essentially synonymous or inseparable. But elsewhere Lopreato and Ness find a distinction between power play and order in Pareto's mind. They affirm

"that there is no question of Pareto's 'approving' the use of the most ruthless force in society. The use of force *may* have positive functions only under special circumstances. Never, however, does Pareto take an ideological position in this respect. The closest he comes to doing so is when he considers the type of utility that may properly be called societal: specifically, when he considers the question of order and 'protection to the citizen' in the society. In this connection Pareto appears to some to be arguing in favor of the type of ruling elite that is capable of using force to maintain itself in power. This is, however, a totally unwarranted interpretation of his position, for his focus is not on power maintenance *per se* but on social order. To be sure, power maintenance by the ruling elite is a crucial expression of social order, but one must understand that, for Pareto the continuing maintenance of power depends also upon the circulation of the elite. For the most stable, the most effective, and the most legitimate ruling elite is that which is open and allows a free flow of talent into it from the governed masses" (Lopreato and Ness, 1966, p. 28).

There are several generally unrelated (or related but presently unimportant) difficulties with such a view. First, the utility of force is circumstantial to Pareto, and he would view the words *stable, effective,* and *legitimate* as begging the question. Power is power, and to the winner goes — and should go, according to Pareto — the spoils. The word *force* may be substituted for the word *power* in the preceding sentence. Second, the "free flow of talent" would take place, of course, on terms as propitious and advantageous to the rulers as they can obtain.

But the important matter here is this. The distinction between power (or power maintenance) and social order should not be pushed too far. From a modern sociological point of view (as Parsons showed in the *Structure of Social Action*), "Pareto's focus is ultimately on social order and citizen protection" in the case discussed by Lopreato and Ness (1966, p. 28), *but* Pareto's analysis was in terms of power play, which included power maintenance. Social order (such as there is) emerged from that power play under the hegemony of the rulers. Indeed, Pareto would consider it mere derivation — the exercise of deception — for a *power player* to assert that his power moves were to ensure social order. Yes, social order, Pareto would say, but social order in his view and on his terms (that is, the power player's). Rather than "power maintenance by the ruling class" being only "a crucial expression of social order," social order *emerges* more or less indirectly from power maintenance efforts by the ruling class, as well as other maneuvers by other players. Power and order are two facets of one process.

The basic Paretian analysis of the problem of freedom and control therefore, already has been given in the discussion of power in chapter four. The next three sections of this chapter will briefly examine the status of the concepts of freedom and of control in the *Treatise*.

## 2. Freedom

Pareto's *Treatise* is not to be included among those works in which "freedom," or "liberty," is gloriously but ambiguously invoked as a presumably precise criterion of policy choices. Pareto himself does use the words *free* and *freedom*, (Secs. 127, 1893, 2096n.1, and *passim*), for example, in differentiating one case from another; and there can be no doubt that Pareto was an aristocratic-elitist libertarian who delighted in denouncing democratic-humanitarian interventions. Indeed, his uses reflect his own specification of the otherwise ambiguous concept, and one may argue that his denunciations reflect a personal inclination toward belief in the omnipotence of words. If cursing is a substitute for aggressive wishes, then certainly his biting and bitter comments upon humanitarianism, democracy, and so forth, reflect similarly aggressive emotions. Moreover, and more important, the *Treatise* was intended by Pareto to deal with the role of subjective ambiguities contained in derivations and to reveal the non-logico-experimental and subjective element in propaganda. But, for whatever reason, Pareto in the *Treatise* did not basically use *freedom* as if it had objective substantive content and as a propaganda slogan. Rather, *freedom* is held to be a meaningless ideal albeit useful for ideological, hence manipulative, purposes.[1]

To Pareto the social scientist, freedom was subjective. It was a semantic, metaphysical, and, above all, emotional phenomenon (Secs. 1553 - 1555, 1561, 1565, 1573, 1708, 2566n.3, and *passim*). One felt free depending, in no small part, upon how one's residues or sentiments had been manipulated, that is, free along the lines one had been induced to prefer, and much less, if at all, upon objective reality. Freedom, in addition, was considered by Pareto to be complex (Secs. 2316, 2609) and contextual (Sec.

142

2316; *cf.* Henderson, 1937, p. 56). Freedom was reciprocal (Sec. 1554) rather than absolute (Sec. 2147). The freedom of one power player was limited by his exposures to the freedom of others, and, among other objectives, power play aimed at minimizing the impact of such exposure. Although Pareto referred to nineteenth century economic individualism as "freedom" and opposed what he considered "crystallization" (involving a distinction not unlike Maine's juxtaposition of contract and status), he nevertheless acknowledged that it was "only a limited freedom" (Sec. 2553; *cf.* 2316). Freedom connoted the absence of limitations (Secs. 617, 1553, 2609), but control and limitation were necessary and inevitable because of the ubiquity of power play and the universality of coercion (of one form or another), and they were necessary because of the exigencies of life in society. If one liked some and disliked other control (because of one's sentiments and/or interests), one would feel free by virtue of the former and coerced by the latter.

With respect to "rights" Pareto considered that claims of the "rights of society" against individual rights were really the claim of one individual(s) versus another (and established, or vested) individual(s) (Sec. 1716). He rejected "rights" arguments as criteria of the distribution of income and wealth, which distribution is, according to him, a function of power.

"So as between the various social classes no principle of 'right' can be found to regulate the division of social advantage. The classes that have the greater strength, intelligence, ability, shrewdness, take the lion's share. It is not clear how any other principles of division could be logically established and even less clear how once they were established logically they could be enforced or applied in the concrete. Every individual certainly has his own principle for a division that would seem ideal to him. But such a principle is nothing more than an expression of his individual sentiments and interests which he comes to conceive as a 'right.' It is just a case of the usual derivation whereby a name is changed to make a thing more acceptable to others" (Sec. 1509; *cf.* 2147).

Rights are sophistries and derivations (Sec. 1689), and, like "justice," ambiguous (Sec. 2147). Arguments over rights are part of the semantics of power play (Sec. 2147, 2316), that is, the use of derivations. Rights, like freedom, are relative (Sec. 2316), and rights arguments, aside from functioning mainly to appeal to sentiments, usually beg the very point at issue. Ultimately they are a matter of the sentiments.

What is also implicit in the *Treatise* is Pareto's elitist theory of freedom. Freedom is given substance in terms, primarily, of the context of the ruling class (Sec. 298; *cf.* Novack, 1933), and secondarily, in terms of Class I and Class II residues. With respect to the former, effective freedom exists for those in the ruling class and those in the subject class on the rise. In this context, also, freedom is extolled but not as freedom; rather, it is seen as necessary and salutary, given the power nature of society. With respect to the latter, the residues, freedom connotes opportunity for speculators and security for rentiers. For Pareto, society has, and must have, both. His proper proportion of Class I and Class II residues (within and between ruling and ruled classes) is paralleled by the opportunity- and security-feelings which freedom in each sense connotes.

Finally, as will be seen briefly in the next section, Pareto also uses freedom in the sense of non-legal social control, a usage related to and perhaps derived from Class II residues. Like many libertarians before and since, Pareto praised both freedom and authority: freedom from deliberate, hence generally legal, social control (actually, from law as a mode of change), and the authority of non-legal or non-deliberative controls such as custom and morality. Freedom thereby connotes primary reliance upon custom and morality as social controls and a "minimum" reliance upon government; the status quo participation by and use of government largely is taken for granted. But this connotation, although strongly implicit in the *Treatise,* is not as developed by Pareto as it is, for example, in such writers as Hayek, Knight, and Leoni. Rather, it is eclipsed by Pareto's theory of the circulation of the elite and related themes (notions generally not stressed by libertarians).

In sum, freedom must be interpreted in the context of dynamic power play. Pareto's definition of the concept is meaningless outside the context of the struggle for power. In addition, freedom is essentially a subjective and emotional phenomenon, its use relating more about the sentiments and interests of the user than about objective reality except as a pointer to trends (for example, complaints about the loss of freedom may indicate the direction of achievement of other power players).

## 3. Control

As already developed *in extenso*, the Paretian model of society is pervaded with control exercised through cunning and force. In the manipulative society, control, not freedom, is stressed, however much society is, in fact, a structure of freedom *and* control, and however much forces in society preach the virtues of freedom as they connote it. In addition to what Pareto had to say on power *per se*, the following further indicates the status of control in the *Treatise*. Again, because of the inseparability of power play and social control in Pareto's analysis, what follows is largely a footnote to chapter four as well as the obverse of the foregoing analysis of freedom.

First, Pareto demonstrably understood the necessity for authority and discipline in society (Sec. 1113; *cf.* 242 - 243 and *passim*) (in the view of many critics, too well, too obsessively, or perversely). Control over conduct is necessary in perhaps all facets of social life, including sex (Sec. 1167; *cf.* 1139). Conduct must be channeled to become a function of rules, the individual becoming disciplined in the ways of his society. Parsons early interpreted the *Treatise* as recognizing the necessity for a framework of order, for channeling coercion, and for processes of conflict resolution (Parsons, 1937, pp. 458, 235; 1936, pp. 256, 260 and *passim*). In addition, the individual is a socialized individual in the sociological sense (Becker and Barnes, 1961, p. 1018; Homans and Curtis, 1934, p. 228). His income and wealth are distributed (or rather, received) in part as a function of the norms and working rules of the framework (Sec. 2147 and *passim*); indeed, the price system itself functions as a system of social control (Parsons, 1937, pp. 234 - 237). Law and economy are both regimes of social control (Timasheff, 1940; Amoroso, 1938, pp. 5 - 6), as is education, including the teaching of history (Secs. 747n.3, 1580ff, 2156ff). In the *Treatise*, one finds the germs of a "social control theory of value." Although not equivalent to Commons' "reasonable value" theory, it points, as did Commons, to non-market resolutions of conflicts of ends which become embodied in what Commons called "working rules" and what Pareto called "norms."[2] For both Commons and Pareto, issues of policy of this variety are much more significant than market questions of resource allocation.

Second, Pareto quite well appreciated that social control involved manipulation of the sentiments, or the residues.[3] Conversely, morality depended upon accord with sentiments (Secs. 361,

1156, and *passim*). Power play, as developed above, was both a function of sentiments and manipulation of sentiments. So also with control, if the two may be distinguished.

Third, although legitimation of authority (Sec. 583 and *passim*) through absolutist formulation (Secs. 1032, 1772, 1878 and *passim*) was prevalent in society, Pareto also insisted that the content of both law and morality was ambiguous (Secs. 398ff, 1716, 1796, 1852, 1893, 1898, 2147). Specific content was attributed by strategically located individuals in accordance with their sentiments and interests.

Fourth, as will be developed more fully at the end of this chapter, Pareto recognized that socio-economic reform ultimately involved the delicate task of changing the pattern of social control (Sec. 2139).

Fifth, Pareto treated non-logical conduct as partially the complex result of social control. Specifically, habit and customary morality as well as the reasonings of economic and political argumentation were comprised mainly of derivations which, as sanctions and as definitions of reality, functioned as non-deliberative social control.[4] Moreover, Pareto applauded social control through non-logical conduct *vis-a-vis* deliberative legal control (Secs. 242 - 243, 364, 365, 400). That is to say, he preferred the operation of the derivations and the non-logical conduct which they promoted, particularly as they manifest Class II residues in the masses, to the deliberative interventionism of the state.

Sixth, this latter point brings the discussion to the group in whom Class II residues generally are dominant, and in which they should be dominant, according to Pareto, as a condition of prosperity and order. This group is the subject class. Two points should be made. First, social control in the Paretian model connotes manipulation by the ruling class of the subject class both in fact and in the view of the governing sector of the former at least. Second, social control also connotes control as the product of interaction between ruling and subject classes, including, of course, circulation of the elite.

In the latter connection, particularly, it is to be stressed again that control was not only *by* but also *over* the ruling class. Freedom was most conspicuous for the elite, particularly the governing group therein, and for the speculator group, but even these were constrained, in part, through Class II residues. The elite, after all, is part of the social system and therefore is both determining and determined, free and exposed, manipulating and manipulated,

146

within itself and with the other class and forces in social equilibrium. The threat, if not the fact, of ambitious elements from the subject class — and thus of forced circulation — was always present. Control, as with freedom, was control within the power structure and the continuing struggle for power.

The questions of whose freedom, whose power, and whose control were elemental in Pareto's theory of social control and in the resolution of the problem of freedom and control in the Paretian model. Just as the mule exercises control over the farmer by his obstinacy, an awkward analogy perhaps, so does the dull grey mass, as some have called the subject class, dominate in a way through its sheer bulk, immobility, and conservatism. More than that, the subject class represents a permanent threat of revolution, and its leaders must be bargained with. Yet, by virtue of their leadership, these leaders tend to become coopted into the ruling class if they are at all bending and obliging. This is social control, or power play, in action.

Seventh, it should be clear that Pareto considered religion — faith — as an instrument of social control, a form of social cement.[5] In addition, religion itself was partly a result of the sentiments (Secs. 626, 1802, and *passim*); as social control, religion operated through the sentiments (Secs. 361, 2375). The sentiments were the sources of morality, and both the specific content of religion and the connotation adduced to the deity were held to be a function of circumstance and power play (Sec. 2349 and *passim*). Moreover, insofar as the members of the ruling class were not believers in but rather users of religion, religion was a device — an opiate — for the social control of the masses (Secs. 313 - 314, 364 - 365).

Eighth, reflecting Pareto's sense of the operation of social control, he wrote of "ties." By these he meant circumstantial constraints upon behavior and choice, including social control both formal and informal (Secs. 127, 237, 242 - 243, 1021ff, 1037, 1853, 1881, 2316, 2609). Ties "regulate the conduct of the individual" (Sec. 2552), and also bind the group (Sec. 1037). In the context of tastes *vis-a-vis* obstacles, ties are checks in the form of obstacles to the acquisition of economic values (Sec. 2079). Social equilibrium is a function of the ties (Secs. 2124, 2128, 2148, 2316n.8), and reform, considered as requiring or reducing to change in the pattern of social control, involves a change in the ties (Secs. 2096n.1, 2097, 2131, 2139, 2175, 2262). Finally, although, as Perry has pointed out, Pareto gave no analysis or exami

147

nation of the ties (Perry, 1935, p. 100), he did define individualism and collectivism in terms of the strength of ties (Sec. 2552), (and in terms of the number of restrictions (Sec. 1702n.3)).

Ninth, in addition to disparaging anarchism as the antithesis of a well-ordered society (this more by innuendo than by explicit discussion), Pareto considered that anarchism was in part a product of particular residues which lead to a failure on the part of the individual to adjust to the requirements of authority and discipline in society (Secs. 1140n.1, 1156, 1215). But he also examined anarchism as the result of the breakdown or failure of social control forces (Secs. 2515n.1, 2609).

Tenth, Pareto greatly denigrated socialism, along with democracy and humanitarianism, but he (as with Marx on capitalism) did not flinch from paying tribute when he thought it was due. Socialism, or at least proletarian as opposed to ascetic socialism, was or had become an important social control force in the disciplining and civilizing of the masses.

"From the standpoint of social utility, the ascetic residues are not beneficial — they are positively harmful. It is very probable, therefore, that the Socialist religion of the lower classes is socially beneficial, while the ascetic Socialism of the upper classes is socially pernicious. Proletarian Socialism may be at bottom revolutionary, but it is not in the least opposed to discipline, in fact stresses it; and the authority of Socialist leaders is often far better respected than the authority of government officials. The Socialist religion is a great school of discipline, and one may even go so far as to say that, from that standpoint, it runs a close second to Catholicism. It has served to strengthen Class V residues (personal integrity) in people of the lower strata of society. Better than any legislative enactment — not excepting compulsory education — it has succeeded in raising the molecules in an amorphous mass of humanity to dignified status as citizens, and in so doing it has increased the capacities for action of society as a whole. Ascetic socialism, on the other hand, tends to debilitate every sort of energy. When at all effective it weakens Class V residues in the higher strata of society, and of the few who accept it in good faith it makes cowards and dolts who are useless to themselves and to others ... Standing apart from real interests, ascetic Socialism prevents social conflicts from finding solutions on the basis of a balance among such interests, and so occasions useless wasting of energies"[6] (Sec. 1858).

As will be seen in the next chapter, Pareto's analysis had a functional, even a respected, place for revolution, although in the quotation just given he appears to be antagonistic to socialist revolution. Revolution and socialism Pareto did not like, particularly the latter. But his theory required him to recognize, first, the social control function of both socialism and revolution; and, second, that with respect to maximizing social utility, including "the capacities for action of society as a whole," circulation of the elite through both revolution and socialism had social utility.

Eleventh, and finally, Pareto had what may be called either a social control or manipulative definition of ethics. The author elsewhere has quoted Bentham's social control oriented definition: "Ethics at large may be defined, the art of directing men's actions to the production of the greatest possible quantity of happiness, on the part of those whose interest is in view" (Samuels, 1966, p. 42). Similarly directed is Adam Smith's proposition that "The great ˉsecret of education is to direct vanity to proper objects" (Samuels, 1966, p. 67). Ethics and virtue are combined in Bertrand Russell's treatment to the same effect:

"Ethics is thus closely related to politics: it is an attempt to bring the collective desires of a group to bear upon individuals; or, conversely, it is an attempt by an individual to cause his desires to become those of his group. ...

Ethics is an attempt to give universal, and not merely personal, importance to certain of our desires. ... ... [The legislator] will then, if he can, so construct his code that conduct promoting ends which he values shall, as far as possible, be in accordance with individual self-interest; and he will establish a system of moral instruction which will, where it succeeds, make men feel wicked if they pursue other purposes than his. Thus 'virtue' will come to be in fact, though not in subjective estimation, subservience to the desires of the legislator, in so far as he himself considers these desires worthly to be universalized" (Russell, 1961, pp. 232, 234; *cf.* Butler, 1940, p. 17 and *passim*).

As Pareto expressed it, society is engaged in an attempt to induce individuals to define their private interest in terms of the

149

social interest (utility) as the latter is defined or given substance by strategic decision makers. These generally are numbered among the ruling class. In particular, the social interest is defined "by theologians and metaphysicists, out of a love for the absolute, ..; by moralists, in order to induce individuals to concern themselves with the good of others; by statesmen, to induce the individual to blend his own advantage with the public advantage; and by other sorts of people for reasons of like character" (Sec. 2115). Therefore, wrote Pareto,

> "It is essential to distinguish the purpose ... that an individual has of his own accord from the purpose ... that others may try to induce him to have. That distinction is of immense importance in human societies because of the conflict the individual feels between his own advantage and the advantage of other individuals or society. The history of morals and law is, one may say, the history of the efforts that have been made to reconcile, by fair means or foul, those two sorts of utility" (Sec. 1877).

> "... for almost always the purpose of a doctrine is to persuade individuals to aim at an objective that yields an advantage to other individuals or to society" (Sec. 1883; *cf.* 1685, 1853, 1884, 1916, and Becker and Barnes, 1961, p. 1021).

Ethics, then, was to Pareto an instrumental phenomenon characterized by its role in power play and, thereby, in social control.


### 4. Private Property

Some of the foregoing is illustrated by Pareto's comments concerning the institution of private property and the controversies surrounding it. The institution was of both practical and emotional importance to Pareto himself. He was rather well aware (to understate the matter!) that the type of society which he preferred was itself partially grounded in and structured by that institution. The juxtaposition of Pareto the human being and citizen and Pareto the social scientist is evident.

As may be expected, Pareto envisioned a psychological character of private property. He located it in two sentiments: the first, to defend and increase the quantity of "one's own," related to the sense of integrity in the individual (Sec. 1207; *cf.* Homans and Curtis, 1934, pp. 119ff; Faris, 1936, p. 666; and Amoroso, 1938, p. 8); the second, the residues of "persistence of relations between a person and other persons and places," "a sense of property" (Sec. 1015; *cf.* 1056ff), *ergo*, a need for continuity. Private property as an institution is thus conservative, connoting status quo rights, that is, rights generally already having legal status (Secs. 1211, 1416, 2553, 2558). The nature of private property therefore leads to conservative social policy — policy promotive of continuity of power structure. Reform, for example, generally is, labelled by Pareto as robbery (Secs. 1345, 1462, 1552, 1716; *cf.* 1416). On the other hand, Pareto went out of his way to note that the argument that tariff protection is robbery is a derivation (Sec. 2208n.1), and he confessed to having made related errors in the analysis of protection in the *Cours* (Sec. 2208n.3).

The treatment of property in society is a function of the sentiments, differing sentiments being aroused in different individuals by the derivations used in controversies over private property (Secs. 7, 113, 585n.1, 1210, 1546, 1716, 1884n.1, 1890, 2022, 2147, 2316). Much of the discussion and controversy simply involves derivations and not objective reality (Secs. 1817 - 1819, 2147, 2566n.3, and *passim*). The law of private property includes rationalization of non-logical conduct (Sec. 256). As Perry has summarized Pareto in regard to the derivations:

> "The words or concepts determine patterns of cooperation which are inventions or constructs. Laws, marriage, money, nationality, property, and similar social facts are the words and ideas in which they are expressed. In one sense they are 'beliefs'; but their relation to reality is not the relation of correspondence; and the social process by which they are established as institutions or conventions must not be identified with the process by which scientific theories are established" (Perry, 1935, p. 102).

In addition, arguments over property rights usually beg "the very point in dispute" (Sec. 2147n.6).

But the regime of private property is itself a system of social control, imposing relationships of limitation and constraint — ties — however much it is viewed as a system of freedom (Secs. 126 - 127, 2147, and *passim*). Although property rights are themselves limited ("We have, in other words, no example of a society

in which the property-right subsists strictly without limitation.")
(Sec. 2316; *cf.* 2147n.6) and although there is the inescapable
question of when private property is private property (Secs. 551,
805ff, 1495n.1, 2147, 2147n.3), private property and inequality
go hand in hand:

> "History shows that in societies in which private property is
> apparently non-existent or reduced to a minimum, in which
> equality seems to prevail, private property, or similar institu-
> tions, along with inequalities, tend to develop. That fact empha-
> sizes the necessity (the experimental necessity) of other ties
> working in a sense opposite to the equalitarian ties. And from
> that to conclude that attacks on private property, and other
> similar institutions, and on inequalities, can be suppressed alto-
> gether would be to go astray and fall into the ... error [of using
> a qualitative instead of a quantitative analysis, of overlooking
> interdependences in social phenomena, of imagining that in
> explaining social phenomena one can confine oneself to a single
> tie among the many ties and modify the one without touching
> the others.] For such things are just another illustration of the
> composite character of the forces that are working upon society"
> (Sec. 2316; the bracketed phrase is from the preceding para-
> graph; *cf.* 254).

Moreover, where theological doctrine denigrates private property, because private property is necessary and (in some form)
inevitable (Secs. 448, 1815), subterfuge is found through which to
interpret theology in a way that would at least "not jar too vio-
lently" the practices of property (Sec. 1815). Theology being
derivations, derivations expressing certain residues, and derivations
also "lacking in definiteness," (Sec. 1800) it is not hard to stretch
them (Sec. 1815).

Pareto thus treats reform as robbery. But the relation between
speculators and *rentiers*, in a property context (in addition to the
psychological, discussed earlier), also involves the robbery, albeit
legal (or not illegal), of the *rentiers*. Through one device or another the real income of the *rentier* group falls prey, according to
Pareto, to the speculators (Secs. 479, 2268, 2310 - 2316). If private property connotes status quo rights, and if power play involves the coerced redistribution of those rights, then the manipulative society becomes, in effect, a system of institutionalized robbery. Conflict between conservative and liberal thus centers

around which robbery is to be sanctioned or allowed. If, further-more, private property is itself robbery, as *Proudhon* argued, and if *Pareto's* analysis is accepted, all social policy is indeed institution-alized robbery. But this is essentially only another way of express-ing the theme that society is a system of mutual coercion and manipulation. The ultimate question in this context, as Pareto seems to have understood it, is: What is one's "own?" That is to say, the decision-making process must evolve workable and accept-able grounds upon which to base and change particular property rights and with which to resolve conflicts of claims through litiga-tion and/or legislation.

Pareto also pointed to a Romanic tendency toward an overcrys-tallization of society when the institution of private property is used to conservatively rigidify the social structure. Private prop-erty, he pointed out, can be associated with open and closed sys-tems. The significance of the meaning and operation of private property as an institution is a function of the larger system of which the concept is a part in any particular society (Secs. 2548 - 2550).

It also may be pointed out that Pareto optimum and Pareto's famous law on income distribution both assume as given or as constant the distribution of property and fundamental property relations, respectively. Finally, attention may be called to Schum-peter's remark "that property relations *per se* are much less in evidence with Pareto than they are with Marx, and that this also constitutes a claim to superiority of the Paretian analysis." This, Schumpeter wrote, was because "with Pareto the historical process is not so much the result of the conflict of comprehensive social classes [in the Marxian sense] as it is the result of the conflict of their ruling minorities" (Schumpeter, 1951, pp. 140 - 141). This latter statement should serve as a reminder that in the Paretian model conflict is not only between ruling and subject class in the large, but also, and most important, between plural elites. These elites not only jockey for position but also appeal to the senti-ments of the masses. Whether property relations are less evident, or less important, with Pareto *vis-à-vis* Marx is quite another ques-tion, however, which need not be examined here.

The institution of private property, then, is bound up with the problem of freedom and control. That is, it is bound up with the power process of society. Pareto recognized this fact and the fact that property, therefore, has a dynamic character. That dynamism, as well as the power structure as a whole, means that the problem of freedom and control is integrally related to the problem of continuity and change.

## 5. Freedom and Control and Continuity and Change

Without examining the matter in detail from the perspective of contemporary social and behavioral science, in which many of the details and basic theorems have not been fully worked out or integrated, it nevertheless may be asserted that the continuing resolutions of the dual basic social problems of freedom and control and of continuity and change are worked out together in and through the same social processes. Not only is one interrelated with the other, but also their resolution emerges from common social phenomena. For present purposes it is unnecessary to go beyond this. Attention need only be directed to the interrelatedness and common genesis of both. What the precise interrelations are and exactly what that common basis is remain unanswered in any final and certainly in any short answer sense.

It is possible, however, to *interpret* each in terms generally of the other, that is, the problem of freedom and control can be specified in terms of continuity and change, and *vice versa.* Controversy over continuity versus change may be envisioned as ultimately involving the distribution of power (the pattern of freedom and control). Moreover, the resolution of continuity versus change may be specified as a function of the power structure. Alternatively, freedom versus control may be interpreted as controversy over the power of choice between continuity and change. There are many semantic difficulties encountered in discussing (particularly, briefly) these questions. For example, the great issues of policy may be generalized as involving either control over the choice of change *or* choice over the control of change (Samuels, 1966, p. 268). But change brings with it and/or requires change in the pattern of control and thereby the mode of choosing. Each problem may be generally defined in terms of the other.

There are, accordingly, implicit elements of both interpretations in the *Treatise.* On the one hand, the problem of resolving freedom versus control is interpreted as being a function of the resolution of continuity versus change: the pattern and/or the problem of freedom and control is a product of the resolution of continuity versus change, ultimately of the power structure. On the other hand, the problem of continuity and change is interpreted as being a function of the resolution of freedom versus control, that is, as a result of the struggle for power. The resolution of this conflict is seen as a twofold function. First and most generally, it is a function of power play. Second, it is a function of the efficacy of social control governing the integration of individuals into the status quo system and adherence to status quo modes of change as opposed to alienation of individuals and groups from the status quo, including simple discontent and active revolution against the status quo as well as anomie.

Dominating both interpretations, however, as would be expected given Pareto's main argument in the *Treatise*, is an emphasis upon the psychological foundation upon which the resolution of each rests. Moreover, in his own way Pareto had each basic problem relate to both the power structure and the question of integration versus alienation. The recognition by Pareto of both the interrelatedness of the two problems and their common psychological basis is apparent in the following statement:

"It is evident that if the requirement of uniformity (residues IV.b) were so strongly active in all individuals in a given society as to prevent even one of them from breaking away in any particular from the uniformities prevalent in it, such a society would have no internal causes for dissolution; but neither would it have any causes for change, whether in the direction of an increase, or of a decrease, in the utility of the individuals or of the society. On the other hand if the requirement of uniformity were to fail, society would not hold together, and each individual would go his own way, as lions and tigers, birds of prey, and other animals do. Societies that endure and change are therefore situated in some intermediate condition between those two extremes" (Sec. 2171).

This statement is found, it is interesting and important to note, at the beginning of his discussion, in chapter twelve of the *Treatise*, of "the use of force in society" (Sec. 2170). It is in the paragraphs that follow (Secs. 2174ff) that the struggle for power, including the use of force, is (a) specified in terms of the problem of continuity versus change of the power structure and (b) made the basis of resolving continuity versus change, that is, continuity and change as a function of freedom and control.

Anticipating, then, some of the discussion of chapter seven, and referring back to the discussion in chapter three concerning

Class I and Class II residues as embodying forces and values for change and continuity, respectively, one of Pareto's major themes is that continuity versus change of the status quo power structure is a function of Class I versus Class II residues. In other words, the resolution of freedom versus control is a function of the resolution of continuity versus change; both, through the latter, are a function of conservative versus innovative sentiments or emotions (Secs. 1716, 1932, 2184, 2375, and *passim*). Pareto, for example, quoted one source discussing another person: "A lover of the unusual, eager for anything new, he was prone, as men of such temperaments are, to fomenting heresies and dissensions" (Sec. 2381n.1).

If innovation is seen as a threat to those who identify with settled ways and who rely upon established ties to reinforce those ways, power may be evoked on the side of continuity. Power play (and thereby the resolution of the problem of freedom and control) is thus a function of the resolution of the problem of continuity and change as the latter is governed by temperament, with temperament connoting the residues as manifestations of the sentiments. (Although it is also possible to say that the resolution of the problem of continuity and change is a function of the resolution of the problem of freedom and control as the latter is governed by temperament.) Notice again, then, that the psychological disaffection with the status quo (a position with respect to continuity and change) is equivalent to a challenge to the status quo power structure (a position with respect to freedom and control).

As Pareto wrote at another point, "in a given society of a certain stability the residues that we find operative will for the most part be residues favourable to its preservation; and they also enable us to predict that in such a society affirmative solutions [to the problem of the relations between observance of the norms of religion and morality and the attainment of happiness] (Sec. 1897) will be the ones most widely current and most readily accepted; ..." (Sec. 1931). What is considered "legitimate," after all, is what is "in accord with ... sentiments" (Sec. 2147).

Furthermore, if the status quo is accepted as "natural," or simply accepted as given or taken for granted, one is, by virtue of the operation of social control, induced to feel happy and thus "free" in its context. Accordingly, *control* is defined in terms of *new* limitations and constraints (that is, new and additional to the limitations and constraints existing in the status quo but which are taken for granted, assumed as "necessary" or sacrosanct, or are the object of personal identity relations), and government activity is seen as "intervention." Resolution of the problem of freedom and control thus becomes, with the status quo pattern of freedom and control remaining at stake, a function of interplay of postures on continuity and change (Sec. 1702n.3), which situation also may be seen as the latter being a function of the former.

Continuity and change, then, are themselves specified as a function of the resolution of freedom and control. For example, Pareto makes virtual movements (change) conditional upon the suppression of existing ties (Sec. 2097), that is, a change in the pattern of freedom and control, a relaxation of social control, and a change in the distribution of power. In this case continuity versus change is a function of control, rather than vice versa.

Elsewhere Pareto (as will be seen again in chapter seven) uses the term *religio* to connote "scrupulous attachment to ties" (Sec. 237), meaning "painstaking, conscientious, diligent attention to duties," "a state of mind in which certain ties wield a powerful influence over conscience" (Sec. 236). If by *duties* one means, as did Pareto in his use of the concept *"ties,"* obligations or constraints imposed by the status quo system of social control (which is to say, the status quo power structure), then it is obvious that scrupulous attention to duties or ties means continuity, therefore the maintenance of existing duties or ties, and *ergo* the status quo power structure. Continuity and change and freedom and control are, in the Paretian model, quite integrally interrelated, and both are dominated by the sentiments, particularly, in the situation quoted, by Class II residues.

As Timasheff has written, "Particular emphasis is given to norms and social control. Social control is almost identical with Pareto's conception of restoration of equilibrium, being understood as the process by which if a person's conduct deviates atypically from a norm ... his behavior is brought back to the typical degree of conformity" (Timasheff, 1957, p. 257). (The conservative character of Pareto's equilibrium analysis will be discussed in chapter seven.) Or, as Lopreato has pointed out, there is in the *Treatise* a "dialectics of stability and change, consensus and coercion ..." "What happens in reality is that social cohesion expresses itself in a process of continual conflict coupled with continual, and sometimes abrupt and radical, social transformation" (Lopreato, 1965, pp. 29, 30). There are those processes which "gnaw" at social cohesion, and there are those which strengthen it. Both of these processes, and their interaction, given what cohesion

157

involves in terms of social control and the power structure, govern the resolution of freedom and control as well as that of continuity and change.

Thus, a few sections after his initial use of the concept *religio*, Pareto interprets *freedom* as the opportunity to change. It is a loss of *religio*, a weakening of ties, a strengthening of forces of innovation. Insofar as discipline (continuity, maintenance of ties, maintenance of status quo power structure, reliance on accepted modes of change) is reconciled with freedom (opportunity to innovate, and so forth) the latter is held in check by ties, that is, by the status quo power structure. The "golden mean" exists, according to Pareto, in a balance of "ties of non-logical conduct and ... forces of innovation" (Sec. 242), a proper proportion of Class I and Class II residues within and between classes. It is that "intermediate state," human societies being "essentially heterogeneous," in which "the requirement of uniformity is very strong in some individuals, moderately strong in others, very feeble in still others, and almost entirely absent in a few" (Sec. 2172). When *uniformity* is understood in terms of existing ties, and thus in terms of the status quo power structure or pattern of freedom and control, how obvious is the blending of freedom and control with continuity and change. But, as has been seen above, the subject does allow for each to be specified in terms of the other, and the resolution of both, according to Pareto, is psychological in character.

# Chapter 7.

# The Problem of Continuity and Change

The problem of continuity and change is coordinated to the problem of freedom and control. As was pointed out in chapter six, each may be interpreted in terms of the other. Considering the problem of continuity and change by itself, every decision-making process confronts the problem of choosing between continuity and change (including and perhaps most especially, between continuity and change of the power structure in part or in whole, or to a smaller or larger extent). The choice is not a simple one. Control over change is not total, as change is generally incremental; an option for continuity may result in change, and *vice versa*. *Inter alia*, continuity may require change from what otherwise might have occurred. Change and continuity, in sum, are not simple concepts. They are multifaceted, complex, and subtle. Yet both are *desiderata*, and the most controversial and arduous social task is agreement upon and achievement of change. No one is totally in favor of continuity and no one wants everything changed.

The process of social choice is largely at the many margins at which change may take place under human instigation, deliberate and non-deliberate, private and public, political and technological, and so on. For several centuries both science and rationalism have been at the service of the deliberate control and direction of social change. Conservatives have been much dismayed by this fact, although business and industry — the Schumpeterian innovator — have been the main engine of reformation. "Interventionism" as a slogan and as a description has thus come to mean, in effect, deliberate (generally legal) change. The quest for power is very much the struggle to control the choice of change, including using the state as either or both a means of change and a formal ratifier and legitimizer of change wrought through other (at least nominally private) means. Policy as choice is, with the *given* character of the status quo, choice of change. The arduous task is the selection and balancing, as it is usually expressed, of continuity and change. The basic or elemental policy questions are, primarily, what change, who chooses, and by what process?

## 1. Continuity and Change in Society

Given the enormous scope of Pareto's undertaking in the *Treatise*, it is not surprising that it not only evidences a theory of freedom and control but also a theory of continuity and change. More specifically, there is in the *Treatise* what amounts or reduces to a theory of how the resolution of the conflict of continuity and change is worked out in society. Although this theory of change is essentially quite clear and, furthermore, is rather general or functional in character, it is influenced (one is tempted simply to say distorted) by Pareto's own perspective on change. The general theory of continuity and change in Pareto's general model will be sketched in this section. The following section will trace several ways in which Pareto's own perspective became incorporated into his otherwise generally objective or functional model.

In general, the *Treatise* reflects Pareto's actual or implicit awareness of the necessity of choosing between or balancing continuity and change (Secs. 2171, 2419, 2553, and *passim*). He rejected the notion that "stability is always beneficial or that change is always beneficial" (Sec. 2195); neither is necessarily or intrinsically beneficial[1] (Secs. 2340, 2420, 2514, and *passim*). He pointed to the limited nature of the actual change possible in society at any time (Sec. 2096n.1). He also noted the limitedness of the utopian or expansive definition of freedom used in his day and of the nineteenth century (also utopian) view of progress. Nevertheless, he recognized that the social system changes. However inadequate from the viewpoint of contemporary social theory, Pareto's model includes both a theory of why the possibilities of change are limited (primarily because of the slowness with which the residues in society change) (Secs. 2417ff) and a theory of the forces which produce change. Thus he repeatedly stressed the epistemologically and socially contingent character of principles of law and morality as a result of social change. Law and morality are not given but are contingent (Secs. 241, 469); change, therefore, including revolution, cannot be conclusively if at all properly judged in their terms (Secs. 2147n.8, 2163, 2177, 2569 - 2572; *cf.* Tufts, 1935). There is conflict, then, between the preachers of "progress" and the "wisdom of the forefathers," (Sec. 933), including conflict between the rule of "living law" and the rule of the law of the past (Sec. 466). This is the stuff of which continuity and change is made (Moore, 1935 - 1936, p. 297).

Although there is some degree — perhaps a good deal — of determinism in the *Treatise* (both metaphysical determinism and, primarily, scientific determinateness), Pareto's model is essentially open ended. Policy is a matter of interplay between forces representing or embodying (although not always, if ever, simply) continuity versus change, involving in part a "choice ... between persistent aggregates and combinations."[2] Moreover, "The maximization of utility is contingent, Pareto's analysis suggests, upon the striking of a proper balance between the forces favorable to stability and those favorable to social circulations and change. In the absence of such balance, disadvantage outweighs advantage" (Spengler, 1944, pp. 121 - 122). But the working out of that balance and the judgment as to what is "proper" is open ended. The resolution of continuity versus change is accomplished primarily non-deliberatively. The scope of logico-experimental decision-making is limited in both theory and practice. Most of the result of human action comes through non-logical conduct and not through rational choice, but the resolution and the judgment come about from and are part of the interplay of forces in society.

Whether, then, one writes of social equilibrium, utility maximization, resolution of continuity and change, or policy, all of which certainly overlap and are largely synonymous in terms of the substantive material involved, the end result is the same. It is the outcome of the interplay that Pareto envisioned between the primary elements of his social system: interests, residues, derivations, social heterogeneity, and class circulation (Secs. 2279ff). There is no simple theory of or formula for social change in the *Treatise*: the sacrifice of continuity to change and of change to continuity comes about through the reciprocal interaction of all of the variables in Pareto's multivariable general social-equilibrium model. Each of the elements or variables represents forces working for change and for continuity. The resolution of continuity and change emerges from the conflict between or among the following: deliberative and non-deliberative forces; logico-experimental and non-logico-experimental knowledge; logical and non-logical conduct; reformist schemes of various varieties; residues; residues and interests as well as between residues, interests and class circulation; derivations; and so on. Not the least of these is the conflict between interests. Change may involve alteration in substance, form, or both, although Pareto insisted that change was primarily, but not exclusively, in form; substance generally remained unchanged or was altered only marginally (Sec. 1008; cf. 172, 230, 232, 244, 875, 1009, 1695, 1702, 1712, and passim).

Expressed another way, the resolution of continuity and change is a function of the interplay of psychology, knowledge, and power in society. On the basis of what has been developed previously, that proposition hardly requires amplification. But given Pareto's deliberate and intentional emphasis upon psychology (which will be taken up in a moment), attention should be directed again to the theme which Pareto essentially took for granted. Society is a system of power, and the resolution of continuity versus change is a function of power play. The evidence already has been developed, largely in chapters four, five and six. Manipulation of continuity versus change is an object of power play in the Paretian model (Secs. 1805 - 1811, and passim).

The balancing of continuity and change results from the resolution of conflict between power players (Sec. 1116; cf. Lopreato and Ness, 1966, p. 30), including conflict between monarch and people, elite and subject class, and the interests of present and future generations (Amoroso, 1938, p. 14). Particularly, Pareto believed the balance came from the conflict between existing and would-be elites, between "new elites" and "old entrenched elites," out of "the fundamental struggle ... for power to be exercised by an elite" (Seligman, 1962, p. 390). The struggle becomes one "between individualists and interventionists" (Clerc, 1942, p. 591), the former being those in power under the status quo regime and the latter being those who would change or displace the old elite. Change, then, is a function of the rise of new elite claimants seeking entry into the ruling class (Sec. 2193n.1).

As Spengler has phrased it, "Mutability and selection originated in the desire and capacity of some men for advancement in the social hierarchy; they flourished when circumstances were favorable, as, for example, when prices were rising. Stability originated

162

in both the institutions of private property and inheritance and the desire of the well-situated groups and aristocracies to perpetuate existing social arrangements of especial advantage to themselves" (Spengler, 1944, p. 121). The conflict of continuity and change is thus fought out in a general context of power play and social conflict, including the universal conflict between those with a speculator and those with a *rentier* mentality (Secs. 2233ff and *passim*; Amoroso, 1938, pp. 6, 14; Ginsberg, 1936, p. 241).

Consideration of the conflict between speculators and *rentiers* brings the discussion once again to the main deliberate thrust of the *Treatise*. According to Pareto, the resolution of continuity versus change, of social equilibrium, is emphatically a function of *psychology*. "One of the principal factors determining the social equilibrium was the relative proportions of Class I and Class II residues in individuals."[3] For example, in the concluding chapter of the *Treatise*, "The Social Equilibrium in History," Pareto considered, *inter alia*, comparisons of relative proportions "(1) between populations of different countries, or populations of a given country in different periods of history; or (2) between social classes, and more particularly between the governing class and the class that is governed; or finally (3) as bearing on class-circulation within a population" (Sec. 2413). Continuity and change as a function of the distribution of residues means that positions on continuity and change with respect to particular social policies derive from the relevance of Class I versus Class II residues.[4] In particular, they derive from innovative as opposed to inertial sentiments,[5] as well as from residues of uniformity (Class IVb) (Secs. 1115ff), including neophobia (Class IVb3) (Secs. 1130 - 1132), and of resistance to alterations in social equilibrium (Class Va) (Secs. 1207 - 1219). But basically these are Class I versus Class II residues, since it will be recalled that Pareto placed the remaining residues with Class II residues for purpose of simplification.

Emphasis upon the psychic basis of the resolution of the problem of continuity and change, especially but by no means entirely as applicable to the redivision of power (the circulation of the elite, in Pareto's term), is the distinctive relevant message of the *Treatise*. Pareto distinguished, as has been seen, "individuals who aimed at undermining group-persistences, at substituting logical for non-logical conduct, at deifying Reason, from individuals who defended group-persistences, stood by tradition, were therefore favorable to non-logical conduct and burned no incense to the goddess Reason" (Sec. 2346; *cf.* 2390, 2139, 2420). Just as important, in stressing that irrational or non-logical conduct was "one of the primary determinants of social change" (Millikan, 1936, p. 326), Pareto minimized the possibility, indeed the desirability, of so-called rational change. Since change is, *pro tanto*, primarily dependent upon the residues, and since the likelihood of major change in the pattern of residues in society was small, then no major deliberate change was possible (Brinton, 1954, pp. 641, 646, 648, 649; Timasheff, 1940, p. 144; and Ginsberg, 1936, p. 245).

This conclusion revolves upon both the meaning of *major* and the actual possibilities allowed by Pareto's theory of the dynamics of psychic states. Therein lies part of the story of Pareto the social scientist and Pareto the conservative citizen. It is one thing to point out objectively and descriptively the limited possibilities of rational change (of substance as distinct from form, to again use Pareto's terms), as economics has pointed to scarcity, even with a "chilling skepticism" (Grampp, 1965, p. 135). It is quite another thing to erect that conclusion to the status of a normative principle of policy so as to further politically limit the possibilities of reform. The conclusion as social science and as social policy are both to be found in the *Treatise*.

But social change consequent to variations in the relative intensity of the residues does take place. The residues in a population change slowly, but they do change. These variations, Pareto found, do not correlate with the forms of government (democratic, aristocratic) (Sec. 2350), nor with the state or level of wealth (Sec. 2351). They do correlate with rapid increases in wealth (Secs. 2351, 2357; Ginsberg, 1936, p. 242), involving "a very rapid increase in economic prosperity and a decline in the residues of group-persistence in the masses at large, but to a still greater extent in the upper classes" (Sec. 2354). Material progress, itself abetted by Class I residues, promotes those very residues. (Yet, as will be seen in a few moments, "Then comes a reaction ... The action and reaction appear therefore in conjunction, and it is their sum as a whole that is to be viewed as correlated with variations in wealth and in class-circulation" (Sec. 2354)).

In addition, as developed extensively earlier in this study, the derivations function as intermediaries in the promotion of continuity and change. In the process of justifying and legitimating positions, derivations support and strengthen particular residues, they thereby engage or disengage psychic support for change and

164

hence change itself (Secs. 1414, 1415, 1536, 2553). The dynamics of psychic states under conditions of power play (chapter five, *supra*) are at the heart of Pareto's theory of continuity and change. Manipulation of the particular residues by circumstance and by power players using derivations is the manipulation, *pro tanto*, of continuity and change. The residues are both constrained and constraining in the processes of social change.

Just as Marx believed the class struggle was a major sociological result of dialetical materialism, so Pareto believed the dynamics of history result in the redistribution of power in society, or, as he expressed it, in the circulation of the elite (Cp. Lopreato, 1965, pp. 30 - 31, with Seligman, 1962, p. 393). Once again Pareto's analysis is in terms of the residues. Given that there should be a "proper proportion" in society between Class I and Class II residues, it is also desirable, he concluded, "that combination-instincts should predominate in leaders and the instincts of group-persistence in subordinates" (Sec. 2427; *cf.* Bongiorno, 1930, pp. 367 - 368). Leaders are such by virtue of their combination-instincts. As for the masses, Pareto approvingly quoted Bayle: "All the masses ask is to be led along the beaten paths; and even if they wanted more than that, they would not be capable of mastering the subject. Their daily occupations [note again, incidentally, the circumstantial — here, occupational — basis of mentality] have not permitted them to acquire sufficient competence for that" (Sec. 1415n.2; *cf.* Larrabee, 1935, p. 513). Elsewhere Pareto wrote that "The masses at large pay little attention to the sources of their rules. They are satisfied so long as society has rules that are accepted and obeyed" (Sec. 1930). However, Pareto argued extensively in the later chapters of the *Treatise*, that, "in the higher stratum of society Class II residues gradually lose in strength, until now and again they are reinforced by tides upwelling from the lower stratum" (Sec. 2048). Pressure for circulation thus is engendered by the existence of elite-claimants in the subject class and by degenerate elements in the ruling class. As Borkenau (1936, p 109) points out, Pareto did "not stress general aptitudes, but special abilities coincident with the special demands of a given society" (at a given time). Included among the emerging failures of the increasingly combinations-rich ruling class are an increasing humanitarianism and a decreasing willingness to use force in order to protect its hegemony (Secs. 2471, 2474, 2521, 2588 - 2589). A decline in Class II residues signifies weakening of the foundation of society (Secs. 2471, 2474, 2521). Class I residues need to pre-

165

dominate in the ruling class, but they need to be tempered — and the power of the ruling class strengthened — by Class II residues. But the tendency, especially, in a prospering society, is for combination residues to strengthen and, moreover, for only people rich in Class I residues to rise (Sec. 2484). This further increases the disproportionality between Class I and Class II residues in the ruling class.[6] Less typical is the case in which an excess of Class II residues in the governing elite may occasion the rise of people with Class I residues (Faris, 1936, p. 667; Amoroso, 1938, p. 11).

"Aristocracies," therefore, "do not last. Whatever the causes, it is an incontestable fact that after a certain length of time they pass away. History is a graveyard of aristocracies" (Sec. 2053). The governing elite decays "not in numbers only. They decay also in quality, in the sense that they lose their vigour, that there is a decline in the proportions of the residues which enabled them to win their power and hold it. The governing class is restored not only in numbers, but — and that is the more important thing — in quality, by families rising from the lower classes and bringing with them the vigour and the proportions of residues necessary for keeping themselves in power. It is also restored by the loss of its more degenerate members" (Sec. 2054).

Circulation restores the vigour of the ruling class by replenishing the diminished stock of Class II residues (Bittermann, 1936, p. 306). "In virtue of class-circulation, the governing *elite* is always in a state of slow and continuous transformation" (Sec. 2056). Stability itself thus requires an optimum degree of change or of circulation (Schumpeter, 1951, p. 140). If the processes of revitalization of the ruling class come to an end, "the governing class crashes to ruin and often sweeps the whole of a nation along with it" (Sec. 2055). When superior elements accumulate in the masses and inferior elements accumulate in the ruling class (Sec. 2055), and when circulation fails as both restorer of the ruling class and as safety-valve for the masses, then conditions are propitious for revolution.

The situation is further aggravated — from the point of view of the ruling elite and, as far as Pareto is concerned, from the point of view of social utility — by the reluctance of the governing class to resort to force. "Notable," wrote Pareto, "is the fact that if a ruling class is unable or unwilling or incompetent to use force to eradicate violations of uniformities in private life, anarchic action on the part of the subject class tends to make up for the deficiency." Here Pareto refers to private vendettas and lynchings. "Whenever the influence of public authority declines, little states grow up within the state, little societies within society. So, whenever judicial process fails, private or group justice replaces it, and *vice versa*" (Sec. 2180).

As with private life, so also with public life and social classes in general:

"Legal violence is the consequence of the norms established in a society and in general resort to it is more beneficial or at least less harmful than resort to private violence, which is designed as a rule to overthrow prevailing norms" (Sec. 2189).

"... the use of force is indispensable to society; and when the higher classes are averse to the use of force, which ordinarily happens because the majority in those classes come to rely wholly on their skill at chicanery, and the minority shrink from energetic acts now through stupidity, now through cowardice, it becomes necessary, if society is to subsist and prosper. that the governing class be replaced by another which is willing and able to use force" (Sec. 1858).

About the French Revolution, which Pareto considered a conservative phenomenon insofar as it represented or issued from the group-persistences and antispeculator mentality of the masses, Pareto wrote:

"If the class governing in France had had the faith that counsels use of force and the will to use force, it would never have been overthrown and, procuring its own advantage, would have procured the advantage of France. Since it failed in that function, it was salutary that its rule should give way to rule by others; and since, again, it was the resort to force that was wanting, it was in keeping with very general uniformities that there should be a swing to another extreme where force was used even more than was required. ... It was a good thing that power should pass into the hands of people who showed that they had the faith and the resolve requisite for the use of force" (Sec. 2191).

[In general, revolutions] "come about through accumulations in the higher strata of society — either because of a slowing-down in class-circulation, or from other causes — of decadent elements no longer possessing the residues suitable for keeping them in power, and shrinking from the use of force; while meantime in the lower strata of society elements of superior quality are coming to the fore, possessing residues suitable for exercising the functions of government and willing enough to use force"[7] (Sec. 2057).

Pareto's theory of the resolution of the problem of continuity and change thus tends to center on the changing distribution of residues and of power in society. The dynamics of the power structure are integrally connected, as both independent and dependent variable (as seen in chapter five), with the dynamics of social psychology. Circulation of the elite is as much a psychological as it is a political phenomenon; circulation of elite elements, and not the turning of the table by the subject class (although elite-claimants from the masses will use derivations appealing to the interests and sentiments of the masses), is very much the social mechanism through which continuity versus change is resolved in society as Pareto saw it.

Pareto also discerned cycles in the predominantly psychologically conditioned substantive path of social equilibrium or policy. According to Pareto, human society manifests cycles of interdependence (Secs. 2203ff), including pendulum effects. Included in his view are cycles of prescriptiveness and permissiveness (patrism and matrism of sorts) or of faith and skepticism. Expressed differently, these cycles reflect a sequence of alternating domination by Class II and Class I residues, respectively. The process of the circulation of the elite is closely but not exactly intertwined with those cycles; in Pareto's view, the various movements generally tend to correspond or correlate (Secs. 2279 - 2396, 2546ff). But any movements traced by Pareto in terms of speculator - *rentier*, Class I and Class II residues, circulation, and the like, are all facets of the same moving path of social equilibrium.

Parsons (1933, p. 577) has written that "Pareto's most important contribution to the concrete interpretation of social phenomena lies in his cyclical theory of social change." Lopreato (1965, p. 30), although he maintains that "Pareto has no real theory of social change," does point out that his "observations about cycles of change" relate to "cycles of change along the axis of the authority structure" of society.

Pareto wrote that "History shows that when the proportions between Class I and Class II residues in the *elite* begin to vary, the movement does not continue indefinitely in one direction, but is

168

sooner or later replaced by a movement in a counter-direction" (Sec. 2221). The path of social equilibrium is rhythmical and undulating (Secs. 1694, 1715, 1718, 1800, 1806, 2329ff, 2550), with waves of incremental (especially in the residues) (Secs. 1143ff) intensification (Sec. 2048). There is a "form of mutual correlation between an undulatory movement in residues and an undulatory movement in derivations, and between both those movements and other social phenomena, among which, very especially, the economic" (Sec. 2329). There are plural waves, and there is "interdependence of waves" (Sec. 2339).

The final two chapters of the *Treatise*, numbering four hundred and seventy-nine pages, are replete with analysis of the interrelations of residues and derivations, the use of force in society, the relation of residues and derivations to social utility, government and its forms, proportions of residues, and activities of speculators and *rentiers*. Also present are discussions of cycles of interdependence, economic periodicity, class circulation, fluctuations in and interdependence between derivations and social facts, and so on, including the documentary descriptions which make up the great bulk of the work.[8]

One example of Pareto's analysis relates to the manner in which tariff protection stimulates the speculator mentality (already noted as exemplifying the circumstantial character of the residues): "After interests have, thanks to protection, brought into the governing class individuals richly endowed with Class I residues, those individuals in their turn influence interests and stimulate the whole country in the direction of economic pursuits and industrialism" (Sec. 2215). Interdependence thus engenders pendulum effects of cumulation.

The impact, moreover, on social utility may not be judged *a priori*. "... the theories of mathematical economics supplied," Pareto pointed out, "a proof that, in general, the direct effect of protection is a destruction of wealth. If one were free to go on and add an axiom, which is implicitly taken for granted by many economists, that any destruction of wealth is an 'evil,' one could logically conclude that protection is an 'evil.' But before such a proposition can be granted," he argued "the indirect economic effects and the social effects of protection have to be known" (Sec. 2208). Thus, "The increase in economic production may be great enough to exceed the destruction of wealth caused by protection; so that, sum total, protection may yield a profit and not a loss in wealth; it may therefore prove (though not necessarily so) that the economic prosperity of a country has been enhanced by industrial protection" (Sec. 2217). But when the intensification of Class I residues in the elite, and the accompanying prosperity (as a general rule), has gone on long enough, "sooner or later [it is] replaced by a movement in a counter-direction" (Sec. 2221). As already indicated, the pendulum effect arising out of interdependence is basically described by Pareto in terms of relative strengthening or weakening of Class I or Class II residues (Secs. 2221ff, 2311; Ginsberg, 1936, p. 247; Parsons, 1933, p. 577).

The multifaceted cycles of interdependence are described by Pareto in another way — but always ultimately in terms of undulations of Class I and Class II residues — that is, in terms of waves of permissiveness and prescriptiveness, or of skepticism and faith. Pareto distinguished between the different attitudes toward conventional or fundamental morality corresponding to Class I and Class II residues. On the one hand are intelligence, cunning, rationality, the absence of religious sentiments, and looseness toward traditional morality; on the other are devoutness, force, and excessive moral strictness and fervor (Secs. 2514, 2538). The cycles may be expressed in terms of alternating phases of (logico-experimental) reason and (non-logico-experimental) superstition (Ginsberg, 1936, p. 242). "Hence those perpetually recurrent swings of the pendulum, which have been observable for so many centuries, between skepticism and faith, materialism and idealism, logico-experimental science and metaphysics" (Sec. 1680). Although he calls the description superficial, inasmuch as it does not specify the underlying transformations in the proportions of Class I and Class II residues, which is how Pareto saw the matter, "one may say that in history a period of faith will be followed by a period of skepticism, which will in turn be followed by another period of faith, this by another period of skepticism, and so on."[9] The derivations of individualism and collectivism, of nominalism and realism, and of freedom and planning (Secs. 2553, 2612), all have an undulatory character "very like the case" of "alternations of 'faith' and 'reason'" (Sec. 2553).

In the *Treatise* Pareto paid attention not only to the grounds, processes, and paths which the moving social equilibrium takes, as seen above, which constitutes his general model of continuity and change, but also to the ways in which continuity and change, respectively, were institutionalized in society. These forces already have been discussed, and only need be given summary attention at this point.

170

Continuity is institutionalized in the sense of duty and in custom, language, religion, and morals. *Religio* functions through the sense of duty which, although non-logico-experimental and metaphysical (Secs. 523, 1400), serves to promote continuity. *Religio* illustrates the distinction between logico-experimental truth and social utility (Secs. 236 - 243). So also do custom and language, which are functions of Class II residues, function to promote continuity (Timasheff, 1940, p. 141; Secs. 256, 400, 1071). Religion and morals, necessary for the survival of society, operate upon Class II residues to promote continuity. To promote stability, order, and the status quo, it is thus instrumental to promote religion (Secs. 1744, 1854 - 1855, 1932, 2534 - 2535; Henderson, 1937, p. 55).

Legitimation is relatively harder for those in favor of change (Secs. 2570, and *passim*). Although they have many derivations and Class I residues at their disposal (Sec. 2147), the status quo is commanding by its very nature. Indeed,

"On the side of those who wish to maintain the present system and are reaping benefits from it, fewer derivations are used, because people who are in the saddle do not need derivations to spur their retainers to action, and resort to them only when it seems advisable to justify their conduct, or in order to weaken opposition on the part of people who bite at such bait. In this case, as usual, their derivations aim at showing that the maintenance of law and order, which is aptly identified with the arbitrary will of the rulers, is a "highest good" for which everything else must be sacrificed. Or else the resort is to the principle that the end justifies the means — and for a person in the saddle what better end can there be than staying there and enjoying the fruits of such eminence?" (Sec. 2147).

The institutionalization of continuity and change, always psychological in character, is related to the institutionalization of authority and thus to the problem of freedom and control. In this connection, it may be noted that Pareto differentiated between Germanic and Latin temperaments. "It is clear enough," he wrote, "that the Latin condition is favourable to groups that are disposed to resist the law or the authority of the government: all they seem to need in order to enforce their will is the courage to get out into the streets and fight. The Germanic condition is favourable to

171

orderliness and respect for law, and also to arbitrary conduct and even crimes on the part of individuals in power" (Sec. 2147).

Some institutions or loci of power (including speculators, *rentiers*, and power players in general) have an interest in continuity or change and, accordingly, work to promote the one or the other as appears prudent. The institutionalization of continuity and of change comes about in other ways through the derivations embodied in the respective theologies of continuity and change. Always, of course, grounded or to be grounded in the sentiments, there are the ideologies, philosophies, and theologies glorifying immobility, the wisdom of the past, and so on, and those glorifying movement, "progress, in one direction or another" (Sec. 2173), and so on (Secs. 933, 1211, 1793 - 1794, 1937, 2175; Moore, 1935 - 1936, p. 297).

Perhaps most fundamental is the institutionalization, if it may be called that, of continuity through the strong tendency for individuals to define their self-identity in terms of some aspect or facet of the status quo. Crucial here, as already has been seen, are the Class V residues, which have to do with the integrity of the individual and his appurtenances and possessions. As Becker and Barnes (1961, p. 1018) have said. "It is these residues " — "closely linked with our everyday words 'just' and 'injust'" — "rather than rational thought, which lead us so strongly to resent every disturbance threatening to ourselves as individuals or to the society of which we are a part." On the other hand, personal identity may be defined, for example, under the influence of Class I residues, in a manner signifying or portending or building in change in society. As noted, alienation from the status quo may be interpreted either as a particular development of personality or as a failure of the socialization (societization) process. In every case, the resolution of continuity versus change may be seen as a product of the internalization process, which is to say that continuity versus change is a function of the interaction of psychic states.


## 2. Continuity and Change: Pareto's Perspective

It is hardly necessary to demonstrate that Pareto was a conservative. It is well known and to some extent obvious from the foregoing that he was an elitist-aristocratic conservative, an aristocratic libertarian, whose personal socio-political predilections supported the concentration of power on the side of established interests. All this and more, of course, is claimed by those who interpret Pareto as a philosopher of fascism. More specifically in terms of the present analysis, Pareto was conservative, first, in respect to freedom and control, upholding a relatively narrow concentration of power; and second, in respect to continuity and change, favoring continuity of established property interests. Pareto himself was characterized, in his own terms, by a blend of logico-experimental capabilities and a strong dosage of Class II and Class V residues. Pareto the scientist thus could recognize and could place in his system the functional contribution to social equilibrium and social utility of innovators, whether businessmen or social reformers, and of socialism. Furthermore, as a good intellectual he preached freedom of thought. Nevertheless, Pareto the private citizen and emotional creature had his own sentiments, and these were strongly of the Class II and Class V variety.

The present author would attempt to show at this point some of the ways in which Pareto's personal conservatism influenced or, more exactly, was embodied in his analysis of social equilibrium. Some of his conservatism related quite obviously to the problem of freedom and control. Examples are his theory of the power structure, elitism, and the use of force, although from an economic viewpoint his analysis can be limited to that of an elitist-dominated "free" market in the libertarian, antistatist, antisocialist, antiegalitarian tradition. It is, rather, in respect to the problem of continuity and change that the conservative elements in his model are relatively unobtrusive but important.

The thrust of Pareto's logico-experimentalism, insofar as he practices it in the *Treatise*, is essentially or approximates an objective, descriptive functionalism. Given that Pareto was a mere mortal with his own predilections, he succeeded quite well, and certainly was no less successful than Comte or Spencer. Notwithstanding his support for the necessity of continuity at the margin, his transformation of the limitedness of change into a normative principle of policy, and his support of the use of force to maintain the status quo (Secs. 2176, 2180, 2189, 2196), Pareto was often, if not typically, quite balanced in his functionalist treatment of continuity and change (Secs. 242, 2139, 2175). In fact, Pareto's own formula, if it may be called that, for the resolution of continuity and change tends to reduce to the combination of conservatism with respect to form and progressivism with respect to substance (Secs. 230, 232, 241, 244; *cf.* 172).

Moreover, as has been seen, Pareto is generally quite functionalist and reasonably objective in his analysis of the use of force and of the claims and conditions of success of both status quo power holders and new elite-claimants. Indeed, he is at times ruthless in his impartiality, although that may serve to cover (intentionally or otherwise) the sarcasm directed at governing elites too inept to maintain their hegemony.

Finally, in his discussion of utility *of* a community, that is, what has come to be called Pareto optimum, he was also quite objective and balanced. He pointed out the existence of many optimal positions, the relevance of the institutional framework, and the necessity to choose when policy questions involve going beyond Pareto optimum. That is, he acknowledged the necessity to "resort to other considerations foreign to economics — to decide on grounds of ethics, social utility, or something else, which individuals it is advisable to benefit, which to sacrifice" (Sec. 2129; *cf.* Samuels, 1972b). But in other respects Pareto's conservatism was embodied in his analysis. Some of these now will be sketched.

First, the impact of Pareto's Aristotelianism now may be fully appreciated. As was indicated (actually asserted) in the first section of chapter two, *supra*, Pareto's theory of knowledge in relation to social policy posits that knowledge is knowledge of what *is* and therefore of what has status because it *is*. This view emphasizes not any ideal potentially derivable from existent reality; rather it stresses the reality itself. Quite contrary to a Platonic philosophy of reform or of potential reformation, it casts luster on the status quo. Pareto's view of science (what he called logico-experimental knowledge and reasoning) thus builds in an emphasis upon what *is*, or, to reiterate Muller's phrasing, on *being* as opposed to *becoming*. Pareto's science, in explaining what exists, incorporates a presumption in favor of the status quo (Tarascio, 1968, pp. 50 - 55).

Perhaps the clearest expression of Pareto's continuity-oriented logico-experimentalism is contained in the following statement:

"We can also say that the fact of the existence of society results from the facts observable within it, that, in other words, these latter facts determine the social equilibrium; and, further again, that *if the fact of the existence of a society is given, the facts arising within it are no longer altogether arbitrary but must satisfy a certain condition, namely, that the equilibrium being*

174

*given, the facts which determine it cannot be altogether arbitrary"* (Sec. 2089, emphasis added).

The last clause represents as clear an expression as can be found of the Aristotelian view with respect to the position of the status quo (the relation of knowledge to social policy). Little wonder that Pareto derided the efforts of reformers who, in formulating ideals and potential social reforms, are only, according to him, trying "to establish relations ... between their pockets and their neighbour's money" (Sec. 479). The existing distribution of property is taken as given; it is an *is* and as such not only is the proper object of science, but also is possessed of normative status because it *is*. So also with reform in general. Whereas the *is* is given and thus has presumptive status, what might be or what ought to be is a function of sentiments: "Social reformers as a rule also fail to notice, or at least they disregard, the fact that individuals entertain different opinions with regard to utility, and that they do so because they get the data they require from their own sentiments. They say, and believe, that they are solving an objective problem: 'What is the *best* form for a society?' Actually they are solving a subjective problem: 'What form of society best fits my sentiments?' " [10]

Pareto prefers "theories that allow themselves to be guided strictly by the facts," to wit, the status quo, to "theories that try to influence the facts ..." (Sec. 521), to wit, to change the status quo. Thus, also, Pareto finds that Class II residues, or rather explanations based upon Class II residues, come "closest to experimental reality ..." (Sec. 2330; *cf.* 2162). In his most elaborate statement on this latter point, however, his position is well-balanced:

"... there are many cases in which conclusions drawn from residues of group-persistence (or, in other words, obtained by 'intuition') come much closer to realities than conclusions that are drawn from the combination-instinct and go to make up the derivations of that pseudo-science which, in social matters, continues to be mistaken for experimental science. And — again in many cases — these latter derivations seem so harmful that the society which is not eager to decline or perish must necessarily reject them. But not less deleterious are the consequences of an exclusive predominance of Class II residues, not only in physical arts and sciences, where their harmfulness is obvious, but in social matters as well, where it is perfectly apparent that but for the combination-instinct and the use of experimental thinking there could be no progress" (Sec. 2340; *cf.* 2262).

This formal statement is more balanced, as has been seen, than is Pareto's own practice. Just as the concept of Pareto optimum may be interpreted conservatively when coupled wiith an Aristotelian view of the status quo, so combinations, and therefore change, may have their functional role in his model. Yet Pareto's science at the margin supports group-persistences and therefore continuity by taking the status quo for granted and giving it preferential status. Still another example is the double connotation given the term *uniformity*. Pareto the scientist meant essentially the widely found, objective tendencies in society; Pareto the conservative, preoccupied with maintaining the status quo, attributed a value-status to uniformity. The uniformities of social science are not merely statements of tendencies; they are, in particular, statements of tendencies descriptive of the status quo, and they thus take on meaning not only as scientific statements but as propositions of received norms. (This is true even though Pareto, when he formally considers the subject, treats norms as relative to time and place.)

Thus, in a statement already quoted above in a different connection, after pointing out that "force is used by those who wish to preserve certain uniformities and by those who wish to overstep them," Pareto identified the use of derivations to weaken opponents of the status quo: "... if a partisan of a governing class disavows the use of force, he means that he disavows the use of force by insurgents trying to escape from the norms of the given uniformity" (Sec. 2174; *cf.* 2170 - 2202, e.g., 2175, 2189, 2196, and *passim*). Note that the concept *uniformity* is not just a tendency; it is a tendency of the status quo which has normative status. The uniformities describe what exists, and, in the conservative mind, they thus have honorific and presumptive status. Pareto undoubtedly tried very hard to establish a logico-experimental sociology, or science of society, but the *is* nature of science took on a luster that is normative and distinctively conservative in character because of Pareto's predilection for continuity or stability. This fact may be further evidenced in his use of the concept *equilibrium* and in the related comparison of real and virtual movements.

Pareto the scientist was quite capable of a technical and non-normative definition of *equilibrium*. For example, in an article on

176

mathematical economics, he wrote: "The position of the individuals concerned will be called an *equilibrium position* if it is such that, according to the given law, the individuals can remain there indefinitely ... A position of economic equilibrium is one in which the individual remains at rest" (Pareto, in Gherity, 1965, p. 376). Moreover, Pareto elsewhere wrote that "When one talks of a disturbed equilibrium which is becoming stable again, one does not, by any means, imply a return to precisely the same conditions as before; ... Economic and social equilibrium is not static but dynamic, and ... one cannot reconstruct a condition of equilibrium as it existed in the past; to restore an equilibrium that has been disturbed means to approach a new condition of equilibrium" (Pareto, quoted in Por, 1923, pp. 23 - 24).

In the *Treatise* Pareto endeavored to construct an equilibrium model; but his notion of equilibrium became conservative (Wollheim, 1954, p. 575). As Perry (1935) has shown, this result stems from the use of two connotations of equilibrium. Also involved is the use of *artificial* in a particular way and the related juxtaposition of real and virtual movements. Timasheff has nicely summarized Pareto's general point of view: "For Pareto, society is a system in equilibrium. This means that there exists, within every society, forces which maintain the form (or configuration) which the society has achieved or which guarantee even and uninterrupted change; in the latter case the equilibrium is dynamic" (Timasheff, 1957, p. 160; *cf.* Secs. 2067ff 2093ff.

Now equilibrium or a state of equilibrium may be understood to mean a condition from which there is no tendency to move. This connotation is seen in the quotations from Pareto cited above. Equilibrium is in this case a state, a condition, or a situation in which matter or society conceptually may exist, and it is quite distinct from the form of the substance in equilibrium. For example, both the market and the plan economy may be in conceptual equilibrium with respect to the allocation of resources, the same equilibrium price may correspond to different levels of equilibrium quantity, and the level of income (GNP) may be in equilibrium at full employment or at less than full employment. In each of these cases equilibrium has to do with a condition and not with the substance involved; in neither of these cases do equilibrium conditions connote anything necessarily normative. In the *Treatise* Pareto gave the following definitional statements:

"If an existing state of social equilibrium is altered, forces tending to re-establish it come into play — that, no more, no less, is what equilibrium means"[11] (Sec. 1210).

"The real state, be it static or dynamic, of the system is determined by its conditions. Let us imagine that some modification in its form is induced artificially (virtual movements). At once a reaction will take place, *tending to restore the changing form to its original state as modified by normal change*" (Sec. 2067, emphasis added).

"We can then say that the state X [equilibrium] is such a state that if it is artificially subjected to some modification different from the modification it undergoes normally, a reaction at once takes place tending to restore it to its real, its normal, state. That gives us an exact definition of the state X" (Sec. 2068).

"If we start in the first place with the definition just given of the state $X_1$ [a particular equilibrium state], we can see that the action of each element having been completed, society cannot of itself assume any form other than the form $X_1$, and that if it were made artificially to vary from that form, it should tend to resume it; for otherwise, its form would not be entirely determined, as was assumed, by the elements considered" (Sec. 2070; *cf.* Russett, 1966, chapter five).

Note, first, the blend of metaphysical determinism and scientifically determinate solutions, which amounts to a deterministic positivism. Deliberate social change is excluded from consideration. Note, second, the blend of equilibrium as a technical result when the forces operating are so constituted or balanced that there is no tendency for change and equilibrium as "the state to which" the system "returns after it has been influenced for a short time by an external or artificial force,"[12] that is, the restoration of form. Notice, also, the change of meaning of *internal*: in Pareto's general model, the term refers to the elements of social equilibrium internal to a society; here it refers to elements other than deliberate social change, which becomes "artificial," non-real, non-normal, *ergo* external. In the case of the first connotation, equilibrium is simply a condition of rest; in the case of the second, equilibrium involves restoration of the status quo prior to the alteration considered external.

Pareto blended a technical usage with a normative one, and the normative one is conservative. The second connotation identified above gives normative status to the substantive form of society to which, after disequilibrium, restoration is directed. Equilibrium thus is used throughout the *Treatise* to build into Pareto's general model a force by which the status quo more or less conclusively and necessarily asserts or reasserts (and restores) itself and through which it is given presumptive status. Just as Pareto's science casts luster on what *is*, his notion of equilibrium, with its tendency to restore what *is*, builds into his model a bias in favor of continuity.

Further and dramatic evidence lies in Pareto's use of the concept *artificial*. At one point in the *Treatise*, Pareto the social scientist pointed to the normative character of *artificial*. He argued that, along with *nature*, *natural*, and *state of nature*, *artificial* is a loaded derivation no less important because it is ambiguous.

> "Those terms are all so vague that oftentimes not even the person who uses them knows just what meaning he is trying to convey. In his daily life the human being encounters many things that are inimical to him, either doing him harm or causing mere annoyance through certain circumstances which he considers artificial. ...If all such circumstances are eliminated, we are left with a nucleus that we will call "natural," as opposed to the "artificial" things we have discarded; and it must necessarily be good, nay, perfect, since we have thrown out everything that was bad in it. That, in fact, is the reasoning of all metaphysicists or theologians, of the followers of the Physiocrats, of Rousseau and other dreamers of that type. ... What they do is to start with a present state, eliminate from it everything they dislike, and then foist the term 'natural' on what is left" (Sec. 1602).

In this author's view, Pareto was substantially correct in his understanding of how substance is adduced to the "natural" and the "artificial" in human discourse in our definitions of reality. But whether what is "natural" is what we like or what we take for granted, and *vice versa* with "artificial," is of no present concern. Indeed, whether Pareto was correct or incorrect is of no present consequence. What is significant is that Pareto used *artificial* in substantially the same way as what he earlier characterized as normative and derivational. Notice how, in statements already quoted, Pareto differentiated between "normal change" and "artificial" alterations. Pareto wrote that "if the system were made artificially to deviate from the line [equilibrium path] $X_1$, $X_2$...it would tend at once to return to it; and that if the effect of

179

the elements is to impel the system along that line, their action would not be complete unless the system were located on that line, and no other" (Sec. 2070). What he was doing was making a distinction between those changes internal and normal to the system and (thereby) to its equilibrium path, on the one hand, and those changes external and artificial to the system, on the other hand. As Homans and Curtis point out, "What is or is not considered outside is determined arbitrarily and by convenience."[13] This means that the concept of *artificial* is inherently normative (however useful for analytic purposes) and, when used with a *restorative* connotation of equilibrium, it is inherently conservative, whatever the status quo in question. The crucial matter is the content — the specific content — of what is considered artificial. This use of the device "artificial" pervades Pareto's entire discussion of equilibrium, as does his connotation of restoration (Secs. 2067 - 2078). Moreover, it pervades his *use* of equilibrium throughout the last two chapters of the *Treatise*.

The distinction — normative at heart — between normal and artificial also enters into and pervades Pareto's differentiation between *real* and *virtual* movements. The distinction thereby also promotes continuity by incorporating the status quo into the nominally neutral concept of real movements. As indicated earlier, Pareto defined *real* and *virtual* movements in the following way: "A transition from one state to another is called a movement ... [if] we assume conditions and active influences as given, the various successive states of the group are determined. Such movements are called *real* ... movements" (Sec. 129). "If, for theoretical purposes, we assume as suppressed ... some condition in a sociological group, ... the sociological group will attain states other than those it really attains. Such movements are called *virtual* ..." (Sec. 130).

Pareto treated as virtual movements those which *might* come about and those which some maintain *should* come about. Real movements involve "the study of what is," and virtual movements "the study of what ought to be (ought to be, if a given purpose is to be realized)" (*Treatise*, p. 1925; *cf.* Secs. 1732n.2, 1732n.3, 1975, 2262). Virtual movements involve artificial alterations, as Pareto points out, roughly equating artificial with virtual movements (Sec. 2067; *cf.* Homans and Curtis, 1934, p. 273). The normative and conservative element here is essentially the same as before. Namely, inasmuch as different people will include in real movements different things — different assumptions as to what

180

"conditions and active influences" are given — at least at the margin, then it becomes a matter of choice, *ergo* normative, as to what is to be treated as a *might be* or *ought to be*. That is, matters are treated as conservative by virtue of incorporating whatever one (Pareto in this case) understands as the status quo into one's connotation of real movements.

Pareto's attitude toward the relation of knowledge and social policy thus is conservative with respect to the status quo. The eminence of the status quo is logically and substantively incorporated into his use of an equilibrium model, his use of "artificial" change *vis-à-vis* equilibrium or "normal" change, and in his distinction between real and virtual movements (which also uses "artificial" *vis-à-vis* "given" as a criterion). Pareto, one feels, suspected that his logico-experimental approach was deficient in these regards, partly because he frequently reassures his reader and himself, it would appear, to the contrary. Whatever the situation, Pareto's conservatism with respect to continuity and change was incorporated into his model. His restorative connotation of equilibrium was intimately related to his belief that "Social stability is so beneficial a thing that to maintain it it is well worth while to enlist the aid of fantastic ideals and this or that theology — among the others, the theology of universal suffrage — and be resigned to putting up with certain actual disadvantages. Before it becomes advisable to disturb the public peace, such disadvantages must have grown very very serious; ..." (Sec. 2184). Little wonder, then, that "It is not the function of theory to create beliefs, but to explain existing ones and discover their uniformities" (Sec. 365).

APPENDIX TO CHAPTER SEVEN: OUTLINE OF THE LAST TWO CHAPTERS OF THE *TREATISE*

### Chapter XII. The General Form of Society

A. The Elements
B. The State of Equilibrium
C. Organization of the Social System
   1. Introductory
   2. Composition of Residues and Derivations
   3. Properties of the Social System
      a. Utility

*Chapter 8.*

# Conclusions: Toward a Positive Theory of Economic Policy

I

This study has had two objectives. The first was to state and better understand Pareto's general sociology (in the light of his economics) as a theory of economic policy. The second was to better comprehend the fundamental constituent elements of a theory of economic policy in either the positive or normative development thereof. Both of these objectives have been substantially accomplished, at least insofar as the model of Pareto is able to serve the latter purpose and insofar as the author is able to achieve both purposes.

The purposes of this study, it should be emphasized, are quite limited. It has not been the intent of this author to critically evaluate the *Treatise* in terms of his own approach to the subject or in light of a half-century of development of the social sciences. In retrospect, it is very easy to say Pareto was incomplete, tautological, and so on: the list of meaningful and perceptive critiques is not short. Indeed, a thorough critical appraisal of the *Treatise* would approach Pareto's *opus* in length and would tend to constitute a resume of the social sciences — if that be possible — in the present day. But the rendering of a serious and thorough critique is outside this author's intent and beyond his competence as well. In addition, it has not been the intent of this author to formulate with Paretian clay his own model of economic policy. Granted that the interpretation of Pareto's *Treatise* has been within the organization of this author's general model of policy, it is beyond his purpose and capacity at this time to elucidate a thorough-going model of economic policy using whatever is deemed appropriate of the insight gained from studying Pareto. That model will have to await additional research, thought, and another volume.

What, then, of Pareto's general sociology considered as a theory of economic policy? What insight does it afford the nature and scope of economic policy and the basic problems of any theory or model of economic policy?


## II

Economic policy is a serious affair. Broader than the market and also more inclusive than government participation, such policy concerns how man makes his living by coping with and endeavoring to overcome scarcity. It encompasses allocation, distribution, and stability and growth factors as well as the organization and control of the economic system. Economic policy, then, ultimately deals with the nature of and constraints upon man's existence and his efforts, both individual and collective, to face the reality of that existence. Serious matters, indeed. Yet it is very much like a game, with players, positions, roles, moves, rules, goals, strategems, and the like. The rules, it is pertinent to note, largely are made and unmade as the game is played — a most fundamental level of policy — as the players struggle not only with each other but also in an effort to comprehend the meaning of the reality of their existence. Needless to say, the stakes are not insignificant. They include the making of man.

Vilfredo Pareto — not alone, to be sure — demonstrated that economic policy was man-made, was a product of the interaction of men in relation to their physical environment and in their efforts to influence each other both directly and indirectly through culture. Out of this interaction emerge social choices which are necessarily collective in impact and effect and complex and incremental in genesis:

"... Pareto makes the transition from individual psychology to sociology proper, that is to say to a study of interactions between individuals. His view does not imply that the course of events is determined by the schemes of individual speculators who rule the world by deliberate and concerted strategem.

Their policy is the resultant of a complex set of forces and an infinite number of acts each initiated by the particular circumstances of the time, but leading collectively to results which individually they do not foresee, despite the fact that they may have a clearer conception of their own interests than the masses have of theirs. Here as elsewhere in the *Treatise* Pareto insists on the great complexity of social interactions and on the need for replacing the notion of one-sided causality by that of mutual dependence of the factors involved" (Ginsberg, 1936, p. 242; *cf.* Muller, 1938, p. 433).

Pareto, it seems almost banal to say, dealt with fundamental matters. Although few will agree with all of his basic contentions, Pareto unquestionably sought, confronted, and identified deep social processes. He laid bare the turmoil and the agony of social choice, the choices worked out through bargains (generally incrementally made) between the generations and between the various subgroups in the population of a society. Generally speaking, Pareto uncovered (there is something of the flavor of the exposé to the *Treatise*), appraised, and described not wholly unrealistically the working of private and public, of market and nonmarket, decision-making in ways typically made unobtrusive and clouded by doctrines, arguments, interests, and emotions.

Pareto, in the view of this author, clearly demonstrated the following: economic policy — indeed, policy in general — is a process of making choices; policy fundamentally connotes choice in a context of conflicting personalities, ends, means, and so on; choice through the market is but one facet, and perhaps a small facet insofar as it is typically specified, of even a nominally market economy; and, *inter alia*, the market must be understood in relation to other forces in society both individual and collective in nature. The *Treatise*, then, was directly concerned with the institutional and motivational forces with and within which the market — insofar as society has a market — operates. Pareto examined the interaction between market forces and interests not only among themselves but also with and within the broader context of his general model of social equilibrium which juxtaposed interests to residues, derivations, social heterogeneity, and class circulation. The *Treatise* evidences the insight that economic policy, particularly in regard to choice governing the structure of the economic decision-making process as distinct from the conventional basic economic problems, must include, for the analyst, far more than orthodox economic theory.

What Pareto made so conclusively clear is that economy and society are systems of power. The central objective characteristic of economy and society which Pareto took for granted and which is articulated throughout the *Treatise* is the basic problem of the distribution of power in society. His four volumes treated from almost every possible angle the processes of formation and reformation of the structure of power. Pareto, perforce, dealt with the problem of order, the reconciliation or resolution of freedom and control and of continuity and change, and thereby with social control and social change. Included within the scope of policy, then, was the structuring and restructuring of the economic decision-making process itself. Pareto's anxiety relating to the public discussion of various themes developed in the *Treatise* attests to his relative affinity for the status quo distribution of power, if not for itself then on the grounds of maintaining social order.

But Pareto went further and demonstrated, in effect, that economic policy (or policy generally) must be interpreted and specified in terms not only of *power* but also of *psychology* and *knowledge*. These are the three great dimensions of policy to whose heuristic usefulness in modeling a theory of policy the *Treatise* attests. In studying the fundamentals of social equilibrium Pareto hit upon what appear to be the crucial variables or dimensions of any theory or model of economic policy.

Now it is to be stressed that Pareto's model includes *all* the elements he acknowledged and their independence; Pareto himself would have had it no other way. But *given* that interests are largely taken for granted in the *Treatise*, and *given* also the relative eclipse but not elimination of knowledge as a main independent variable, it is also to be stressed that psychology and power are the main elements or dimensions stressed by Pareto in the *Treatise*. At least these are the elements concentrated upon by him because he believed they — particularly psychology — were misunderstood by other sociologists. Given, therefore, the subordinate but not totally dependent position of knowledge; power and psychology (the latter including interests, inasmuch as Pareto put sentiments and interests both in the psychic category) are Pareto's crucial variables, or, more accurately, psychology in the context of power play.

It is not neccessary to summarize the Paretian theories and themes which have been presented in the preceding chapters in terms of policy as a function of knowledge, psychology, power, and their interrelations and of policy as embodying the resolution

186

of freedom and control and of continuity and change. Still it may be worthwhile to point to the contribution of Pareto in regard to the identification of pseudo-knowledge.

Like Robinson's *Mind in the Making* and Arnold's *Symbols of Government*, among others, the *Treatise* heightened awareness of the rationalizations or derivations in terms of which so much thought, both conscious and subconscious, is undertaken. As such, Pareto's contribution was in the same direction as empiricism, positivism, operationalism, logical positivism, and so on. If anything, Pareto certainly neglected the fact that while derivations include value statements, which are unlike statements which may be operationally true or false (verified or refuted), such value statements are an important part of man's valuational process, however much they are influenced by the psyche. But Pareto also certainly pointed, as did Freud, to man's deception and self-deception through the invocation of and reliance upon meaningless or at best ambiguous propositions or phrases. In other words, much of policy making was a function of aspiration, delusion, wishful thinking, and subjective feelings.

Although Pareto perhaps discounted too much the communicative value of terms and phrases (the words *property*, *freedom*, *justice* and so forth, *do* connote and communicate meaning in terms of policy alternatives in concrete situations), nevertheless he put them in epistemological perspective. What this means, *inter alia*, is that since policy-making (choice of change) is incremental in character and ultimately must deal with specific content, the derivations or rationalizations both obscure the fact of, yet provide contextual substance for, the marginal choices to be made. Since all policy making involves choice and the necessity to discriminate, which by at least one criterion in each particular case would appear arbitrary, derivations (biases) function to obscure the fact that a choice has been made (as well as provide the choice itself) or at least to make the choice appear as one made upon reasonable classification or grounds. There is thus a built-in tautology between the definition of reality embodied in rationalizations and the policy alternatives and choices to which they help give rise.

The contribution of Pareto in respect to the derivations is twofold. First, he identifies part of our definition of reality as a function of interests and emotions; second, he identifies derivations as means of providing the specific content to incremental choices under the guise of more grand propositions. In general terms, this latter means that the solution to the problem of specific content is at least partially resolved in two ways. One is the identification process of personality and motivation development as the psyche (both the interests and sentiments, to use Pareto's classification) comes to define itself and its security in terms of this or that specificity in the world around it. The other is through the interaction between power players, each of whom has identified in such a way as to support one or another substantive specific content. Economic policy relates most fundamentally, in both determined and determining ways, to the processes of socialization and individuation of the individual.

The problem of specific content is but one of the elemental questions of policy manifest in the *Treatise*. Whose interests, whose freedom, whose capacity to coerce, whose injury, whose rights, and who decides, all these questions are resolved (in terms of specific content) in the processes of social equilibrium or policy making as spelled out in the *Treatise*. Also made clear are several other elemental questions of policy, including: which knowledge, or whose knowledge?; which emotions, or whose emotions?; and who is to be sacrificed for whom?

## III

Pareto's theory of derivations has just been commented upon with respect to the identification of pseudo-knowledge, the valuation process, and the provision of specific content to general problems of policy. Commentators' reactions to Pareto's theory — to Pareto's theory of policy as a function of knowledge but with belief a function of accord with sentiments (and interests) — generally have been those of rejection or cynicism: rejection of Pareto and his theory as a threat to security (identity), or cynicism concerning human nature and the human condition. A common charge has been that Pareto was anti-intellectual and anti-rationalist. His rather complex views were examined in chapter two, *supra*; exactly where he stood *at the margin* must remain a mystery.

It is true that reason will always be fused with emotion and that policy consciousness — deliberate confrontation with problems of choice, control, and change — may be but a phase in history (as Pareto contended). Yet, the fact remains that these very problems may be interpreted as conditions which must be faced in the formulation of both positive and normative theories of economic policy. To reject the existence of emotion, and thereby to reject the psychic facet of belief, is naive and delusionary. To become a cynic is largely to give up the game and exist like the proverbial vegetable, while the game continues regardless. Unless the writing of the *Treatise* is considered as mere balm to its author's ego, which it undoubtedly was *in part*, Pareto's apparent reaction was that however great the obstacles imposed by non-logico-experimental reasoning, the possible gains from an ascendency of reason over emotion and faith were worth the effort.

While the extent of logico-experimental knowledge obtainable *may* be slim, the possibility remains of widening that area. At the same time it must be remembered that values are largely in another category (only somewhat capable of reduction to testable hypotheses) and that even reason — particularly in the hands of the haughty and arrogant — may well be tempered by certain contextually beneficent emotions. Herbert J. Muller has nicely expressed this author's viewpoint:

"Yet to regard Pareto as an enemy of reason is on the face of it absurd. What he attacks is Reason, the capitalized abstraction, with its retinue of false appearances, fantastic claims, and despotic commands. ... His position is fundamentally that of Freud. Neither regards intellect as primary; neither for that reason scorns it or joins the crusaders who for some paradoxical reason fiercely attack this despised power even while they proclaim its powerlessness. As thinkers, both put their trust in it and refuse to prostrate themselves before its triumphant rival — be this called the Unconscious or the Residue. What Pareto maintains is simply that man's behavior is governed primarily by sentiments, that these sentiments are not necessarily contemptible, and that it is folly to ignore or despise them in theorizing about human society or working for its welfare" (Muller, 1938, pp. 434 - 435; *cf.* Lopreato and Ness, 1966, pp. 22 - 23).

In other words, man's emotions are a limitation, and man's efforts to understand and control them are themselves limited by the emotions. Man has emotions and emotional needs. So far as policy making and policy analysis is concerned, that is something to be reckoned with. Whether Pareto would have agreed or disagreed, in whole or in part, is presently irrelevant. Man has chosen to eat of the tree of knowledge; whatever score is run up in the contest of reason with emotion, it will be an agonizing process, as it has been and as Pareto has made clear. However, that is a fact with which to contend; to reject it, as was noted, is naive and delusionary, and to become a cynic is to give up the game and become disengaged while the game continues. Once again this author would echo Muller:

"Ultimately life is, for both the individual and society, an experiment in values. Yet on this ground I should make my last word a recommendation of Pareto. 'The Mind and Society' throws a steady, often brilliant, light upon the terms of this experiment, the possibilities of experience; and the reader whose head is clear and whose stomach strong, who can take Pareto's truths without getting drunk on his heady negations, may be enabled to carry on the experiment more realistically, more intelligently, and even more wholeheartedly" (Muller, 1938, p. 439).

But, one may interpose, it is precisely Pareto's point that it is seldom that the "head is clear." True enough: that point defines the nature of the vicious circle of human entrapment about which one may be optimistic or pessimistic, risk seeker or risk avoider, heroic or routinist. What Pareto's analysis functions to reinforce are the *difficulties* of elevating reason over emotion, of securing peaceable change, and, indeed, of securing peaceable continuity. But that is merely to state the *terms* of the game that man must play. While one man may disengage, mankind may not, or at least never has. One consequence of rejection and withdrawal is totalitarianism, fascist or otherwise. The alternative is the one already suggested: realism tempered by liberality, humanism, self-knowledge, and humility.

But what of the cynical practice of power?


IV

Reactions to Pareto become much more pregnant and much more heated when the subject turns to his theory of power. Thurman Arnold (1962, p. 250) has written that "the net practical result of Pareto's writing, as a governmental philosophy, is to make everything appear cynical and unsentimental except the ideal of power itself." Pareto has been called the "theoretician of

190

totalitarianism" (Popper, 1950, p. 40), the Marx of the middle class (Novack, 1933), and the "Machiavelli of the middle class" (Faris, 1936, p. 668).

The general question is: what is the policy analyst to make of *power*? The specific question is: what is the policy analyst to make of power, as exercised by the cynic or otherwise, in a world of deliberate policy making, in a world, that is, in which the deliberate exercise of reason tends to substitute for blind faith and unreasoning emotion as the mode of policy making?

As Knight has pointed out in poignant terms (Knight, 1960, chapter one and *passim*), for several centuries man has been trying to base policy upon knowledge rather than upon tradition, faith, and emotion. One direct result has been to make more obtrusive (not simply to engender or cause to exist for the first time) the play of power or coercion in society. At the margin, policy consciousness has meant the elevation not only of reason over emotion (as a tendency) but also of deliberative over non-deliberative forces of social control (particularly state action over custom with private action remaining a fusion), of secular over sacred. Consequently, there is more command (or more apparent command) and less tradition in the making of economic policy, that is, in the economic decision-making process. The result has been not necessarily more social control; rather there has been a change in the mix, although amounts barely are measurable.

Apparently, the world increasingly has become Pareto's manipulative society. Motivation research (and other techniques) for example, and its application to consumer advertising, politics, and government and business administration has resulted in the psychic packaging of products, images, platforms, and governments, as well as the making of policy itself. The world is a deliberate and managerialist one. In such a world the question of whether management should concentrate on efficiency and control or on developing human resources may appear to reduce to a choice between one thrust of despotism and another. The problem is all the more serious because the question is inevitable.

Coercion and the practice of power must be taken as they are found by the policy analyst. These, too, are conditions of the human predicament. The situation is not new; it is largely only more obtrusive. However distasteful, mutual manipulation has been and must be central in economic policy making. Patently less manifest in traditional economies, it exists nonetheless. In nominally market economies, notwithstanding the model of wide diffusion of power, plural alternatives and opportunities, and *ergo* no opportunity for despotism, the reality has been one of power structure and power play in more or less Paretian terms. In any social system, choices must be made; conflicting views and interests will engender power play of one sort or another, cunning if not force.

Marshall (1920, p. 6) wrote that "It is deliberateness, and not selfishness, that is the characteristic of the modern age." Up to a point, Marshall was correct. But the larger picture would appear to be that deliberateness was only less obtrusive and perhaps more confined in pre-modern times. Today, particularly in matters of economic policy, including governmental policy, deliberateness and not tradition, reason and not emotion, deliberative and not nondeliberative deployment of power, all dominate and also are more obtrusive. Both state and church government, one would think, always have been deliberate, however colored by emotion and faith. Oriental despotism, no less than the rule of the Borgias and no less than modern statism, was deliberate, however much rational government administration (in the Max Weber sense) has been a relatively recent development. So the human predicament with which the policy analyst is confronted is not the advent of power play and mutual manipulation, but perhaps only the more extensive and certainly more obtrusive exercise of power, whether private or public, economic or political.

Power, then, must be a central dimension of a *positive* theory of economic policy. So far as the analyst is concerned, the exercise of power may be taken properly, indeed, necessarily, as a fact, a subject to understand. It is only for the analyst as citizen that the exercise of power may become a normative principle of power, a scientific Machtpolitik, approached cynically or otherwise (Cf. Larrabee, 1935, p. 508; Hacker, 1955, pp. 328 - 331; Novack, 1933, p. 259; Faris, 1936, p. 668).

So far as a *normative* theory of economic policy is concerned, the problem is *not* manipulation versus no manipulation, but rather manipulation within what type of institutional or power structure. If economic policy making is a process of mutual manipulation or mutual coercion, the normative problem becomes one of creating that evasive condition of a balance of power, of power as a check upon power, of procedures for the redress of grievances (that is, the procedures rather than the substance of the judgments reached become more significant for policy analysis and democratic theory (Jones, 1962, p. 761 and *passim.*)). In other words,

192

power play is tempered in order to reduce if not eliminate the adverse consequences of power play. With respect to specific content, such a proposition is admittedly only to state and not solve the problem. It is in this amelioration that reason in the employ of power must be softened by sentiments, Smith's moral sentiments.

If moreover, society (still considered as a system of mutual manipulation) is a class society, the normative problem becomes that of creating and maintaining an open mobility with respect to leadership selection, resisting efforts and trends toward class stratification. If pluralism is to have any meaning in a normative theory of policy under conditions of class structure, it must be effectuated through measures which enable both the elevation of the masses and the selection of leaders from as wide a base as possible.

The application of Pareto's doctrine of truth versus social utility to Pareto's own obsession with power suggests that the exercise of power may well be tempered and made at least civil by a propaganda for freedom, however much freedom will be ambiguous, conservatively understood, or misused. If the "divine right of kings" could promote order by securing obedience, then perhaps "freedom" can promote pluralism by curbing power. Certainly the analysis of power need not be as stark and obsessive as Pareto's.


V

Without any pretension or intention to develop either a critique of Pareto's theory of power or a model of power for a general theory of policy, several other specific insights of Pareto's analysis may be noted. First, and in no special sequence, Pareto not only put his finger on the important yet delicate problem of choosing society's (and economy's) leaders, but, also, and what amounts to the same thing, put his finger on the importance of eliciting organizational energy both for innovation and for conservation. This thought has become quite apparent in economic development theory through the recognition of the necessity for some group in society with an interest in and the power to seek economic development. Of course, the result is coercion versus the traditional status quo and the deliberate employment of power. But the eliciting and marshaling of organizational energy, translated into leadership or power, however seen, is crucial in any society. Indeed, the masses are substantial beneficiaries of the often neurotic efforts of their leaders, although their gains are not without costs, and any judgment of social utility is presumptive.

Second, Pareto's analysis of power and of freedom and control places in perspective, although it hardly resolves, conservatism's dilemma. It must appeal on the one hand to freedom and on the other to authority, a dilemma shared by liberalism. Both extremes may be approached through these questions: Whose power? Whose freedom? Whose authority? For what purpose?

Third, Pareto's analysis clearly reveals to what extent policy making involves the identification of particular private interests with alleged social interests, and the labeling of a particular leader's (or leaders') policy as national (or company) policy, both for purposes of legitimation. Conversely, impiety, blasphemy, heresy, and treason (as disbelief and nonattention to sacrosanct notions, if not more) really connote "violations" of proprieties of the elite or establishment which, by virtue of their efforts plus custom (helped along, to be sure, Pareto would say), come to be equated and identified with either truth or country or both. The conduct of policy is as much semantics as it is anything else. Still, it is serious business, and as Pareto's theory of the dynamics of psychic states suggests, the words may have an influence of their own.

Fourth, Pareto's analysis facilitates the placing in perspective of conservative strategems. These strategems include: ignorance as a normative principle of policy; universal consent as a requirement of change to avoid coercion; taking the status quo for granted and, through tautological conclusions, casting luster on the status quo, in part through the predictive power of theories presuming the status quo; defining freedom in terms of status quo rights and/or in terms of non-deliberative (generally non-legal) change; and so on. On the other hand, Pareto's analysis does point to the *fact* of the status quo; after all, *it* does exist. He recognized the difficulties of adjusting the status quo to desired changes, with success along any one line being probabilistic at best, especially in view of the necessity of bargaining between competing views of what and how to change. He also was aware of the emotional attachment to the status quo embodied in identity formation (with selective alienation also existing) and of the tenuousness of social peace as a requirement for orderly if not also rational change. The practice of power with respect to continuity and change is, in short, a complex matter.

Finally, Pareto's analysis considered as a theory of policy, including the exercise of power with respect to continuity versus change, is put into relief by Galbraith's juxtaposition of the modernizing and conserving sectors.

"The modernizing sector of the American community sets much store by rational accommodation to change and its warmest praise for a man is to say that "he has ideas." But it is only a part of the American community. Set against it is the large — I think by instinct much larger — sector which sets store not by ideas but by faith. It is conservative and it tests men not by the originality of their mind but by the quality of their character. And character is closely associated with constancy of commitment to a secular faith — to a particular view of economics, a particular attitude toward government, a particular conception of foreign policy, a particular assessment of the nature or threat of Communism."

"This faith is not inviolable. On the contrary, it is constantly yielding to the modernizing sector — to its evangelism or to the practical compulsions of more employment, more public education, more public spending, less poverty, or peace. It is this constant yielding which explains the endemic sense of betrayal on the American right. This feeling has a certain foundation. Men of established faith are, indeed, constantly being weaned away by the march of modernizing ideas" (Galbraith, 1967, pp. 10 - 11).

Galbraith, interestingly enough, went beyond the juxtaposition of innovative and conservative postures with respect to policy and pointed to the semantics of policy in a manner reminiscent of Pareto's roles of derivations:

"Here we have the explanation of much of our official expression. It is suspended between the modernizing sector, those whose views reflect an accommodation to change, and those who are committed to existing belief as to a faith. Sometimes it shares the conservative faith. More often it reacts to it with prudence or fear. Thus the divergence between what is avowed and what is done. Keynesian economics and the welfare state entered the United States through the liberal intellectual community. Had they been forthrightly avowed there would have been a hideous row. And since the majority adhered to the ancient economic faith they might have been rejected. So the new action was taken and the old faith avowed. I do not especially applaud this resolution; I am partial to candor. But my purpose here is to explain, not judge" (Galbraith, 1967, p. 11).

The processes of continuity and change, always subtle and complex, and probed by Pareto in his own fashion, are no better underscored than by Galbraith's description.

"On other occasions, though an eventual change in policy is inevitable, it has to wait until the modernizing forces gain the requisite power. ...

We also have here much of the explanation of the trite character of expression on American foreign policy and the tendency for that expression to be more retarded than the reality. ... Subjectively [Washington] recognizes the sources of the pressures for modernization. But concessions are made to the older faith. And men would not be human if they did not, on occasion, resist by their own oratory the admission of their own obsolescence.

... For it follows from what I have said that anyone who is guided by official expressions of American policy will be rather poorly guided as to the present and much misguided as to the future. For it is inevitable that our official expression will be addressed at least partly to the world not of fact or of change but of faith. Meanwhile, much of the present and all of the future will belong to the forces of modernization.

... If everything were evident from the official statements, no such scholarship would be needed" (Galbraith, 1967, pp. 11, 12, 13).

## VI

Particularly significant to this author is the confirmation which the foregoing chapters afford to the general model of economic policy, and the general conception of the nature and scope of that policy. Pareto's *Treatise* amply illustrates the fundamentals to which either a positive or normative theory of economic policy must relate. In particular, Pareto's analysis supports the addition of the dimensions of knowledge and psychology to that of power. As Parsons found, the *Treatise*, with due respect and attention to the original thrust of the author, is eminently suitable as a subject of reinterpretation. With the help of later insight, new insight may be derived from an earlier original work, and the meaningfulness of new analyses may be explored in the context of earlier studies.

In such a way the history of thought and the analysis of policy can be mutually constructive and enlightening endeavors (Samuels, 1965b, pp. 146 - 147).

But Pareto's efforts in the *Treatise* also attest to some of the difficulties which must be encountered in constructing a positive theory or model of economic policy. A few of these simply may be enumerated. It is hard to develop general models of freedom and control and of continuity and change, that is, of social control and social change, including meaningful definitions of power, and so forth. It is difficult to disentangle the strands of power, knowledge, and psychology, in part because what can be developed in terms of one generally readily can be developed in terms of another. It is not easy to be positivistic; one unwittingly can build in one's own normative positions concerning power, psychology, knowledge, freedom, control, continuity, and change.

Concerning the third item above, as specific examples of the introduction of personal prejudices masquerading as principles, Pareto first developed a general theory of the social utility of non-logico-experimental reasoning and knowledge. At times, therefore, he did not discriminate between liberal and conservative derivations. A derivation is a derivation, period. But at other times, he was devastatingly critical of the derivations used by humanitarian, democratic, socialist, and generally left-wing reformers which use merely attests to their sentiments. Pareto then developed a social control definition of *ethics.* At times he applied it indiscriminately, but at other times he was manifestly critical of reformers attempting to effectuate *their* norms. Next Pareto developed a general theory of the dynamics of social change, of the resolution of continuity versus change in society. Here again, although he often treated both continuity and change, he both built continuity into his model and adopted as normative principles what were conditional facts, to wit, the limitedness of possible deliberate change and the fact of ignorance.

Once again this author would approach these particular subjects not as normative principles, insofar as positive theory of policy is concerned, but as limitational conditions, that is, as descriptive principles not as canons of policy. This would be not substantially different from treating Malthus' law of population not as a statement of inevitable adversity (with all sorts of policy implications, as were drawn in the first half of the nineteenth century in particular), but as a statement of conditions necessary for improvement of living conditions (Samuels, 1966, p. 70). This type of analysis is hardly novel; for example, Harry V. Ball and associates interpreted Sumner's theory of law and social change along similar lines (Ball et al. 1962).

Finally, particularly relevant in the case of Pareto was the use of capstone concepts. Necessary when maximizing or optimizing models are employed, they build in much ambiguity and normativism. This author has in mind Pareto's concept of *social utility*. Like many of the terms whose use he chastised on identical grounds, such as "good" and "the greatest happiness for the greatest number," *social utility* leaves much to be desired. As can Bentham's formula and the concept of the *public interest*, the term can be interpreted and applied one way or another depending upon the specification or twist given it by the user. Pareto himself seemed to be sensitive to these difficulties. As Hutchison has pointed out, "maximizing formulas must depend for their significance, except as analytical *tours de force*, on the significance and content of the 'maximand.' As Mitchell and Keynes saw, the problem of the content of the maximand has never been very satisfactorily solved, and social science would be ominously simple if it could be."[1]

Pareto's *Treatise* is significant, then, not necessarily for its answers but for the questions posed and the problems probed, even if they need to be restated and redirected. Moreover, it makes it abundantly clear that a positive theory of economic policy must draw on such fields as linguistics, epistemology, historiography, political sociology, and so on.


## VII

What, then, is the relation between Pareto's neoclassical economics and the broader subjects formally considered by him in the *Treatise*?

Pareto generally is treated in the history of economic thought as a member of the Lausanne or mathematical economics "school," thereby as a member of neoclassical economics, and as a founder of welfare economics. Indeed, he was a pre-eminent contributor to neoclassicism in economics.

Pareto's sociological *Treatise*, however, illuminates the nature of institutional economics and the relation of institutional to neoclassical economics (microeconomic theory), when all are considered as facets of the theory of the organization and control of the economic system, *ergo* of economic policy. As the preceding chapters make abundantly clear, Pareto considered, at least in effect, that economic policy included more than market allocation of resources, that is, more than the market, more than resource allocation, and more than micro-economic equilibrium. Accordingly, he analyzed the forces governing the distribution of power in society, and economy, the operation of the institutional and motivational forces and framework within which market activity takes place, and the interaction between market, institutions, and socio-economic forces. Moreover, he analyzed the institutional and motivational framework not just as it bears on the allocation of resources but primarily as it constitutes the structuring of the economic decision-making process, that is, the power structure.

Like Knight (1960, p. 82), Pareto was both a neoclassical economist and, as sociologist, an institutionalist, however much he, again like Knight, did not share the typical institutionalist's (for example, Commons) enthusiasm for reform. Institutionalism, particularly of the Commons' variety, has been interested in much the same problems which Pareto analyzed in the *Treatise*: the operation of the market, the operation of legal and customary institutions, and their interaction; the resolution of the problems of freedom and control and of continuity and change; and thereby the basic economic problem of the structuring and restructuring of the economic decision-making process in a changing economy (cf. Clark, 1939). This is as true of Pareto as it is of Hayek, Mises, and Knight and of the institutionalists proper, including Veblen, Clark, and Commons. All of these economists, as did the classicists and other neoclassicists, including Marshall and Pigou, studied "the disposal of scarce means within the framework of our developing economic system" (Gruchy, 1957, p. 13; *cf.* Gruchy, 1947, pp. 550ff). That is, they studied in isolation and/or in conjunction the resolution of the basic economic problems of resource allocation, income distribution, income level determination, and the organization and control of economic activity, in sum, the distribution of power, the structuring of the economic decisional process (Samuels, 1972a). Pareto's *Treatise* serves to clarify that much of what is now in the fields of comparative systems and economic development always has been within the domain of the analysis of economic policy, if not within that of formal economic theory. Both in his distinction between "pure" and "applied" economics and in the *Treatise* as a whole (Secs. 2011, 2014; *cf.* 1732n.3 and *passim*), Pareto makes clear that the economy and economic policy include more than resource allocating market forces, whether abstractly considered or not.

What this author would include within the compass of the concept "theory of economic policy," Pareto divided and dichotomized into economics and general sociology (with his "applied" economics standing ambiguously between "pure" economics and general sociology.) His field of general sociology, therefore, bears much the same relation to formal neoclassical economic theory as institutional economics bears to neoclassicism. The relation concerns not (or not so much) method as scope. Both positive and normative theories of economic policy tend to encompass both resource allocation and the distribution of power. The theory of economic policy as a field includes analysis of market, institutions, and their interaction, as well as analysis of power, knowledge, psychology, and polity and economy narrowly defined.

One may speculate that Pareto would have sympathized with Ayres' view that

"... the object of dissent is the conception of the market as the guiding mechanism of the economy or, more broadly, the conception of the economy as organized and guided by the market. It simply is not true that scarce resources are allocated among alternative uses by the market. The real determinant of whatever allocation occurs in any society is the organizational structure of that society — in short, its institutions. At most, the market only gives effect to prevailing institutions. By focusing attention on the market mechanism, economists have ignored the real allocational mechanism" (Ayres, 1957, p. 26).

Although perhaps in sympathy with this view, Pareto most certainly, and at a minimum, would have specified the residues as a "real determinant."

## VIII

The *Treatise* also provides insight into the character and significance of what has come to be called "Pareto optimum" in general micro-economic theory and welfare economics.[2] Pareto optimum may be formulated as a (equilibrium) situation in which no change can be made to benefit some Alpha without injuring some Beta. As Vickrey expresses it, the criterion of Pareto optimality is a

200

situation in which "it will not be possible to modify the result in any way so as to make some people better off without at the same time making others worse off."[3] It is a situation in which the original distribution of resources is taken for granted (Blaug, 1962, p. 536; Vickrey, 1964, p. 212), and with respect to which there is no necessary *unique* Pareto optimum but, rather, an infinite number of possible optima.

Pareto optimum is essentially a solution to the problem of reconciling continuity and change concerning the distribution of sacrifice, a decision rule governing the condition under which change is permissible. What Pareto optimum does is to allow change if and only if there is no visitation of injury on some Beta for the advantage of some Alpha or as a necessary consequence of the benefit given some Alpha. As Blaug (1962, p. 538) points out, "An unwillingness to make interpersonal comparisons of utility means that the only changes that can be evaluated are those that make everyone better or worse off. An improvement in some people's welfare at someone else's expense cannot be judged."

What Pareto optimum functions to probe, then, is the distribution of sacrifice in the process of reconciling continuity and change in society. But Pareto optimum assumes the existing distribution of resources and the existing distribution of power in society, including the system of property relations and distribution of property rights. It takes as given the existing distribution of sacrifice in society. Inasmuch as Pareto optimum assumes the existing status quo, it is obviously inherently conservative.

Moreover, Pareto optimum may be and has been specified and employed conservatively so as to thwart change through deliberate (generally legal) policy, in effect treating the status quo as if it were a unique Pareto optimum situation. Thus, Buchanan defines Pareto optimum such that "any situation is 'optimal' if all possible moves from it result in some individual being made worse off. The definition may be transformed into a rule which states that any social change is desirable which results in (1) everyone being better off or (2) someone being better off and no one being worse off than before the change." Buchanan then acknowledges that the Pareto rule "is itself an ethical proposition," one which "specifically eliminates the requirement that interpersonal comparisons of utility be made," but in which there remains "a fundamental ambiguity:" "Some objective content must be given to the terms 'better off' and 'worse off': This is accomplished by equating 'better off' with 'in that position voluntarily chosen'" (Buchanan, 1959, p.

125; *cf.* Vickrey, 1964, p. 209). This formulation functions, at least as a tendency, to preclude or disengage law as a mode of altering vested rights. Thus, Campbell has interpreted Smith in the light of Buchanan's formulation of the Pareto rule: "For Smith a change (an action) cannot be called socially beneficial if it involves injury or harm to other individuals. Such actions should be discouraged by means of the formulation of legal and moral rules."[4] Others, however, are willing to alter existing relationships (including property relationships and rights) upon a (mere) showing of presumptive benefit to society (*cf.* Nicols, 1967, p. 346; Demsetz, 1967, p. 348, and *passim*; and Coase, 1960).

Yet Pareto optimum theoretically can have a change-promotive role. Insofar as the situation prior or up to that of Pareto optimum is a positive sum game (with or without actual compensation payments), the logic of Pareto optimum is a call, albeit a conservative call, for change up to the point of Pareto optimum. Although militating against change at that point, it is a conservative but not wholly non-reformist solution to the problem of reconciling continuity and change, that is, of the claims of existing and proposed rights-beneficiaries (Samuels, 1966, pp. 284 - 285; Schumpeter, 1951, p. 131; Blaug, 1962, p. 542).

Pareto optimum, then, is at least inherently conservative in one respect and liberal in another, and it rather easily functions to discredit and minimize deliberate legal change of the existing distribution of rights and thereby power and claims to income. On balance, Pareto optimum would appear to narrow the range of possible alterations in the distribution of sacrifice in society. In part, this is done by implicitly assuming that the status quo is already in a condition of Pareto optimum and, therefore, desirable. Needless to say, change resulting from technological innovation and power play in the private sector is not restricted to situations in which either everyone is better off or, if someone is better off, no one else is worse off after the change. This latter is the problem of externalities which can be analyzed in a Paretian or non-Paretian context. (See Samuels, 1972b.)

In the *Treatise*, Pareto specified that "When the community stands at a point, Q, that it can leave with resulting benefits to all individuals, procuring greater enjoyments for all of them, it is obvious that from the economic standpoint it is advisable not to stop at that point, but to move on from it as far as the movement away from it is advantageous to all. When, then, the point P, where that is no longer possible, is reached, it is necessary, as regards the advisability of stopping there or going on, to resort to other considerations foreign to economics — to decide on grounds of ethics, social utility, or something else, which individuals it is advisable to benefit, which to sacrifice" (Sec. 2129). Pareto's own formulation in the *Treatise*, then, did not formally define Pareto optimum as *the* decision rule — as the presumptive resting place. Rather, he viewed it only as a readily identifiable, objectively (Vickrey, 1964, p. 209) definable (albeit still formal) situation which he *coupled with* the possibility of change supported by *other* decision rules, based on ethical or power factors and so forth. The fact that Pareto characterized choice of change to a point beyond Pareto optimum as a function of "no criterion save sentiment" (Sec. 2135; *cf.* 2137 and *passim*) points to the psychological, value clarification, and power facets of policy making discussed in preceding chapters. The use of Pareto optimum as *the* optimum is thus incomplete and, functionally, conservative. Pareto's own conservatism, as developed above, is echoed in the conservative so-called new welfare economics of Pareto optimality.

What can be said, then, of Pareto optimum as a decision rule with respect to continuity versus change in the context of normative and/or positive theories of economic policy? First, it is clear that, although Pareto optimum reasoning could establish a theoretical or a priori mandate for change to the Pareto optimum condition, it primarily functions to conservatively limit the scope of possible change by requiring no visitation of injury, eliminating interpersonal-utility-comparison or normative-judgment cases, and generally disengaging legal change either of relative rights' relations or (what amounts to the same thing) of the structure of the economic decision-making process.

Second, Pareto optimum reasoning generally does not allow consideration of the status quo distribution of power, nor does it generally allow consideration of change in the pattern of sacrifice. This means that when used conservatively (that is, as *the* decision rule or as a presumptive criterion), although it has Paretian social utility through functioning to disengage change, it is analytically barren with respect to most issues of policy and certainly the crucial and most controversial ones, to wit, the ones redistributing the imposition of cost and the ones restructuring the economic decision-making process.

Third, Pareto optimum must be interpreted as operative within the existing social framework of moral and legal rules (Buchanan, 1962; Morgenstern, 1964). Change in the framework, that is, in the moral and legal rules, means change in the coefficients of Pareto optimum, but these changes are beyond the capacity of Pareto optimum reasoning to contribute direction as to choice of moral or legal rules. It is change of these rules which tends to be at the heart of the crucial policy questions. It is by assuming the pre-eminence of the existing rules that Pareto optimum functions conservatively.

Fourth, economic policy cannot avoid the problem of the distribution or redistribution of sacrifice unless it is to assume a substantially if not totally conservative posture or else selectively and presumptively reenforce certain interests and not others, which is the case with certain normative theories of economic policy and/or the uses to which they are put. The columnist Sydney J. Harris has written: "Politics is the art of pretending that everybody will be better off if the politician's party is in power, whereas it is perfectly plain that no matter which party is in power, some elements will be better off and some will be worse off" (*Miami Herald*, June 8, 1967). As Pareto recognized (Sec. 1497) society and economy involve combinations of relationships of individuals to each other and to the common weal. Whether a particular relation is "better" or "worse" is a function of extra-Pareto optimum considerations of the nature of interpersonal utility judgments, definition of reality and of interests, and ethical criteria, or, as Pareto would put it, of the sentiments.

Fifth, Pareto optimum is not the only logic of welfare economic reasoning to be found in the *Treatise*. There is also cost-benefit reasoning along what are essentially Pigovian lines, although the analysis is not stressed (Secs. 1496, 1479, 1554, 1898, 1975ff, 1987n.2). Moreover, even in the *Treatise*, consideration of Pareto optimum is subsumed under and eclipsed by the forces of psychology, knowledge, and power play.

Sixth, although Pareto optimum is limited, it is nevertheless an important criterion of policy, an important social decision rule. Its function, not unlike that of orthodox economic analysis generally, is to force the analysis and consideration of alternatives and opportunity costs. It is thus of considerable power and significance with respect to maximizing allocative efficiency and thereby social efficiency. Now, as Blaug has pointed out, "The belief that 'efficiency' and 'equity' can somehow be separated represents one of the oldest dreams of economics," and relates to the quest to establish a purely positive, non-normative, value-free economic theory. "The value of Pareto's definition of welfare was to make

204

the separation of efficiency from distribution crystal clear. But Pareto continued to believe that significant pronouncements about economic policy could be laid down solely on the basis of considerations of efficiency. Recent developments in the 'new' welfare economics have cast doubt upon that belief" (Blaug, 1962, p. 540).

But Pareto optimum is essentially a general equimarginal condition. So far as production is concerned, then, Pareto optimum functions with respect to output maximizing co-efficients of production which are, it is important to note, a function of technology and whose change is a function of technological change. This change, it is also important to note, is at least partially independent of the no-injury rule and normative with respect to distribution. But, given the existence of normative elements in resource allocation and production, Pareto optimum does have a crucial economizing function in the usual application of the rule in which marginal cost is to be made equal to marginal revenue, and so forth. Much the same thing can be said with respect to household equilibrium, in which Pareto optimum or the equimarginal principle functions with respect to satisfaction maximizing coefficients of consumption. These ultimately are still a function of taste, and they change as taste changes, and they take the distribution of income, wealth, and claims to income as given. Here also Pareto optimum considerations — again, the equimarginal principle — have a function with respect to social efficiency.

It is, however, with respect to institutional organization, relative rights, the structure of power, and the redistribution of costs (injuries) that Pareto optimum considerations — otherwise generally strong and open-ended — have severe limitations. Pareto optimum reasoning will function to maximize social efficiency, promoting maximum satisfaction-yielding output, with respect to deliberate policy making, under the condition of a given distribution of sacrifice or injury. It is with respect to this use that the limitations enumerated above apply: Pareto optimum not only contains no rule with which to consider changes that incur loss in relative position but also actually tends to postulate them out of consideration. It is these normative changes in relative rights, relative power status, the distribution of income and wealth and of opportunity to attain income and wealth, as well as change toward the pluralizing of institutions and opportunity as well as power with which Pareto optimum is unable to deal.

Indeed, the new welfare economics has its very origin in self-effacing attempts to avoid the necessity for making interpersonal utility comparisons, ultimately to avoid making judgments of value or sentiment. Using Pareto optimum as a moral rule enables policy making to beg the major issues of policy and for this and other reasons promotes continuity of the status quo. In doing so it implicitly makes an interpersonal utility or ethical judgment favorable to the status quo. Pareto optimum requires an antecedent specification of rights, and in assuming the status quo rights structure and its propriety, it operates conservatively. Whereas Pigovian welfare economics may be said to have opened the door to change (Platonic), the new welfare economics may be said to have largely closed the door to significant change (Aristotelian). Pareto optimum is thus well named.

Yet even in these cases Pareto optimum's no-injury requirement would force careful analysis of the relative gains and costs of change. Even though non-deliberative decision-making knows little of Pareto optimum in the real world, deliberative or legal policy (choice) should be reasoned choice based upon careful weighing of opportunity costs. This should be facilitated by a carefully reasoned Pareto optimum analysis, though not necessarily a conservatively utilized one. As Knight has pointed out, the liberation of the mind (deliberative over non-deliberative) has given rise to the quest for rational norms (Knight, 1960, chapters four and six). Pareto optimum as a norm can be very useful, but, as strong as it is, it is still severely limited. It is *a* norm, not *the* norm. It is at least a presumption that change beyond the Pareto optimum situation should not be attempted without careful consideration of ethical and sentimental bases of judgment. This place for the use of other norms by which to go beyond the norm of Pareto optimum was part of Pareto's analysis of optimum.


## IX

The foregoing indicates it obviously is difficult to construct a positive theory or model of economic policy because of the ease with which normative elements may be incorporated therein. Yet this is but another way of saying that much of thought is non-logico-experimental rather than logico-experimental. In the decades since Pareto's *Treatise* appeared, however, it is much clearer that part of the non-logico-experimental is metaphysics with respect to the definition of ultimate reality, part of it is sentiments or emotions,

206

and part of it relates to the process of value clarification, confrontation, and selection, all of which are vital experiences and efforts. The construction of a theory of economic policy itself faces many of the predicaments and perplexities with which economic policy making is involved. If normative elements cannot be wholly eliminated, the effort can be made to at least identify them. The course of development of welfare economics, for example, has comprised just such efforts.

Pareto's *Treatise*, whether or not considered as a theory of economic policy, was penetrating and perceptive. But it also was perverse, reflecting or seeming to reflect an obsession with power and authority, and an antagonism toward permissiveness. After the plurality of hells which the half century since the publication of the *Treatise* has witnessed, no longer should it require so perverse a reminder that at the heart of economic policy is the problem of power, that it is often aggravated by neurosis, and that knowledge is an instrument of power play.

As a professor of law eloquently has formulated the problem, not entirely prematurely, man has learned to live with the truth, has lost his fantasies, and has begun to conquer his world, his body, and his mind (Ehrenzweig, 1965, p. 1331). Another study of policy has concluded that policy formation is not an intellectual process but is a social process with intellectual elements (Bauer, 1966, p. 935). The recognition that policy is a function of power, and psychology means that "we are stripped both of easy virtue and omnipotence" (Bauer, 1966, p. 934). Pareto took equilibrium for granted, both as a technique of analysis and as a social process. Yet his own analysis suggests that "the drive and search for equilibrium is our human, superhuman task in law, as it is in esthetics, in economics — and, indeed, in all endeavors at all times" (Ehrenzweig, 1965, p. 1359), and points to the inherent personal and social agony. The result will appear and may well be more agonizing as the drive is more obtrusively deliberative and managerialist, regardless of whether or not the managers are on public or private payrolls. But that is the human condition; out of it man is made.

# Notes

## Chapter one

1. All citations will be by author and date except for Pareto's *Treatise on General Sociology*. Following customary practice all references to the *Treatise* will be by section number wherever possible. Complete citations are listed at the end of the volume under "References."
2. Muller, 1938, p. 433. "Each acts upon all the others, is in turn acted upon, and itself again reacts." (p. 436.)
3. Perry, 1935, p. 104. "In one place he defines the state of equilibrium of a system at any time as the state which is determined at that time by the factors of the system." (p. 104.) "Pareto furnishes another definition of equilibrium, according to which the state of equilibrium of a system at a specified time is the state to which it returns after it has been influenced for a short time by an external or artificial force." (p. 105.)
4. Sec. 2066. "The system changes both in form and in character in course of time. When, therefore, we speak of 'the social system' we mean that system taken both at a specified moment and in the successive transformations which it undergoes within a specified period of time." (Sec. 2066. *cf.* Sec. 2061 and *passim*.)
5. Spengler, 1944, p. 129; Timasheff, 1957, pp. 159 - 160. For critiques, *cf.* Perry, 1935, pp. 104ff; Murchison, 1935, pp. 57ff; and Parsons, 1937, *passim.*
6. Martindale (1960, p. 466.) considers Pareto "a voluntaristic organicist. At the same time, he is a transitional figure between organicism and sociological functionalism." Stark (1963a, p. 125.) considers the *Treatise* "as the most massive and impressive statement of the mechanistic conception of social life." Lopreato, (1965, p. 3) argues "that Pareto's functionalism is highly developed, systematic, and in many respects free of the snares, that bedevil most current functionalist conceptions" (*cf.* Lopreato, 1964, p. 646).
7. *Cf.* Parsons, 1936, pp. 257, 260, and Parsons, 1937, *passim*; Mihanovich, 1953, p. 193; Stark, 1963b, p. 108; DeVoto, 1933a, p. 579; Lopreato,

209

1965, p. 18; and, *inter alia*, Pareto, in Hamilton, 1962, p. 50; and Sec. 883.

8. Indeed, it can be argued that Pareto has central organicist components in his *Treatise* (as would be possible, for example, by following Schneider's analysis of Hayek, among others.) (Schneider, 1962, pp. 497 and *passim*.)

9. "Interests ... reflect underlying sentiments, just as do residues ..." (Spengler, 1944, p. 124n.1.)

10. "Living in a given milieu impresses on the mind certain concepts, certain modes of thinking and of acting, certain prejudices, certain beliefs, which are antithetical to those that are formed in other environments, and which by this antithesis are strengthened, persist, and acquire an objective existence." (Amoroso, 1938, p. 8.)

11. "Though of course not entirely devoid of empirical elements, Pareto's sociology is in reality a philosophy of society, a social creed, determined mainly by violent political and even purely personal passions" (Borkenau, 1936, p. 165. *cf.* Henderson, 1937. p. 42).


## Chapter two

1. In addition, the question arises, how should history be written, i.e. for what purpose? *cf.* secs. 1580ff.

2. Concerning Platonic reform via reason alone, *cf.* sec. 2348.

3. For brief summaries of Pareto's theory of science, *cf.* Perry, 1935, pp. 96 - 97, and Tufts, 1935, p. 65. DeVoto called Pareto the "Newton of sociology" (DeVoto, 1933a, p. 546).

4. "Faith and metaphysics aspire to an ultimate, eternal resting-place. Science knows that it can attain only provisory, transitory positions. Every theory fulfills its function, and nothing more can be asked of it" (Sec. 2400; *cf.* secs. 52, 97, 829, and p. 1924).

5. *Cf.* Perry, 1935, pp.96 - 97; Bousquet, 1928, p. 9; Millikan, 1936, p. 331; and Pareto, in Hamilton, 1962, pp. 49, 59; and Secs. 2176, 2397 - 2399.

6. "We have no knowledge whatever of what *must* or *ought to* be. We are looking strictly for what *is*. That is why we have to be satisfied with one judge at a time" (Sec. 28).

7. "On all that we can know nothing *a priori*. Experience alone can enlighten us." (Sec. 14, *cf.* sec. 28)

8. "From our point of view not even logic supplies *necessary* inferences, except when such inferences are mere tautologies. Logic derives its efficacy from experience and from nothing else." (Sec. 29, *cf.* Sec. 97, and p. 1924.)

9. "Non-logico-experimental theories usually arrive in one bound at a state which those who accept them believe must *obviously* be immutable, though as a matter of fact it varies from writer to writer, from believer to believer." (*Treatise* p. 1925.)

10. "Metaphysicists generally give the name of 'science' to knowledge of the 'essences' of things, to knowledge of 'principles.' If we accept that defini-

tion for the moment, it would follow that this work would be in no way scientific. Not only do we refrain from dealing with essences and principles: we do not even know the meaning of those terms." (Sec. 19). "Blessed indeed are they knowing the essences of things and the necessary relations between facts. We, much more modest, are simply trying to discover such relations as experience discloses; and if those good souls are right, it only means that we shall be discovering with great effort and after laborious investigations things that were revealed to them by metaphysical enlightenment. If the relations they talk about are really *necessary*, we cannot possibly find different ones," (Sec. 530 *cf.* secs. 62, 1086).

11. Secs. 452, 582, 1066ff. "Theology and metaphysics do not wholly disdain experience, provided it be their servant. ... In their explorations in the realm beyond experience they satisfy a hankering that is active and even tyrannical in many people for knowing not only what has been and is, but also what ought, or must necessarily, be; ..." (Sec. 613.)

12. "For the metaphysicist [truth] designates something independent of experience, beyond experience; for the experimental scientist it designates mere accord with experience." (Sec. 1778n.2.)

13. "At bottom he is exhorting rather than proving." (Sec. 42. "... the metaphysicist fashions the abstraction to suit himself, ... the mind creating the theory appears as both pleader and judge." (Sec. 594, *cf.* sec. 2147.)

14. "To ascribe an attribute of 'necessity' to the proposition, one has to add to it a something that is non-experimental — an act of faith." (Sec. 976.) "Hitherto sociology has nearly always been expounded dogmatically." The sociology of Comte and Bossuet "is a case of two different religions, of religions nevertheless; ..." "Faith by its very nature is exclusive." (Sec. 6, cf. sec. 1621.)

15. "We in no wise assert that the logico-experimental proof is superior to the other and is to be preferred. We are saying simply — and it is something quite different — that such proof alone is to be used by a person concerned not to abandon the logico-experimental field." (Sec. 47, *cf.* secs. 70, 346.)

16. Secs. 6, 476, 486, 506, 512, 524, 848, 979, 2340. "The positivism of Herbert Spencer is nothing but a metaphysics." (Sec. 112.)

17. See generally Millikan, 1936, pp. 331ff; MacPherson, 1937, pp. 458ff, 470 - 471; Moore, 1935 - 1936, p. 294; Ascoli, 1936, pp. 81, 83; Stark, 1963b, pp. 103ff; Hook, 1935, p. 747; Larrabee, 1935, pp. 508ff. *Per contra*, cf. Bittermann, 1936, pp. 306ff; Muller, 1938, pp. 434 - 5; Lopreato and Ness, 1966, pp. 22 - 23. *Cf.* also Bongiorno, 1930, p. 352; Clerc, 1942, pp. 588 - 589; Bogardus, 1955, p. 515; House, 1935, p. 81; Suranyi-Unger, 1931, p. 26; and Schumpeter, 1951, p. 138.

18. Sec. 149; *cf.* secs. 304, 447, 516. Empiricism has its limitations also; *cf.* secs. 2400ff.

19. Secs. 129 - 130. For examination of examples of virtual movements, *cf.* secs. 517 - 519, 1825 - 1895, 2067 - 2072, 2088, 2093 - 2096.

20. Timasheff, 1957, p. 161; *cf.* secs. 153, 249, 1404, and generally chapters two and three. See also Lerner, 1935, p. 136; House, 1935, pp. 84 - 85, 88; Faris, 1936, p. 665; DeVoto, 1933b, pp. 570 - 572; Bongiorno, 1930,

p. 356; Lindeman, 1935, p. 454; Lopreato and Ness, 1966, p. 22; and Ginsberg, 1936, p. 238.

21. Sec. 151 where Pareto presents a classification of "genera and species;" *cf.* MacPherson, 1937, p. 460; Bongiorno, 1930, p. 354; and Ginsberg, 1936, p. 223.

22. "... the social importance of religion lies not at all in the logical value of its dogmas, its principles, its theology, but rather in the non-logical actions that it promotes." Sec. 365; *cf.* secs. 256. 345, 383n.1. *Cf.* House, 1935, pp. 85 - 88; Schumpeter, 1951, p. 138; Tufts, 1935, p. 77; Faris, 1936, pp. 658, 665, 666; De Voto, 1933b, p. 572; and Borkenau, 1936, p. 23.

23. *Cf.* Bogardus, 1955, pp. 513, 515; Stark, 1963b, p. 106; Muller, 1938, pp. 429, 432, 434, 435; and Schumpeter, 1951, pp. 139 - 140. *Per contra, cf.* Ginsberg, 1936, pp. 244, 245.

24. *Cf.* Parsons, 1933, p. 577; 1936, pp. 247, 248, 261; and 1937, chapters five and six, particularly pp. 187, 190 - 191, 217.

25. See, generally, Perry, 1935, pp. 106 - 107; Suranyi-Unger, 1936, p. 141; Bongiorno, 1930, pp. 353 - 355; Beardsley, 1944, 86ff; Ascoli, 1936, pp. 81 - 82; Larrabee, 1935, p. 511; Borkenau, 1936, pp. 24, 28, 91ff; Ginsberg, 1936, pp. 223, 225, 227, and *passim*; and Lopreato and Ness, 1966, p. 22.

26. Hundreds of examples are examined and analyzed by Pareto in chapters two through five and nine and ten of the *Treatise.*

27. Ginsberg, 1936, p. 222; *cf.* secs. 180, 251, 583, 1498, 1690; and Timasheff, 1957, p. 161; Borkenau, 1936, p. 78; Ascoli, 1936, p. 82; Hook, 1935, p. 748; Tufts, 1935, p. 67; Bongiorno, 1930, pp. 362 - 363; and DeVoto, 1933b, p. 577.

28. As Timasheff, among others, has pointed out, the categories overlap. Timasheff, 1957, p. 163.

29. "In one and the same treatise Cicero sways back and forth between the various demonstrations, so betraying the fact that it is not the conclusions that follow from the demonstrations, but that the demonstration is selected for the purpose of obtaining the conclusions." (Sec. 412; *cf.* secs. 1710, 1802; and Timasheff, 1957, pp. 161, 162; Borkenau, 1936, p. 80; and Schumpeter, 1951, p. 138).

30. "To restate in that language an observation that we have many times made, we may say that the social value of a doctrine, or of the sentiments which it expresses, is not to be judged extrinsically by the mythical forms that it assumes (they assume), which is only its means (their means) of action, but intrinsically by the results that it achieves (they achieve)." (Sec. 1868). "As a matter of fact many fallacies that are current in a given society are repeated in all sincerity by people who are exceedingly intelligent and are merely voicing in that way sentiments which they consider beneficial to society." (Sec. 1397n.2, *cf.* Lopreato and Ness, 1966, p. 34.)

31. Sec. 2105, *cf.* the following summaries of Pareto's theory of utility: Borkenau, 1936, pp. 130 - 132; Lopreato, 1965, pp. 4, 11, 13ff; Homans and Curtis, 1934, pp. 278ff; Parsons, 1937, chapter six, and 1936, pp. 255 - 256; Spengler, 1944, pp. 114 - 115, and Tarascio, 1968.

32. Sec. 2130. "The utilities of various individuals are heterogeneous quantities, and a sum of such quantities is a thing that has no meaning; there is

no such sum, and none such can be considered. If we would have a sum that stands in some relation to the utilities of the various individuals, we must first find a way to reduce those utilities to homogeneous quantities that can be summed." (Sec. 2127.)

33. "... leaving unanswered the question *which* is really to be maximized, the number or percentage of (more or less) happy people, or the intensity of the happiness of those most largely benefited." Taylor, 1960, p. 134.

34. "The utility of today is frequently in conflict with the utility of days to come, and the conflict gives rise to phenomena that are well known under the names of providence and improvidence in individuals, families, and nations." (Sec. 2119.)

35. "The reader should remember, however, that the positions of these maxima depend upon the choice of norms, that different judges and critics will choose different norms, that each choice is arbitrary, and that there is no known logical operation which yields a choice between these arbitrary choices." (Henderson, 1937, p. 50.) "He distinguishes first between subjective and objective utility. The latter supposes the existence of some objective rule and as a consequence can never be applied to individuals who do not accept the rule concerned." Borkenau, 1936, p. 130.

36. "This basis of unity Pareto finds in the last analysis to lie in the necessary existence of an 'end the society pursues.' That is, the ultimate ends of individual action systems are integrated to form a single *common system of ultimate ends* which is the culminating element of unity holding the whole structure together." (Parsons, 1937, p. 249 (italics in original); also quoted by Spengler, 1944, p. 114n.7.)

37. *Cf.* secs. 72 - 74, 401, 445 - 446, 965, 219, 598, 603n.1, 616, 843, 936, 965, 1219, 1336, 1382, 1896ff, 171, 304, 312, 855, 1226, 1349, 1678 - 1683, 2001 - 2002, 2340ff, 2440, 2566n.3, 1397n.2, 1586, 1621, 1772, 1689n.2, 1695n.1, 1716n.2, 1775, 1823n.1, 1868, 1895ff, 1882, 2113n.1, 2162, 2184, 2239, 2340, 2400n.1, 2400n.2, p. 1921. See also Muller, 1938, p. 434; Lopreato, 1965, pp. 15 - 16; Tufts, 1935, pp. 65, 66, 74ff; Larrabee, 1935, 513; Borkenau, 1936, p. 169; Henderson, 1937, p. 54n.; Ascoli, 1936, p. 86; Perry, 1935, p. 103; Clerc, 1942, p. 590; Bongiorno, 1930, pp. 358 - 359; Novack, 1933, p. 260.

38. Sec. 1932; *cf.* Tufts, 1935, p. 65; "A measure that is reprehensible from the ethical standpoint may be altogether commendable from the standpoint of social utility; and, *vice versa,* a measure commendable from the ethical point of view may be deleterious from the standpoint of social utility. But in that connexion it is better for the subject portion of the population to believe that there is an exact identity between the ethical value of a measure and its social utility." (Sec. 2274.)

39. Muller, 1938, p. 425. "Despite his many brilliant, provocative observations, the contribution of Pareto lies chiefly in his destructive criticism. He serves more as an antidote than as a tonic," (p. 432.)

40. Sec. 1755. "The religious spirit, moreover, is ordinarily stronger in heretics than in the followers of an established orthodoxy protected by a government," a few lines after, "The proposition 'A person can be religious only if he has the sentiments of a specified religion' is completely discredited by experience, and many practical men know that, even if they see fit not to admit as much in public." (Sec. 1851.)

41. Sec. 1583; *cf.* 2341. "Furthermore, it will be just as well if the doctrine here stated be not very generally known to the masses who are to be influenced, for the artifice, to be fully efficient, has to remain concealed. It loses little if any of its efficiency, however, if it is known to some few scholars; for daily experience shows that people continue to believe assertions that stand in flattest contradiction with the known results of logico-experimental science." (Sec. 2440.)

42. Sec. 2176. "Experimental researches, even if imbibed or practised by the masses at large, have proved beneficial; whereas ethical researches have, under the same circumstances, proved harmful in that they are for ever shaking the foundations of the social order. And in that we have proof and counter-proof of the consequences that ensue when experimental truth and social utility coincide or diverge." (Sec. 2002; *cf.* secs. 240n.1, 2048n.1, 2345n.5, 2345n.8; cp. 1737n.1; and see also Tufts, 1935, pp. 76 - 77.)

43. "Curiously enough, Pareto thinks that ethical discussions, though logically futile, have had great influence on social life: 'they are forever shaking the foundations of the social order' (2002). A philosopher might say that this was no mean achievement for mere 'derivation.'" (Ginsberg, 1936, p. 228.) The role of derivations in social equilibrium through their influence upon the residues is discussed at length in chapter five, *infra*.

44. Muller, 1938, p. 439; *cf.* pp. 433, 438, wherein Muller sees the necessity for the disinterested checking of values given the inseparability of action from unverifiable ideals, *cf.* sec. 2254.

45. Parsons' analysis is presented and/or summarized in Parsons, 1937, chapters six and seven, and pp. 454 - 460 and 704 - 708; and in Parsons, 1933, and 1936.

46. Parsons, 1936, pp. 255 - 256; Parsons, 1937, e.g., pp. 222, 247, 460. *Cf.* sec. 2143, and also 379.

47. Parsons, 1933, p. 577. *Cf.* McDougall, 1935, p. 45; Lopreato, 1965, pp. 8, 9, 25, 30; Spengler, 1944, pp. 132 - 133; Brinton, 1954, pp. 645 - 646; Amoroso, 1938, pp. 12, 13; Borkenau, 1936, p. 80; and Tufts, 1935, p. 68.

48. On the individualist character of economic theory employing utility analysis, *cf.* sec. 2271.


## Chapter three

1. Generally, *cf.* Homans and Curtis, 1934, pp. 88, 90; Henderson, 1937, pp. 105ff; Faris, 1936, pp. 662 - 663; Ginsberg, 1936, p. 229; DeVoto, 1933b, p. 573; Lerner, 1935, p. 135. Bogardus, 1955, pp. 507 - 509; Spengler, 1944, p. 122; MacPherson, 1937, p. 466; McDougall, 1935, pp. 39, 41; Hughes, 1958, p. 263; Muller, 1938, pp. 430, 431. It is instructive that McDougall was highly critical of Pareto's analysis and procedures.

2. "Personality and social system are very intimately interrelated, but they are neither identical with one another nor explicable by one another; the

214

social system is not a plurality of personalities." Parsons and Shils, 1962, p. 7.

3. "... Pareto's analysis of social change ... is an analysis in terms of shifts in the proportion, distribution, and importance of traits regarded as invariant." "But in his explicit analysis Pareto makes no provision for a schematism for relating specific residues to conditions determining the time, manner, or degree of their expression." (Perry, 1935, pp. 101, 99.)

4. The enumeration which follows in the text and the subclassifications of the individual classes listed below are adopted from Sec. 888.

5. "And this is the critical point at which the notion of conflict (and eventually coercion) comes in, for societies are essentially heterogeneous, meaning among other things that the need of uniformity is not equally strong in all members of society." (Lopreato, 1965, p. 26; *cf.* secs. 1115ff, 2170ff.)

6. Secs. 1116, 1126. "The need of uniformity is much more strongly felt among uncivilized than among civilized peoples." (Sec. 1115.)

7. "It is very very powerful among uncivilized or barbarous peoples, and shows a very considerable strength among civilized peoples, being surpassed only by the instinct for combinations (Class I residues)." (Sec. 1130.)

8. "Ordinarily such sensations belong to the vague categories known as the 'just' or the 'unjust.' When a person says: 'That thing is unjust,' what he means is that the thing is offensive to his sentiments as his sentiments stand in the state of social equilibrium to which he is accustomed." (Sec. 1210.) "At bottom what is expressed is a feeling, vague and instinctive to be sure, that it is a good thing that resistance to disturbances of the social order should not stand in direct ratio to the number of individuals affected, but should have a considerable force independent of any such number." (Sec. 1216.) "Where a certain kind of property exists it is 'unjust' to take it away from a man. Where it does not exist it is 'unjust' to bestow it on him. Cicero would have those who are in power in the state refrain from that type of liberality which takes away from the ones in order to give to the others. ... That principle, on the other hand, is fundamental to the so-called social legislation that is so dear to the men of our time." (Sec. 1211.)

9. Sec. 1213. "If that sentiment did not exist, every slight incipient alteration in the social equilibrium would meet little or no resistance, and could therefore go on growing with impunity until it came to affect a sufficiently large number of individuals to provoke their resistance from a direct concern to avoid the evil. That is what happens to a certain extent in every society, however highly civilized. But the extent to which it happens is minimized by the interposition of the sentiment of resistance to any alteration in equilibrium, regardless of the number of individuals directly affected. As a consequence the social equilibrium becomes much more stable, and a much more energetic action develops as soon as any alteration sets in." (Sec. 1214, *cf.* Timasheff, 1957, p. 160.)

10. See Livingston: "The general effect of the sex residue in combination with others is to intensify those others, so that if a sex slant can be introduced into a non-logical impulse, the latter flares on high." (Sec. 1396n.1.)

11. On the principle of indirection in regard to prostitution, *cf.* secs. 1382n.4, and 1383n.3.
12. *Cf.* generally, Taylor, 1954, pp. 77, 79, 134, 312 - 314, and *passim, cf.* secs. 2514, 1715n.1, and *passim.*
13. *Cf.* MacPherson, 1937, p. 463; Spengler, 1944, p. 123; Parsons, 1937, p. 279; Borkenau, 1936, pp. 35ff; Millikan, 1936, p. 327; Amoroso, 1938, pp. 7 - 8; and Livingston, in *Treatise*, Sec. 889n.a.

## Chapter four

1. In his *Trasformazione della Democrazia,* Pareto wrote that, "Always in every human community two forces stand in opposition; one, which may be called centripetal, tends to a concentration of power at the centre; the other, which may be called centrifugal, tends to its partition." Moreover, "It is difficult for a civil population to get on without laws; they may be written, fixed by custom, or decided in any other way, but they must exist; there must be a theory behind every Society. The present condition of things, therefore, can only be transient when the old law is dying and the new one not yet born; but this new law is bound to come. If the Trade Unions conquer it will be a Trade Union law." (Quoted in Por, 1923, pp. 25, 64).
2. *In re* religion as power play, *cf.* secs. 1810, 1928n.2, 2188, and *passim; in re* politics as power play, *cf.* secs. 1524, 1714n.1, and *passim.*
3. There is a substantial body of literature on Pareto's theory of the ruling class; *cf.* generally, Homans and Curtis, 1934, pp. 248ff; Borkenau, 1936, pp. 106 - 163; Meisel, 1958, and 1965; Sereno, 1962 and Finer, 1966.
4. Compare Pareto's own recognition that elitist theories themselves may be derivations: "Ruling-class theories, when the requirement of logic is not too keenly felt, appeal simply to sentiments of veneration for holders of power, or for abstractions such as 'the state,' and to sentiments of disapprobation for individuals who try to disturb or subvert existing orders." (Sec. 2182; *cf.* 2184).
5. For example, such fields as class, power, status, social structure, social control, social change, symbols, authority, conflict, and so on.
6. It perhaps needs to be emphasized that Pareto's theory is not a simple class struggle theory in the Marxist sense. *Cf.* Meisel, 1965: "... the class struggle is understood in terms of individual rather than collective psychology, so as to strengthen the conviction that class conflict is enduring, under all skies and in all societies," p. 119. See also Hughes, 1958, pp. 81 - 82; and Homans and Curtis, 1934, p. 248.
7. *Cf.* the many references to Machiavelli in the *Treatise*. See chapter eight, *infra.*
8. It may be pointed out in passing that Pareto's analysis of the interaction of power players encompasses what Boulding has called reaction processes, "processes in which a movement on the part of one party so changes the field of the other that it forces a movement of this party, which in turn changes the field of the first, forcing another move of the second, and so on," (Boulding, 1962, p. 25). Private governments, being power

concentrates, behave in the manner of oligopolies and oligarchies, as contrasted with perfect competitors. Thus, in the words of Lopreato, "if the units constituting the system are interdependent, the repercussions of action or movement in one unit combine with movements in other units, modifying these to some extent and thus producing certain effects that in some degree differ from the effects that would have been observed if the individual units had been autonomous." (Lopreato, 1965, p. 16. *cf.* Parsons, 1937, pp. 235 - 236; and secs. 2092, 2568, and 1557.)

9. This continues in a note: Facts without number serve to show that for many people in the governing classes politics is simply the art of looking out for the interests of certain voters and the representatives they elect." (Sec. 1713n.3, *cf.* Lopreato, 1965, p. 29; and Tufts, 1935, p. 77) "Ministers ... have to look over the field of business with a discerning eye to discover subtle combinations in economic favouritism, neat ways of doing favours to banks and trusts, of engineering monopolies, manipulating tax assessments, and so on; and in other domains, influencing courts, distributing decorations, and the like, to the advantage of those on whom their continuance in power depends." (Sec. 2268; *cf.* secs. 2255ff.)

10. "At the promptings of religious myths, which were once pagan, were then Christian, and are now nationalistic, individuals are induced to hand over their savings in the hope of winning favours from their gods ..." (Sec. 2316.)

11. "If it is true that governments which are incompetent or unable to use -force fall, it is also true that no government endures by depending entirely upon force." (Sec. 2202.)

## Chapter five

1. "How many words just to describe how he feels. He might have done that in the first place without such a long detour." (Sec. 2147n.6.)
2. "As the various religions succeed one another in history, their forms may be as different as one please, but after all they are all expressions of religious sentiments that vary but slightly. The same may be said of the various forms of government, each of which explicitly or implicitly has its own 'divine right.' ... Nor is there any very appreciable difference, either, in the derivations by which the imperative and absolute character of all such ethical systems is justified." (Sec. 1695.)
3. Sec. 1710, which continues: "So the variety that the derivations seem to show, but which is only apparent, disappears, only the substance being left, which is much more constant than the derivations, and is in fact the underlying reality. It often happens, in general, that statesmen ascribe to their conduct in public utterances causes that are in no sense the real ones; and that is especially the case when they allege general principles as motives." (*Cf.* secs. 598, 2147.)
4. "We may, therefore, conclude that certain circumstances which we may designate by the term 'strength', or its opposite 'weakness,' raise or lower the general level of this or that residue." (Sec. 1691.)
5. "Better than any legislative enactment — not excepting compulsory education — it has succeeded in raising the molecules in an amorphous mass

of humanity to dignified status as citizens, and in so doing it has increased the capacities for action of society as a whole. Ascetic Socialism, on the other hand, tends to debilitate every sort of energy." (Sec. 1858.)

6. Here Pareto is certainly at least ambiguous, for his general notion includes disengaging and weakening residues by precluding their activity through eliminating the derivations that strengthen them. Essentially what he is calling for appears to be this: a more careful and efficient manipulation of derivations and thereby of residues than perhaps an anxious and pressed regime is capable of, (cf. Sec. 1747.)

7. Pareto's text continues, "It must not however be forgotten that that holds true only for non-logical conduct, not for conduct of the logical variety." (Sec. 1746.) Earlier in the *Treatise* Pareto had written, "The situation may be stated, inexactly to be sure, because too absolutely, but nevertheless strikingly, by saying that in order to influence people thought has to be transformed into sentiment." (Sec. 168.)

8. The distinction between, on the one hand, the user, author, and invoker, and, on the other, the acceptor, recipient, and believer, of derivations is very important. The user chooses the derivations which will — he intends — accord with the sentiments of his audience so as to induce the desired response. The individual psychic state, being comprised of numerous variable dispositions — including ambivalences — is channeled by the adroit use of derivations by the invoker. On the distinction, cf. secs. 427, 431, 442, 1543, 1843, and *passim*.

9. Timasheff, after noting that the sentiments "are indefinite but seemingly basic biopsychic states," perhaps "instincts or innate human tendencies," goes on to say that, "On the other hand, [Pareto] admits that residues are correlated with the changing conditions under which human beings live, that action in which the sentiments express themselves reenforce such sentiments and may even arouse them in individuals lacking them, that sentiments are engendered or stressed by the persistence of groups and, in their turn, may help such groups to survive." (Timasheff, 1957, p. 161; cf. Timasheff, 1940, p. 143.)

10. Pareto insisted that to argue that conduct should be logical is to state an *ought* and must be considered in light of the social utility of non-logico-experimental knowledge and non-logical conduct; cf. sec. 253; also 1786, 1932.

11. Perhaps the better formulation is "that the art of government consists in knowing how to take advantage of the residues one finds ready to hand." (Sec. 1857.)


## Chapter six

1. The only exception to the argument of this paragraph is freedom of thought which Pareto avidly supported but which he also analyzed in functional terms (as a manifestation of Class I residues); cf. secs. 568, 570, 618, and *passim*.

2. Secs. 1877ff, 1307ff, 1897ff, 1930, 2001, 2196; cf. Parsons, 1937, p. 256;

Ginsberg, 1936, p. 234; Stark, 1963a, p. 111. On the casuistic interpretation of precepts and norms, *cf.* secs. 1919ff and 1799.
3. Secs. 167 - 168, 1126 - 1127, 1206, 1854, 1918, 1936, 2145; *cf.* Lopreato, 1965, p. 25; Homans and Curtis, 1934, p. 228; Becker and Barnes, 1961, p. 1018; Novack, 1933, p. 259; Moore, 1935 - 1936, p. 296; Ginsberg, 1936, p. 234; and Stark, 1963a, p. 111.
4. *Treatise,* chapters 2 - 5, 9 - 10, and *passim*; *cf.* Perry, 1935, p. 102; Moore, 1935 - 1936, p. 295. On the definition of reality as social control, see secs. 196ff, 442, 445, and *passim.*
5. Secs. 383nl, 747, 1027, 1032ff, 1037, 1630, 1799ff, 1817n.3, 1854ff, 1931, 1932, 2048nl, 2184, 2375; *cf.* Moore, 1935 - 1936, p. 295.
6. On socialism as a religion, *cf.* secs. 616, 1073, 1081, 1857 - 1858.

# Chapter seven

1. Pareto also pointed out that "Where sentiments of group-persistence are not very strong, people readily surrender to the momentary impulse without giving adequate thought to the future, forgetting the larger interests of the community under the sway of uncontrolled appetites." (Sec. 2443.)
2. Ginsberg, 1936, p. 245; *cf.* sec. 242. Concerning determinism, see Secs. 132, 2069, and 2094; and Lopreato, 1965, pp. 6, 20, and *passim*; Perry, 1935, p. 104; Homans and Curtis, 1934, p. 275; and Russett, 1966, p. 98.
3. Sec. 2413; on the necessity of balanced, proper proportions, *cf.* 2419 - 2420, 2443, 2522, and *passim.*
4. Secs. 889 - 1088, 1931 - 1932, 2048ff, 2227ff, 2350ff, 2413ff, 2419 - 2420, 2556; *cf.* Moore, 1935 - 1936, p. 297; Clerc, 1942, p. 591; Lopreato and Ness, 1966, p. 30; Perry, 1935, p. 100; and Spengler, 1944, p. 126.
5. Becker and Barnes, 1961, pp. 1017, 1018; Faris, 1936, p. 665; Timasheff, 1940, p. 142; Ginsberg, 1936, pp. 240, 241; Bittermann, 1936, p. 306; and Secs. 1126, 2235, and *passim.*
6. Lopreato, 1965, pp. 28 - 29; Borkenau, 1936, pp. 142ff; MacPherson, 1937, pp. 465 - 466; and Secs. 1143, 2048, 2170ff, 2187, 2191, 2309, 2471, 2521 - 2522.
7. *Cf.* Lopreato, 1965, p. 29; Bogardus, 1955, pp. 513 - 514; Bogardus, 1935, pp. 172 - 173; Ginsberg, 1936, p. 241; Amoroso, 1938, p. 13; Bongiorno, 1930, p. 370; and Mihanovich, 1953, p. 192.
8. In the appendix to this chapter there is an outline of the major subjects in chapters twelve and thirteen of the *Treatise.*
9. "Such descriptions are not in themselves bad; but the terms 'faith' and 'skepticism' may be misleading, if they are thought of as referable to any particular religion or group of religions." (Sec. 2341.)
10. "The reformer, of course, is certain that his sentiments have to be shared by all honest men and that they are not merely excellent in themselves but are also in the highest degree beneficial to society. Unfortunately

that belief in no way alters the realities." (Sec. 2145; *cf.* 2235. See also Bogardus, 1955, p. 511.)

11. The forces, he points out, are chiefly the sentiments.
12. Perry, 1935, p. 105; *cf.* Timasheff, 1957, p. 160; Russett, 1966, pp. 99 - 100, 163; and Wollheim, 1954, p. 575.
13. Homans and Curtis, 1934, pp. 275 - 276. "... why do people who think that they can improve a community by taking certain measures find so often that the measures not only fail to improve the community but even render it worse off than it was in the beginning? ... The answer ... is: because the community is in equilibrium," (p. 258) Not every interpreter of Pareto would put "the" Paretian answer that way, but that is very close and certainly is *one* interpretation. Homans and Curtis also pose the question, "how, then, is a community ever led to better its condition?", to which the Paretian answer is, "by means of residues and derivations making up myths or ideals," (p. 258; see the remainder of their chapter nine.) *Cf.* Russett, 1966, pp. 98ff, for criticism of the distinction between "artificial" and "normal" change.

## Chapter eight

1. Hutchison, in Burns, 1952, p. 297. For Pareto's acknowledgement of the vagueness of utility, see secs. 2111, 2143, and *passim*.
2. It should be made clear that the discussion in this section is not intended to be, nor is it, a thorough discussion — description and/or evaluation — of Pareto optimum in welfare economics. See Samuels, 1972b, for an extended critical analysis.
3. Vickrey, 1964, p. 209; *cf.* Bach, 1966, p. 571; Samuelson, 1967, p. 609; Rothenberg, 1961, pp. 62 and *passim*; and Blaug, 1962, pp. 538 and *passim*.
4. Campbell, 1967, p. 575. For a different interpretation, see Samuels, 1966, chapter five. Injury or harm — determination thereof — is itself a function of legal and moral rules. For analysis of Pareto optimality in terms of injury, and the related ethical ambiguity of the Pareto rule in regard to antecedent non-Pareto optimal change, see Samuels, 1972b.

# References

Amoroso, L. (1938). "Vilfredo Pareto," *Econometrica* 6, 1 - 21.

Aron, R. (1970). *Main Currents in Sociological Thought II*. Garden City: Doubleday Anchor.

Arnold, T. (1962). *The Symbols of Government*. New York: Harcourt, Brace & World.

Ascoli, M. (1936). "Society Through Pareto's Mind." *Social Research* 3, 78 - 89.

Ayres, C.E. (1957). "Institutional Economics: Discussion." *American Economic Review, Papers and Proceedings* 47, 26 - 27.

Bach, G.L. (1966). *Economics*. Englewood Cliffs: Prentice Hall, Fifth Edition.

Ball, H.V. et al. (1962). "Law and Social Change: Sumner Reconsidered." *American Journal of Sociology* 67, 532 - 540.

Barnes, H.E. ed. (1948). *An Introduction to the History of Sociology*. Chicago: University of Chicago Press.

Barzun, J. (1958). *Darwin, Marx, Wagner*. New York: Doubleday Anchor.

Bauer, R.A. (1966). "Social Psychology and the Study of Policy Formation." *American Psychologist* 21, 933 - 942.

Beardsley, M.C. (1944). "Rationality in Conduct: Walras and Pareto." *Ethics* 54, 79 - 95;

Becker, H., and Barnes, H.E. (1961). *Social Thought from Lore to Science*. New York: Dover, Third Edition, Volume 3.

Bell, J.F. (1967). *A History of Economic Thought*. New York: Ronald, Second Edition.

Berger, B. (1967). "Vilfredo Pareto and the Sociology of Knowledge," *Social Research* 34, 265 - 281.

Bittermann, H.J. (1936). "Pareto's Sociology." *Philosophical Review* 45, 303 - 313.

Blaug, M. (1962). *Economic Theory in Retrospect*. Homewood: Irwin.

Bobbio, N. (1956). "Liberalism Old and New." *Confluence* 5, 239 - 251.

Bogardus, E.S. (1935). "Pareto as a Sociologist." *Sociology and Social Research* 20, 167 - 175.

Bogardus, E.S. (1936). "Pareto and Social Objectives." *Sociology and Social Research* 20, 312 - 316.

Bogardus, E.S. (1955). *The Development of Social Thought*. New York: Longmans, Green and Co., Third edition.

Bongiorno, A. (1930). "A Study of Pareto's Treatise on General Sociology." *American Journal of Sociology* 36, 349 - 370.

Borkenau, F. (1936). *Pareto*. New York: Wiley.

Boulding, K.E. (1962). *Conflict and Defense*. New York: Harper & Row.

Bousquet, G.H. (1928). *The Work of Vilfredo Pareto*. Hanover, N.H.: Sociological Press.

Brinton, C., (1954). "The Residue of Pareto." *Foreign Affairs* 32, 640 - 650.

Buchanan, J.M. (1959). "Positive Economics, Welfare Economics, and Political Economy." *Journal of Law and Economics* 2, 124 - 138.

Buchanan, J.M. (1962). "The Relevance of Pareto Optimality." *Journal of Conflict Resolution* 6, 341 - 354.

Burns, A.F., ed. (1952). *Wesley Clair Mitchell: The Economic Scientist*. New York: National Bureau of Economic Research.

Butler, N.M. (1940). *True and False Democracy*. New York: Scribner's.

Campbell, W.F. (1967). "Adam Smith's Theory of Justice, Prudence and Beneficence." *American Economic Review, Papers and Proceedings* 57, 571 - 577.

Clark, J.M. (1939). *Social Control of Business*. New York: McGraw-Hill, Second edition.

Clerc, J.O. (1942). "Walras and Pareto: Their Approach to Applied Economics and Social Economics." *Canadian Journal of Economics and Political Science* 8, 584 - 594.

Coser, L.A. and Rosenberg, B. (1957). *Sociological Theory*. New York: Macmillan.

Creedy, F. (1936). "Residues and Derivations in Three Articles on Pareto." *Journal of Social Philosophy* 1, 175 - 179.

Coase, R.H. (1960). "The Problem of Social Cost." *Journal of Law and Economics* 3, 1 - 44.

Croce, B. (1935). "The Validity of Pareto's Theories." *Saturday Review of Literature* 12, 12 - 13.

Demsetz, H. (1967). "Toward a Theory of Property Rights." *American Economic Review, Papers and Proceedings* 57, 347 - 359.

DeVoto, B. (April 22, 1933a). "A Primer for Intellectuals." *Saturday Review of Literature* 9, 545 - 546.

DeVoto, B. (1933b). "Sentiment and the Social Order." *Harper's* 167, 569 - 581.

DeVoto, B., (May 25, 1935). "The Importance of Pareto." *Saturday Review of Literature* 12, 11.

Ehrenzweig, A.A. (1965). "Psychoanalytical Jurisprudence: A Common Language for Babylon." *Columbia Law Review* 65, 1331 - 1360.

Einaudi, M.M. (1935). "Pareto As I Knew Him." *Atlantic Monthly* 156, 336 - 346.

Faris, E. (1936). "An Estimate of Pareto." *American Journal of Sociology* 41, 657 - 668.

Finer, H. (1964). *Mussolini's Italy*. Hamden, Conn: Archon Books.

222

Finer, S.E., ed. (1966). *Vilfredo Pareto, Sociological Writings.* New York: Praeger.

Friedrich, C.J. (1943). *The New Belief in the Common Man.* Boston: Little, Brown.

Galbraith, J.K. (May 12, 1967). "A Beginner's Guide to American Studies." Address at the opening of the Institute of United States Studies of the University of London, 1 - 13.

Gerth, H.H., and Mills, C.W., eds. (1946). *From Max Weber: Essays in Sociology.* New York: Oxford University Press.

Gherity, J.A., ed. (1965). *Economic Thought: A Historical Anthology.* New York: Random House.

Ginsberg, M. (1936). "The Sociology of Pareto." *Sociological Review* 28, 221 - 245.

Grampp, W.D. (1965). "On the History of Thought and Policy." *American Economic Review,* Supplement 55, 128 - 135.

Gruchy, A.G. (1947). *Modern Economic Thought.* New York: Prentice-Hall.

Gruchy, A.G. (1957). "Institutional Economics: Discussion." *American Economic Review, Papers and Proceedings* 47, 13 - 15.

Hacker, A. (1955). "The Use and Abuse of Pareto in Industrial Sociology." *American Journal of Economics and Sociology* 14, 321 - 333.

Hamilton, E.J. et al., eds. (1962). *Landmarks in Political Economy.* Chicago, University of Chicago Press, volume 1.

Henderson, L.J. (1927). "The Science of Human Conduct." *The Independent* 119, 575 - 577, 584.

Henderson, L.J. (May 25, 1935). "Pareto's Science of Society." *Saturday Review of Literature* 12, 3 - 4, 10.

Henderson, L.J. (1937). *Pareto's General Sociology.* Cambridge: Harvard University Press.

Homans, G.C., and Curtis, C.P. (1934). *An Introduction to Pareto.* New York: Knopf.

Hook, S. (1935). "Pareto's Sociological System." *The Nation* 140, 747 - 748.

House, F.N. (1935). "Pareto in the Development of Modern Sociology." *Journal of Social Philosophy* 1, 78 - 89.

Hughes, H.S. (1958). *Consciousness and Society.* New York: Vintage Books.

Hutchinson, T.W. (1953). *A Review of Economic Doctrines, 1870 - 1929.* London: Oxford University Press.

Jones, H.W. (1962). "Law and the Idea of Mankind." *Columbia Law Review* 62, 753 - 772.

Keller, A.G. (1935). "Pareto." *The Yale Review* 24, 824 - 828.

Knight, F.H. (1960). *Intelligence and Democratic Action.* Cambridge: Harvard University Press.

Larrabee, H.A. (1935). "Pareto and the Philosophers." *The Journal of Philosophy* 32, 505 - 515.

Lerner, M. (June 12, 1935). "Pareto's Republic." *The New Republic,* 135 - 137.

Lindblom, C.E. (1958). "Policy Analysis." *American Economic Review* 48, 298 - 312.

Lindeman, E.C. (1934). "Pareto vs. The Paretians." *The Survey* 70, 363 - 364.

Lindeman, E.C. (1935). "The Pareto Parade." *Survey Graphic* 24, 453 - 4.

223

Livingston, A. (May 25, 1935). "Vilfredo Pareto: A Biographical Portrait." *Saturday Review of Literature* 12, 12.

Lopreato, J. (1964). "A Functionalist Reappraisal of Pareto's Sociology." *American Journal of Sociology* 69, 639 - 646.

Lopreato, J. (1965). *Vilfredo Pareto.* New York: Crowell.

Lopreato, J., and Ness, R.C. (1966). "Vilfredo Pareto: Sociologist or Ideologist?" *The Sociological Quarterly* 7, 21 - 38.

Loria, A. (1923). "Vilfredo Pareto." *Economic Journal* 33, 431.

MacPherson, C.B. (1937). "Pareto's 'General Sociology': The Problem of Method in the Social Science." *Canadian Journal of Economics and Political Science* 3, 458 - 471.

Mannheim, K. (n.d.) *Ideology and Utopia.* New York: Harcourt, Brace.

Marshall, A. (1920). *Principles of Economics.* New York: Macmillan, Eighth edition.

Martindale, D. (1960). *The Nature and Types of Sociological Theory.* Boston: Houghton Mifflin.

McDougall, W. (1935). "Pareto as a Psychologist." *Journal of Social Philosophy* 1, 36 - 52.

Meisel, J.H. (1958). *The Myth of the Ruling Class.* Ann Arbor: University of Michigan Press.

Meisel, J.H., ed. (1965). *Pareto and Mosca,* Englewood Cliffs: Prentice-Hall.

Merton, R.K. (1949). *Social Theory and Social Structure.* Glencoe: Free Press.

Mihanovich, C.S. (1953). *Social Theorists.* Milwaukee: Bruce Publishing Co.

Millikan, M. (1936). "Pareto's Sociology." *Econometrica* 4, 324 - 337.

Moore, H.E., and Bernice, M. (1935—1936). "Folk Implications in Pareto's Sociology." *Social Forces* 14, 293 - 300.

Morgenstern, O. (1964). "Pareto Optimum and Economic Organization," in Kloten, Norbert, et al, (eds.), *Systeme and Methoden in den Wirtschafts- und Sozialwissenschaften.* Tubingen: Mohr (Siebeck).

Muller, H.J. (1938). "Pareto, Right and Wrong." *Virginia Quarterly Review* 14, 425 - 439.

Murchison, C. (1935). "Pareto and Experimental Social Psychology." *Journal of Social Philosophy* 1, 53 - 63.

Nagel, E. (1961). *The Structure of Science.* New York: Harcourt, Brace & World.

Nicols, A. (1967). "Stock versus Mutual Savings and Loan Associations: Some Evidence of Differences in Behavior." *American Economic Review,* Papers and Proceedings 57, 337 - 346.

Northrop, F.S.C., (1959). *The Logic of the Sciences and the Humanities.* Cleveland: World.

Novack, G.E. (1933). "Vilfredo Pareto: The Marx of the Middle Class." *The New Republic* 75, 258 - 261.

Pantaleoni, M. (1923). "Vilfredo Pareto." *Economic Journal* 33, 582 - 590.

Pareto, V. (1910). "Walras." *Economic Journal* 20, 137 - 140.

Pareto, V. (1963). *A Treatise on General Sociology.* (The Mind and Society). New York: Dover, Two volumes.

Parsons, T. (1933). "Vilfredo Pareto." *Encyclopaedia of the Social Sciences* 11, 576 - 578.

Parsons, T. (1936). "Pareto's Central Analytical Scheme." *Journal of Social Philosophy* 1, 244 - 262.

Parsons T. (1937). *The Structure of Social Action.* New York: McGraw-Hill.

Parsons, T. (1951). *The Social System.* Glencoe: Free Press.

Parsons, T. (1960). *Structure and Process in Modern Societies.* Glencoe: Free Press.

Parsons, T., and Shils, E.A., eds. (1962). *Toward a General Theory of Action.* New York: Harper & Row.

Perry, C. (1935). "Pareto's Contribution to Social Science." *Ethics* 46, 96 - 107.

Popper, K.R. (1950). *The Open Society and its Enemies.* Princeton: Princeton University Press.

Por, O. (1923). *Fascism.* New York: Knopf.

Prezzolini, G. (1943). Book Review. *Journal of Philosophy* 40, 356 - 361.

Racca, V. (1935). "Working with Pareto." *Virginia Quarterly Review* 11, 375 - 382.

Ricci, U. (1933). "Pareto and Pure Economics." *Review of Economic Studies* 1, 3 - 21.

Robinson, J.H. (1921). *The Mind in the Making.* New York: Harper.

Roll, E. (1956). *A History of Economic Thought.* Englewood Cliffs: Prentice-Hall, Third edition.

Rothenberg, J. (1961). *The Measurement of Social Welfare.* Englewood Cliffs: Prentice-Hall.

Russell, B. (1961). *Religion and Science.* New York: Oxford University Press.

Russett, C.E. (1966). *The Concept of Equilibrium in American Social Thought.* New Haven: Yale University Press.

Samuels, W.J. (1965a). "Legal-Economic Policy: A Bibliographical Survey." *Law Library Journal* 58, 230 - 252.

Samuels, W.J. (1965b). "History of Economic Thought: Discussion." *American Economic Review, Papers and Proceedings* 55, 145 - 147.

Samuels, W.J. (1966). *The Classical Theory of Economic Policy.* Cleveland: World.

Samuels, W.J. (1972a). "The Scope of Economics Historically Considered." *Land Economics* 48, 248 - 268.

Samuels, W.J. (1972b). "Welfare Economics, Power, and Property," in Wunderlich, G. and Gibson, W.L., Jr., eds., *Perspectives of Property.* University Park: Institute for Research on Land and Water Resources, Pennsylvania State University.

Samuelson, P.A. (1967). *Economics.* New York: McGraw-Hill, Seventh Edition.

Schneider, L. (1962). "The Role of the Category of Ignorance in Sociological Theory: An Exploratory Statement." *American Sociological Review* 27, 492 - 508.

Schumpeter, J.A. (1951). *Ten Great Economists from Marx to Keynes.* New York: Oxford University Press.

Seligman, E.R.A. (1930). "Pareto and Pantaleoni: Personal Reminiscences of Two Italian Economists." *Political Science Quarterly* 45, 341 - 346.

Seligman, B.B. (1962). *Main Currents in Modern Economics.* New York: Free Press.

Sereno, R. (1962). *The Rulers.* New York: Praeger.

225

Spengler, J.J. (1944). "Pareto on Population, I - II." *Quarterly Journal of Economics* 58 - 59, 571 - 601, 107 - 133.

Spengler, J.J. (1948). "The Problem of Order in Economic Affairs," *Southern Economic Journal* 15, 1 - 29.

Spiegel, H.W. (1952). *The Development of Economic Thought.* New York: Wiley.

Stark, W. (1963a). *The Fundamental Forms of Social Thought.* New York: Fordham University Press.

Stark, W. (1963b). "In search of the True Pareto." *British Journal of Sociology* 14, 103 - 112.

Suranyi-Unger, T. (1931). *Economics in the Twentieth Century.* New York: Norton.

Tarascio, V.J. (1968). *Pareto's Methodological Approach to Economics.* Chapel Hill: University of North Carolina Press.

Taylor, G.R. (1954). *Sex in History.* New York: Vanguard.

Taylor, O.H. (1960). *A History of Economic Thought.* New York: McGraw-Hill.

Timasheff, N.S. (1940). "Law in Pareto's Sociology." *American Journal of Sociology* 46, 139 - 149.

Timasheff, N.S. (1957). *Sociological Theory,* New York: Random House, Revised Edition.

Tufts, J.H. (1935). "Pareto's Significance for Ethics." *Journal of Social Philosophy* 1, 64 - 77.

Vander Zanden, J.W. (1959 - 1960). "Pareto and Fascism Reconsidered." *American Journal of Economics and Sociology* 19, 399 - 411.

Vickrey, W.S. (1964). *Microstatics.* New York: Harcourt, Brace & World.

"Vilfredo Pareto on Italy." *Fortnightly Review* 71 (n.s. vol. 65). (1899). 475 - 483.

Welk, W.G. (1938). *Fascist Economic Policy.* Cambridge: Harvard University Press.

Wicksteed, P.H. (1933). *The Common Sense of Political Economy.* London: Routledge & Kegan Paul, volume two.

Wollheim, R. (1954). "Vilfredo Pareto: A Case in the Political Pathology of Our Age." *Occident* 10, 567 - 577.

226

# Name Index

# Subject Index

229

230

231

Printed in the United States
by Baker & Taylor Publisher Services